taste of home
Christmas

taste of home
BOOKS

taste of home

© 2011 Reiman Media Group, LLC
5400 S. 60th St., Greendale WI 53129
All rights reserved.

Taste of Home and Reader's Digest are registered
trademarks of The Reader's Digest Association, Inc.

Editor-in-Chief: **Catherine Cassidy**

Vice President, Executive Editor/Books: **Heidi Reuter Lloyd**

Creative Director: **Howard Greenberg**

Food Director: **Diane Werner, RD**

Senior Editor/Books: **Mark Hagen**

Editor: **Janet Briggs**

Associate Editor: **Amy Glander**

Craft Editor: **Jane Craig**

Associate Craft Editor: **Shalana Frisby**

Associate Creative Director: **Edwin Robles Jr.**

Content Production Manager: **Julie Wagner**

Layout Designers: **Catherine Fletcher, Emma Acevedo**

Copy Chief: **Deb Warlaumont Mulvey**

Copy Editors: **Susan Uphill, Marybeth Jacobson**

Recipe Asset System Manager: **Coleen Martin**

Food Editors: **Karen Scales, Wendy Stenman**

Recipe Testing & Editing: **Taste of Home Test Kitchen**

Food Photography: **Taste of Home Photo Studio**

Set Stylist: **Melissa Haberman**

Administrative Assistant: **Barb Czysz**

North American Chief Marketing Officer: **Lisa Karpinski**

Book Marketing: **Dan Fink**

Creative Director/Creative Marketing: **Jim Palmen**

The Reader's Digest Association, Inc.

President and Chief Executive Officer: **Tom Williams**

Executive Vice President, RDA, & President,
North America: **Dan Lagani**

International Standard
Book Number (10): 0-89821-949-3

International Standard
Book Number (13): 978-0-89821-949-4

Library of Congress Control Number: 2011929962

Cover Photography

Photographers: **Dan Roberts, Rob Hagen**

Food Stylists: **Kaitlyn Besasie, Diane Armstrong**

Set Stylist: **Melissa Haberman**

Pictured on front cover (clockwise from top left):
Chocolate-Hazelnut Pinwheels (p. 109); Surf & Turf
(Lobster only, p. 35); Ricotta Sausage Triangles (p. 11);
Cinnamon Snowflake Ornaments (p. 126); and Peppermint
Candy Cheesecake (p.153).

Pictured on back cover (from left to right):
Chocolate Cherry Martini, (p. 104); Drinking Glass Charm/
Bracelet (p. 209); and Chicken and Artichoke Fettuccine
Alfredo (p. 92).

Additonal photography used:
Comstock/Punchstock, #KS12505, Couple w/tree (p. 176).

Printed in the U.S.A.

"Cooking, Caring, Sharing" is a registered trademark of
Reiman Media Group, LLC

For other Taste of Home books and products,
visit **ShopTasteofHome.com**.

Contents

Ring in the Holidays with *Fabulous* Food, *Sparkling* Decorations and *Heartfelt* Crafts.

There's so much to do before December 25th and so many things to plan, it's no wonder that readers from coast to coast are turning to Taste of Home Christmas for inspiration! This keepsake is brimming with party ideas and 217 never-before published recipes for savory entrees, delectable cookies, heavenly desserts, snacks and so much more.

Plus, there are more than 50 crafts and decorating ideas to help turn your home into a holiday showplace and guarantee you always have the ideal hostess gift on hand. So give yourself an early Christmas present with Taste of Home Christmas.

Party Starters & Beverages. Set the mood with fabulous appetizers, dips and drinks like Chicken Tempura Rolls, Hot Dog Sliders and Midnight Cocktails. Serve these snacks at an open house or to whet your guests' appetites before the main meal.

Plan-Ahead Party Fare. Don't stress about preparing a large meal for company. Turn to these make-ahead foods, which simply require a few last-minute touches or some reheating. Many of these items can be made up to 3 months in advance!

Christmas Dinners. Choose one of the complete menus in this chapter or mix-and-match the entrees with the extra sides and desserts that are provided.

Seasonal Get-Togethers. Celebrate the season with theme parties, such as Winter Solstice, '50s Bash and St. Lucia's Feast. Each one offers a complete menu and directions to add a festive accent to your affair.

Light Christmas. After the holidays, do the scales say you've added a few pounds? These delicious, lower-in-calorie recipes, such as Turkey in Cognac Cream Sauce, Hoisin Pork Chops with Fennel Slaw and Chocolate Espresso Cake, help keep off seasonal weight.

Carefree Entertaining. Chicken and Artichoke Fettuccine Alfredo, Amaretto-Peach Cheese Spread and Strawberries with Vanilla Mascarpone and Balsamic Drizzle are impressive, sensational and easy! Less-fuss menus mean more time to celebrate with guests!

Cookies for Santa. Not just for Santa, but for everyone—it's time for yummy, buttery, crispy and chewy cookies! The delectable selection includes: Caramel-Walnut Star Cookies, Iced Holiday Ornament Cookies, Chocolate-Hazelnut Pinwheels and Hot Chocolate Linzer Cookies.

Spices of the Season. The holidays wouldn't be the same without the wonderful aroma of spices wafting through your home. Cinnamon, allspice, cloves, cardamom, ginger and nutmeg are some of the spices that flavor tasty treats, such as Gingerbread House Sandwich Cookies, Cardamom-Walnut Pound Cake and Cherry Spice Cake.

Enchanting Endings. Desserts make a superb finale to a festive get-together. Fudge Fantasy Cake, Golden Walnut Caramel Squares and Bananas Foster Pie are just some of the luscious treats to choose from.

Wrapped Up for the Holidays. Here, homemade kitchen goodies are packed in unique gift baskets. Choose the Teacher's Coffee Bag gift for a favorite instructor, the backpack filled with survival foods for the college student or the special food bowl for your favorite pooch.

Deck the Halls. Add touches of wonder and enchantment to your home this season. Make simple covers for throw pillows, create a dreamy wreath or line the walkway with glittering votives.

Gifts to Give. When you give a handmade craft, you're offering a thoughtful gift from the heart. A Quilted Tote, Comfy Shrug, Dangle Bracelet and Buttonhole Scarf are just some of the presents you can make.

Create special memories this holiday season. Let Taste of Home Christmas show you how with spectacular decorating items, easy-to-do crafts and absolutely sensational recipes!

Party Starters
& BEVERAGES

Savory Cheese Ball

PREP: 15 MIN. + CHILLING   **YIELD:** 2 CUPS

Blue cheese contributes a pleasant, tangy bite and olives add saltiness to this creamy cheese ball. For optimum taste, let the cheese ball stand at room temperature for 20 minutes before serving it.

Jan Stawara ★ Howell, Michigan

  1   package (8 ounces) cream cheese, softened
  1   cup (4 ounces) crumbled blue cheese
1/4   cup butter, softened
  1   can (4-1/4 ounces) chopped ripe olives
  1   tablespoon minced chives
1/4   cup chopped walnuts
Assorted crackers

In a large bowl, beat the cream cheese, blue cheese and butter until smooth. Stir in olives and chives. Cover and refrigerate for at least 1 hour.

Shape cheese mixture into a ball; roll in walnuts. Wrap in plastic wrap; refrigerate for at least 1 hour. Serve with assorted crackers.

TO MAKE AHEAD: The cheese ball can be made a day in advance; cover and refrigerate. Remove cheese ball from the refrigerator 20 minutes before serving.

Chicken Liver Pate with Walnuts and Figs

PREP: 30 MIN. + STANDING   **YIELD:** 2-1/3 CUPS

Adults will enjoy the sophisticated flavors in this rich pate. The appetizer is fabulous to serve at a wine tasting party.

Wanda Griess ★ Eagle, Nebraska

  1   cup dry red wine *or* chicken broth
3/4   cup dried figs
  1   pound chicken livers
  1   cup reduced-sodium chicken broth
  1   small onion, sliced
  1   cup butter, softened
3/4   cup chopped walnuts, toasted,
  2   tablespoons Cognac brandy
1/2   teaspoon salt
Thinly sliced green onions
Red leaf lettuce
  1   French bread baguette (10-1/2 ounces), sliced and toasted

In a small saucepan, bring wine to a simmer. Remove from the heat; add the figs. Let stand for several hours or overnight; drain. Cut figs into quarters. Transfer to a small bowl; cover and refrigerate.

Line a 3-cup bowl with plastic wrap and spray with cooking spray. In a large saucepan, combine the chicken livers, broth and onion. Bring to a boil. Reduce heat; cover and simmer for 10 minutes or until meat is no longer pink, stirring occasionally. Drain.

Transfer to a food processor; cover and process until chicken mixture is coarsely chopped. Add the butter, 1/4 cups walnuts, Cognac and salt. Cover and process until smooth. Transfer to prepared bowl. Cover and refrigerate until firm, at least 3 hours.

To serve, unmold pate onto a serving platter. Press remaining walnuts onto sides of pate. Arrange green onions and a few figs on top. Place lettuce around pate. Sprinkle remaining figs over lettuce. Serve with baguette slices. Refrigerate leftovers.

TO MAKE AHEAD: The pate can be made a day in advance; cover and refrigerate until serving.

Basil Mascarpone Torte

PREP: 20 MIN.　**BAKE:** 50 MIN. + CHILLING
YIELD: 16 SERVINGS

This decadent torte has a creamy texture and is perfect to take along to your next potluck or holiday meal.

Lisa Renshaw ★ Kansas City, Missouri

1-1/2　cups dry bread crumbs
　　1　cup pine nuts, toasted
　1/2　cup cold butter, cubed
1-1/2　cups Mascarpone cheese
　　1　cup ricotta cheese
　1/4　cup grated Romano cheese
　　2　tablespoons whole milk
　1/2　teaspoon salt
　1/4　teaspoon ground nutmeg
　　2　eggs, lightly beaten
　1/4　cup minced fresh basil

Place bread crumbs and pine nuts in a food processor; cover and process until nuts are finely chopped. Add butter; cover and process until blended. Press onto the bottom and 1 in. up the sides of a greased 9-in. springform pan; set aside.

In a large bowl, beat the cheeses, milk, salt and nutmeg until smooth. Add eggs; beat on low speed just until combined. Stir in basil. Pour into crust. Place pan on a baking sheet.

Bake at 350° for 50-60 minutes or until puffed and golden brown. Cool on a wire rack for 10 minutes. Carefully run a knife around edge of pan to loosen; cool 1 hour longer. Refrigerate overnight. Remove sides of pan before slicing.

Polenta Mushroom Appetizers

PREP: 40 MIN. + COOLING　**BAKE:** 15 MIN.
YIELD: 32 APPETIZERS

Simple ingredients (you probably have most, if not all, in your kitchen) are used to create a fantastic appetizer.

Meta West ★ Abilene, Kansas

　　2　cups chicken broth
　　2　cups 2% milk
　1/2　teaspoon salt
　　1　cup cornmeal
　1/4　cup grated Parmesan cheese
MUSHROOM TOPPING:
　1/2　pound thinly sliced fresh mushrooms
　　3　tablespoons olive oil
　　1　tablespoon butter
　　6　garlic cloves, minced

　　1　teaspoon minced fresh thyme *or* 1/4 teaspoon
　　　dried thyme
　1/2　teaspoon salt
　1/4　teaspoon pepper
　　2　tablespoons white wine *or* additional chicken broth
　　1　tablespoon lemon juice
　1/4　cup grated Parmesan cheese

In a large heavy saucepan, bring the broth, milk and salt to a boil. Reduce heat to a gentle boil; slowly whisk in cornmeal. Cook and stir with a wooden spoon for 15-20 minutes or until polenta is thickened and pulls away cleanly from the sides of the pan. Stir in cheese.

Spread into a greased 11-in. x 7-in. baking dish. Cool to room temperature, about 30 minutes. Cut polenta into 16 pieces, then cut each diagonally in half to make 32 triangles; place on a greased baking sheet. Bake at 350° for 12-15 minutes or until light golden brown.

For mushrooms, saute mushrooms in oil and butter until tender. Add the garlic, thyme, salt and pepper; cook 1 minute longer. Add wine and lemon juice; cook and stir until liquid is almost absorbed.

Top each triangle with 1-1/2 teaspoons mushrooms; sprinkle appetizers with cheese. Serve warm.

Fruited Punch

PREP: 20 MIN.　**COOK:** 10 MIN. + CHILLING
YIELD: 26 SERVINGS (3/4 CUP EACH)

I've been making this for more years than I care to say, and I think it is the best punch ever!

Marlene Meimann ★ Queensbury, New York

1-1/2	cups sugar
1-1/2	cups water
3	cups strong brewed tea, chilled
3	cups orange juice, chilled
3	cups unsweetened pineapple juice, chilled
1/2	cup lemon juice, chilled
3	cups thinly sliced fresh or frozen strawberries
1	bottle (2 liters) ginger ale, chilled

In a small saucepan, combine sugar and water. Bring to a boil over medium heat. Reduce heat; simmer, uncovered, for 3-4 minutes or until sugar is dissolved, stirring occasionally. Remove from the heat; cool to room temperature. Cover and refrigerate for at least 1 hour.

In a punch bowl, combine the tea, juices and sugar mixture. Stir in strawberries. Just before serving, stir in ginger ale.

Cranberry Brie Pinwheels

PREP: 20 MIN.　**BAKE:** 15 MIN.　**YIELD:** 1 DOZEN

People will think you really fussed when you present these crisp, flaky pinwheels....but they're easy to make. The filling is bursting with savory goodness and a touch of sweetness.

Marcia Kintz ★ South Bend, Indiana

1	sheet frozen puff pastry, thawed
2	tablespoons Dijon mustard
2	tablespoons honey
1	cup finely chopped fresh spinach
1/2	cup finely chopped Brie cheese
1/2	cup finely chopped walnuts
1/4	cup dried cranberries, finely chopped

Unfold pastry. Combine mustard and honey; spread over pastry. Layer with spinach, cheese, walnuts and cranberries. Roll up jelly-roll style; cut into 12 slices. Place cut side down on an ungreased baking sheet.

Bake at 400° for 15-20 minutes or until golden brown.

Drain and discard marinade; pat pork dry. Place honey and sesame seeds in separate shallow bowls. Roll pork in honey, then sesame seeds. Place on a rack in a shallow roasting pan. Bake at 350° for 40-45 minutes or until a meat thermometer reads 160°. Let stand for 5 minutes before slicing.

Meanwhile, in a small bowl, combine sauce ingredients. Serve with pork.

Sesame Pork Appetizers

PREP: 15 MIN. + MARINATING **BAKE:** 40 MIN.
YIELD: 2 DOZEN (1/2 CUP SAUCE)

The honey marinade gives this hearty pork appetizer added flavor. It's served with an Asian-inspired dipping sauce that is quite delicious.

Joyce Moynihan ★ Lakeville, Minnesota

- 1/2 cup sherry *or* chicken broth
- 1 tablespoon reduced-sodium soy sauce
- 2 pork tenderloins (3/4 pound)
- 1/2 cup honey
- 1/2 cup sesame seeds

DIPPING SAUCE:
- 1/3 cup reduced-sodium soy sauce
- 1 green onion, finely chopped
- 1 tablespoon sherry chicken broth
- 1 tablespoon sesame oil
- 1 garlic clove, minced
- 1/2 teaspoon minced fresh gingerroot

In a large resealable plastic bag, combine sherry and soy sauce; add pork. Seal bag and turn to coat; refrigerate for 8 hours or overnight.

One-of-a-Kind Serving Pieces

You can create fun, unique serving dishes for a buffet with items you have on hand. Also look for interesting pieces at the clearance area in home goods stores or at garage sales. Select bases of varying height.

Here we used a martini glass, drinking glass and a votive holder, and plates of different sizes and shapes. To permanently adhere the plates to the bases, use waterproof glass glue or permanent glue dots. To temporarily adhere the pieces together, use removable glue dots or tacky wax (look for it in craft stores). Once they are glued together, the dishes should only be hand washed.

Skewered Chicken with Peanut Sauce

PREP: 30 MIN. + MARINATING **GRILL:** 10 MIN.
YIELD: 2-1/2 DOZEN

Sate-style chicken is a popular choice for parties. Here, the golden-brown poultry is served with a scrumptious peanut sauce. You'll find that these will be devoured in no time!

Nancy Stec ★ Upperco, Maryland

  3 pounds boneless skinless chicken breast halves
1/2 cup orange juice
1/2 cup reduced-sodium soy sauce
1/4 cup lime juice
  2 tablespoons chunky peanut butter
  2 garlic cloves, minced
  2 teaspoons curry powder
  1 teaspoon ground cumin
  1 teaspoon ground ancho chili pepper

SAUCE:
3/4 cup coconut milk
1/2 cup chunky peanut butter
1/4 cup lemon juice
  2 tablespoons reduced-sodium soy sauce
  1 tablespoon brown sugar
  2 garlic cloves, minced
  1 teaspoon grated fresh gingerroot
  1 teaspoon crushed red pepper flakes
1/2 cup heavy whipping cream
Minced fresh cilantro

Flatten chicken to 1/4-in. thickness; cut lengthwise into 1-in.-wide strips. In a small bowl, combine the orange juice, soy sauce, lime juice, peanut butter, garlic, curry powder, cumin and chili pepper.

Pour 1 cup mixture into a large resealable plastic bag. Add the chicken; seal bag and turn to coat. Refrigerate for at least 4 hours or overnight. Cover and refrigerate remaining mixture.

Drain chicken and discard marinade. Thread chicken onto 30 metal or soaked wooden skewers. If grilling the chicken, moisten a paper towel with cooking oil, and using long-handled tongs, lightly coat the grill rack. Grill chicken, covered, over medium heat or broil 4 in. from the heat for 3-4 minutes on each side or until no longer pink, basting with reserved juice mixture.

Meanwhile, in a small saucepan, combine the coconut milk, peanut butter, lemon juice, soy sauce, brown sugar, garlic, ginger and pepper flakes. Cook and stir over medium heat until smooth. Cool slightly. Transfer to a food processor; add cream. Cover and process until smooth. Sprinkle chicken with cilantro. Serve chicken warm with sauce.

Place one sheet of phyllo dough on a work surface with a short end facing you. (Keep remaining phyllo covered with plastic wrap and a damp towel to prevent it from drying out.) Spray sheet with cooking spray; repeat with one more sheet of phyllo, spraying the sheet with cooking spray. Cut into three 14-in. x 3-in. strips.

Place a rounded teaspoonful of filling on lower corner of each strip. Fold dough over filling, forming a triangle. Fold triangle up, then fold triangle over, forming another triangle. Continue folding, like a flag, until you come to the end of the strip.

Spritz end of dough with spray and press onto triangle to seal. Turn triangle and spritz top with cooking spray. Repeat with remaining phyllo and filling.

Place triangles on baking sheets coated with cooking spray. Bake at 375° for 15-20 minutes or until golden brown. Serve warm.

TO MAKE AHEAD: Unbaked triangles may be frozen in a single layer on baking sheets; when frozen, transfer to resealable plastic bags. Bake frozen triangles for 25-30 minutes or until golden brown.

Ricotta Sausage Triangles

PREP: 1 HOUR   **COOK:** 15 MIN./BATCH   **YIELD:** 12 DOZEN

Savory pockets filled with cheese, sausage and seasonings... what's not to like? This recipe makes a lot so it's ideal for parties or potlucks. If you don't need the entire amount, they do freeze well.

Virginia Anthony ★ Jacksonville, Florida

- 1 carton (15 ounces) part-skim ricotta cheese
- 1 package (10 ounces) frozen chopped spinach, thawed and squeezed dry
- 1 jar (7 ounces) roasted sweet red peppers, drained and chopped
- 1/3 cup grated Parmesan cheese
- 3 tablespoons chopped ripe olives
- 1 egg
- 1 tablespoon minced fresh basil *or* 1 teaspoon dried basil
- 1 teaspoon Italian seasoning
- 1/4 teaspoon salt
- 1/4 teaspoon pepper
- 1 pound bulk Italian sausage
- 1 medium onion, chopped
- 96 sheets phyllo dough (14 inches x 9 inches)

Olive oil-flavored cooking spray

In a large bowl, combine the first 10 ingredients. In a large skillet, cook sausage and onion over medium heat until meat is no longer pink; drain. Stir into cheese mixture.

Making Phyllo Triangles

1. Place a rounded teaspoonful of filling, in lower corner on each strip.
2. Fold dough over filling, forming a triangle.
3. Fold triangle up, forming another triangle. Fold triangle over and continue folding like a flag, until you come to the end of the strip.

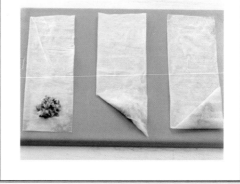

Chicken Tempura Rolls

PREP: 1 HOUR + STANDING **YIELD:** 3 DOZEN

Not only are these appetizers delicious, but they're simpler to make than you might think. An inexpensive bamboo mat and sticky rice are key to making them. Your guests will truly be impressed when you serve this scrumptious treat.

       2 cups sushi rice
     1/2 cup rice vinegar
     1/4 cup sugar
       1 teaspoon salt
     1/2 pound frozen breaded chicken tenders
     2/3 cup thawed orange juice concentrate
       2 tablespoons reduced-sodium soy sauce
       1 teaspoon minced fresh gingerroot
     1/2 teaspoon crushed red pepper flakes
     1/2 teaspoon sesame oil
Bamboo sushi mat
   1-1/2 cups sliced almonds, chopped and toasted
       3 green onions (green portion only)
       1 small sweet red pepper, julienned
       1 large navel orange, peeled, sectioned and cut into
          thin strips

In large bowl, wash rice in several changes of cold water until water is clear. Transfer to a large saucepan; add 2 cups water. Let stand for 30 minutes.

Cover saucepan and bring to boil over high heat. Reduce heat to low; cook for 15-20 minutes or until water is absorbed and rice is tender. Remove from the heat. Let stand, covered, for 10 minutes.

Meanwhile, in small bowl, combine the vinegar, sugar and salt, stirring until sugar is dissolved.

Transfer rice to a shallow bowl; sprinkle with 1/3 cup vinegar mixture. Set aside remaining vinegar mixture for assembly. With a wooden paddle or spoon, stir rice with a slicing motion until cooled. Cover with a damp cloth to keep moist. (Rice mixture may be made up to 6 hours ahead and stored at room temperature, covered, with a damp towel. Do not refrigerate.)

Bake chicken according to package directions; cool. Cut into long thin strips. In a large bowl, combine the juice concentrate, soy sauce, ginger, pepper flakes and sesame oil; set aside 1/2 cup for serving. Add chicken to remaining orange mixture; toss to coat.

Cover the sushi mat with plastic wrap. Spread 1/4 cup almonds in an even layer over plastic wrap to a 9-in. x 6-in. rectangle. Moisten hands with reserved vinegar mixture; press rice in a thin even layer over almonds.

Arrange a small amount of chicken mixture, green onion, red pepper and orange strips about 1-1/2 in. from bottom edge of rectangle. Holding the bamboo mat, roll the rectangle away from you, being careful to enclose the filling with rice. Use the mat to help you squeeze the roll into a compact log. Remove mat; set tempura roll aside. Repeat,

creating six tempura rolls. Cut each into 1-1/2 in. slices. Serve with reserved sauce.

Making Tempura Rolls

1. Cover sushi mat with plastic wrap as directed in recipe. Spread nuts evenly over plastic wrap, then spread cooked rice evenly over nuts.

2. Arrange filling ingredients in a tight pile in the lower third of the rectangle.

3. Using the sushi mat and rolling away from you, roll up the tempura roll.

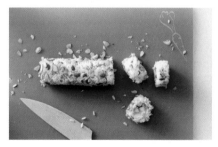

4. Press roll into a compact rectangular log. Cut into slices, as directed in the recipe.

Double-Chocolate Martini

PREP/TOTAL TIME: 5 MIN.   **YIELD:** 1 SERVING

Is it a beverage or a dessert? It could be either! Don't let its looks fool you, this chocolate martini is potent but good!

Deb Williams ★ Peoria, Arizona

Grated chocolate
    1 maraschino cherry
Ice cubes
2-1/2 ounces half-and-half cream
1-1/2 ounces vodka
1-1/2 ounces chocolate liqueur
1-1/2 ounces creme de cacao

Sprinkle grated chocolate on a plate. Moisten the rim of a martini glass with water; hold glass upside down and dip rim into chocolate. Place cherry in glass.

    Fill a mixing glass or tumbler three-fourths full with ice. Add the cream, vodka, chocolate liqueur and creme de cacao; stir until condensation forms on outside of glass. Strain into glass; serve immediately.

Editor's Note: To coat the rim of a glass with grated chocolate, dip the rim in water, and then in grated chocolate.

Spanakopita Bites

PREP: 20 MIN. + FREEZING   **BAKE:** 35 MIN.
YIELD: 10-1/2 DOZEN

For an easy spanakopita, try this version that is made in a pan, then cut into squares. It has all the wonderful taste of the classic version...buttery phyllo with a spinach-cheese filling, but is so simple to do.

Barbara Smith ★ Chipley, Florida

    1 egg
    1 package (10 ounces) frozen chopped spinach, thawed and squeezed dry
    2 cups (8 ounces) crumbled feta cheese
    1 cup (8 ounces) 4% small-curd cottage cheese
3/4 cup butter, melted
 16 sheets phyllo dough (14 inches x 9 inches)

In a large bowl, combine the egg, spinach and cheeses; set aside.

    Brush a 15-in. x 10-in. x 1-in. baking pan with some of the butter. Layer eight sheets of phyllo dough in prepared pan, brushing each with butter. (Keep remaining dough covered with plastic wrap and a damp towel to prevent it from drying out.) Spread with spinach mixture. Top with remaining phyllo dough, brushing each sheet with butter.

    Cover and freeze for 30 minutes. Using a sharp knife, cut into 1-in. squares. Bake at 350° for 35-40 minutes or until golden brown.

TO MAKE AHEAD: Cover and freeze until ready to use. May be frozen for up to 2 months. Cut and bake as directed.

Hot Dog Sliders

PREP: 50 MIN. + RISING   **BAKE:** 15 MIN.
YIELD: 3-1/2 DOZEN

An American favorite, miniature hot dogs can easily be turned into a fun treat that is simply ideal for a casual party any time of the year. They get three special treatments in this recipe: Chicago-style, Bavarian and South-of-the-Border. Try them all, and let guests decide which one they like best!

21 frozen bread dough dinner rolls, thawed
1 egg
1 tablespoon water
3/4 teaspoon poppy seeds
3/4 teaspoon caraway seeds
3 tablespoons shredded Mexican cheese blend
1 package (16 ounces) miniature hot dogs

CHICAGO DOGS:
1/3 cup prepared mustard
1/3 cup sweet pickle relish
1/3 cup chopped sweet onion
1/3 cup chopped tomato
2 whole dill pickles, juilenned

BAVARIAN DOGS:
1 can (14 ounces) Bavarian sauerkraut, rinsed, drained and chopped
1 small apple, diced
1/3 cup chopped sweet onion
1/4 cup chopped celery

CHIHUAHUA DOGS:
1 cup green chili salsa
1 can (8 ounces) unsweetened crushed pineapple, drained
1/4 cup minced fresh cilantro
2 teaspoons chopped seeded jalapeno pepper
1 teaspoon grated lime peel

Cut each roll in half; roll each into an oblong shape. Arrange rolls in two greased 13-in. x 9-in. baking pans. Cover and let rise in a warm place until doubled, about 30 minutes.

In a small bowl, whisk egg and water; brush over rolls. Sprinkle a third of the buns with poppy seeds, another third with caraway seeds and the remaining buns with cheese. Bake at 350° for 14-16 minutes or until golden brown. Remove to wire racks to cool.

Meanwhile, place hot dogs in a 15-in. x 10-in. x 1-in. baking pan. Bake at 350° for 12-14 minutes or until heated through.

Place a hot dog in a poppy seed bun. Top with a teaspoonful of mustard, relish, onion and tomato. Repeat. Top each with pickles.

In a small bowl, combine the sauerkraut, apple, onion and celery. Place a hot dog in each caraway seed bun; top with sauerkraut mixture.

In another small bowl, combine the salsa, pineapple, cilantro, jalapeno and lime peel. Place a hot dog in each cheese bun; top with salsa mixture.

Mushroom Cheese Mini Cups

PREP: 25 MIN. **BAKE:** 20 MIN. **YIELD:** 32 APPETIZERS

If you're looking for a finger food with mass appeal, look no further than these mini cups. They are loaded with onion, mushrooms and cheese. Your guests will love them.

Lynn Severns ★ Carnegie, Pennsylvania

- 1 pound finely chopped fresh mushrooms
- 1 cup finely chopped sweet onion
- 1 tablespoon olive oil
- 3/4 cup shredded part-skim mozzarella cheese
- 1/4 cup shredded Swiss cheese
- 1/2 cup minced fresh parsley
- 2 egg yolks, beaten
- 1 tablespoon Italian seasoning
- 1/2 teaspoon salt
- 8 slices white bread, crusts removed
- 1/4 cup butter, melted

In a large skillet, saute mushrooms and onion in oil until tender. Transfer to a large bowl; stir in the cheeses, parsley, egg yolks, Italian seasoning and salt. Set aside.

Flatten bread with a rolling pin; cut each slice into four pieces. Place butter in a shallow dish; dip both sides of bread in butter, then press into ungreased miniature muffin cups. Spoon mushroom filling into cups, about 1 tablespoon in each.

Bake at 350° for 20-25 or until golden brown. Serve warm.

Orange-Chicken Endive Boats

PREP/TOTAL TIME: 30 MIN. **YIELD:** 2-1/2 DOZEN

This tasty appetizer is great any time of year, but is especially appropriate during the Christmas season with the splash of red from the dried cranberries.

Tracy Anderson ★ Lincroft, New Jersey

- 2 cups finely chopped cooked chicken
- 1 celery rib, finely chopped
- 1/2 cup dried cranberries
- 1/3 cup mayonnaise
- 1/4 cup sour cream
- 1 shallot, finely chopped
- 1 tablespoon grated orange peel
- 1/2 teaspoon salt
- 1/4 teaspoon pepper
- 30 endive leaves

In a large bowl, combine the first nine ingredients. Spoon about 1 tablespoon onto each endive leaf.

Midnight Cocktails

PREP: 15 MIN. + CHILLING **YIELD:** 2 SERVINGS

This unique variation on the popular mojito uses blackberry spreadable fruit, which gives it a deep-purple color and a bit of sweetness in every sip.

- 1/3 cup seedless blackberry spreadable fruit
- 2 tablespoons water
- 1/4 cup fresh mint leaves
- 3 tablespoons lime juice
- 1/3 cup rum brandy
- 1 cup club soda

GARNISH:
Mint sprigs

In a small saucepan, combine spreadable fruit and water. Cook and stir over medium heat until smooth; transfer to a small bowl. Refrigerate until chilled.

In a small pitcher, muddle mint leaves and lime juice. Add blackberry syrup and rum. Divide between two cocktail glasses. Stir in club soda; garnish with mint sprigs.

Onion Brie Bowl

PREP: 40 MIN. **BAKE:** 25 MIN. + STANDING
YIELD: 18 SERVINGS

Golden caramelized onions are paired with buttery, silky brie in this warm spread. Make sure to have enough bread cubes or crackers to use up every gooey bit.

- 3 cups sliced onions
- 2 tablespoons canola oil
- 1 tablespoon brown sugar
- 1 tablespoon balsamic vinegar
- 1/2 teaspoon salt
- 1 round loaf (1 pound) sourdough bread
- 1 round (8 ounces) Brie cheese

In a large skillet, saute onions in oil until softened. Reduce heat to medium-low; add the brown sugar, vinegar and salt. Cook, stirring occasionally, for 30-35 minutes or until onions are deep golden brown.

Cut top third off loaf of bread; hollow out enough bread from the bottom to make room for cheese. Cube removed bread; set aside. Using a knife, make 2-in. cuts into loaf around edge of bread at 1-in. intervals. Remove rind from cheese; cut cheese in half horizontally. Layer half of the cheese and onions in bread. Repeat layers.

Transfer to an ungreased baking sheet. Bake at 350° for 25-30 minutes or until cheese is melted. Let stand for 10 minutes. Serve with bread cubes.

Blue Cheese Stuffed Walnuts

PREP: 30 MIN. + CHILLING **YIELD:** 4 DOZEN

Set a plate of these nutty, one-bite snacks out and watch them disappear. They're so easy to make.

Charlotte Rogers ★ Virginia Beach, Virginia

- 1 package (8 ounces) cream cheese, softened
- 1/2 cup crumbled blue cheese
- 1-1/2 teaspoons minced chives
- 1/2 teaspoon garlic powder
- 1/4 teaspoon kosher salt
- 1/4 teaspoon coarsely ground pepper
- 96 walnut or pecan halves (about 2-1/2 cups)

In a small bowl, beat the first six ingredients until blended. Shape into 1/2-in. balls. Place each between 2 walnut halves; gently press together. Cover and refrigerate for at least 1 hour or overnight.

TO MAKE AHEAD: The stuffed walnuts can be made a day in advance; cover and refrigerate until serving.

Poppin' Cheese Dip

PREP: 15 MIN.   **BAKE:** 25 MIN.   **YIELD:** 3 CUPS

I love jalapeno peppers and created this dip to showcase them. It makes a lot and is affordable, so it is a perfect choice when you're feeding a crowd.

Julie Roush ★ Woodstock, Illinois

- 2 packages (8 ounces *each*) cream cheese, softened
- 2 cups (8 ounces) shredded cheddar cheese
- 1/4 teaspoon garlic salt
- 1 can (12 ounces) pickled jalapeno peppers
- 1 cup panko (Japanese) bread crumbs
- 2 tablespoons butter, melted

Tortilla chips

In a large bowl, beat the cream cheese, cheddar cheese and garlic salt until blended; set aside. Drain peppers and discard juice. Cut peppers lengthwise; open and lay flat. Remove seeds if desired; finely chop peppers. Stir into cheese mixture. Spread into a 9-in. pie plate.

In a small bowl, combine bread crumbs and butter; sprinkle over top. Bake at 350° for 25-30 minutes or until topping is lightly browned. Serve with tortilla chips.

TO MAKE AHEAD: The cheese mixture can be prepared a day in advance; cover and refrigerate. Remove from the refrigerator 30 minutes before baking. Sprinkle with the bread crumb mixture just before baking.

Curried Chicken Cheese Log

PREP: 25 MIN. + CHILLING   **YIELD:** 3 CUPS

Curry and cooked chicken team up in this unique cheese log. The curry is very mild, so everyone is sure to enjoy this flavorful spread.

Karen Owen ★ Rising Sun, Indiana

- 2 packages (8 ounces *each*) cream cheese, softened
- 1-1/2 cups finely chopped cooked chicken
- 1/3 cup finely chopped celery
- 2 tablespoons minced fresh parsley
- 1 tablespoon steak sauce
- 1/2 teaspoon curry powder
- 1/2 cup sliced almonds, toasted and coarsely chopped

Butter-flavored crackers

In a large bowl, beat cream cheese until smooth. Stir in the chicken, celery, parsley, steak sauce and curry powder. Shape into a 9-in. log. Roll in almonds. Wrap in plastic wrap; refrigerate for at least 2 hours. Serve with crackers.

Pesto Dipping Oil

PREP/TOTAL TIME: 10 MIN.   **YIELD:** 1 CUP

This is absolutely my favorite and easiest appetizer for entertaining. It is simply delicious with its combination of balsamic vineger, pesto and Parmesan cheese. The oil can also be used to marinate cubes of cheese and mushrooms for another simple appetizer.

Alice Schucard ★ Carlsbad, California

- 1/2 cup olive oil
- 1/4 cup balsamic vinegar
- 1/4 cup prepared pesto
- 1/4 teaspoon salt
- 1/8 teaspoon pepper
- 1/4 cup grated Parmesan cheese
- 1 French bread baguette (1 pound), thinly sliced

In a small bowl, whisk the oil, vinegar, pesto, salt and pepper. Pour into a shallow serving bowl; sprinkle with Parmesan cheese. Serve with bread.

Mediterranean Masterpiece Pizza

PREP: 40 MIN.   **BAKE:** 10 MIN.   **YIELD:** 12 SERVINGS

This meatless pizza has a lovely combination of vegetables, cheese and rosemary.

Charlene Chambers ★ Ormond Beach, Florida

- 1   medium red onion, halved and sliced
- 1   teaspoon sugar
- 3   tablespoons olive oil,
- 1   cup balsamic vinegar
- 1   prebaked 12-inch thin pizza crust
- 1   cup crumbled goat cheese
- 1/2   cup chopped Greek olives
- 1   jar (7-1/2 ounces) roasted sweet red peppers, drained and sliced
- 1   medium tomato, seeded and chopped
- 1-1/2   cups cubed fresh mozzarella cheese
- 1   tablespoon minced fresh rosemary *or* 1 teaspoon dried rosemary, crushed

In a large skillet, saute onion and sugar in 1 tablespoon oil until softened. Reduce heat to medium-low; cook, stirring occasionally, for 30 minutes or until deep golden brown.

Meanwhile, in a small saucepan bring vinegar to a boil; reduce heat. Simmer, uncovered, for 15-20 minutes or until reduced to 1/3 cup.

Place crust on an ungreased 12-in. pizza pan or baking sheet. Combine goat cheese and olives; spread over crust. Top with peppers, tomato, caramelized onion and mozzarella cheese.

Bake at 450° for 8-10 minutes or until cheese is melted. Drizzle with remaining oil; sprinkle with rosemary. Serve with vinegar reduction.

Crab Cakes with Chesapeake Bay Mayo

PREP: 20 MIN. + CHILLING   COOK: 10 MIN./BATCH
YIELD: 16 APPETIZERS

I placed my personal stamp on my Aunt Ellie's crab cake recipe by changing up some of her ingredients. They're served with a tart and tangy cream sauce. You can serve them on an appetizer spread or as a terrific first-course at a dinner.

Michelle Critchell ★ Moon, Virginia

1/2   cup sour cream
1/2   cup mayonnaise
2   tablespoons sweet pickle relish
1   tablespoon spicy brown mustard
1/4   teaspoon seafood seasoning

CRAB CAKES:

1   egg, beaten
1/4   cup grated Parmesan cheese
1/4   cup seasoned bread crumbs
1/4   cup mayonnaise
2   tablespoons finely chopped onion
1   tablespoon minced fresh parsley
1   tablespoon spicy brown mustard
1/2   teaspoon seafood seasoning
1/8   teaspoon pepper
3   cans (6 ounces) lump crabmeat, drained
1/4   cup canola oil

In a large bowl, combine the first five ingredients. Cover and chill until serving. For crab cakes, in a large bowl, combine the egg, cheese, bread crumbs, mayonnaise, onion, parsley, mustard, seafood seasoning and pepper. Fold in crab. Refrigerate for at least 30 minutes.

With floured hands, shape mixture by 2 tablespoonfuls into 1/2-in.-thick patties. In a large skillet over medium heat, cook crab cakes in oil in batches for 3-4 minutes on each side or until golden brown. Serve with sauce.

Nutty Artichoke Spread

PREP/TOTAL TIME: 30 MIN.   YIELD: 4 CUPS

I keep a can of artichoke hearts in my pantry so I can quickly make my signature appetizer at a moment's notice. I find wheat or whole grain crackers nicely complement the artichokes. Everyone likes this warm spread.

Susan Kruspe ★ Shortsville, New York

2/3   cup mayonnaise
1   tablespoon lemon juice
1   tablespoon finely chopped onion
1   can (14 ounces) water-packed artichoke hearts, rinsed, drained and quartered
2   cups (8 ounces) shredded cheddar cheese
1/2   cup finely chopped pecans, toasted
4   bacon strips, cooked and crumbled
Assorted crackers

In a large bowl, combine the mayonnaise, lemon juice and onion. Stir in the artichokes, cheese, pecans and bacon. Spoon into a greased 9-in. pie plate.

Bake at 350° for 15-20 minutes or until cheese is melted. Serve with crackers.

Plan~Ahead
PARTY FARE

Plan-Ahead Party Fare

The holiday season is a busy time filled with family, friends, parties and a large to-do list. And with shopping, wrapping and decorating taking priority, cooking and baking often fall to the bottom of that list. That's why we're offering the scrumptious recipes in this section—each is ideal for making ahead and freezing! Most can be frozen for up to 3 months, so you can whip up a recipe in October, then store it in the freezer. When you need a last-minute bite, just defrost and, if necessary, reheat. The recipes offer exact instructions, so you can expect wonderful results no matter how busy your schedule becomes!

Make-Ahead Turkey and Gravy

PREP: 4 HOURS + FREEZING   **BAKE:** 1 HOUR
YIELD: 14-16 SERVINGS (2-1/2 CUPS GRAVY)

Relax on Christmas by preparing your turkey ahead of time. With this recipe the turkey is cooked, sliced and ready to serve in a nicely seasoned broth. It is also a great way to bring a turkey to a potluck.

- 1 turkey (14 to 16 pounds)
- 2 teaspoons poultry seasoning
- 1 teaspoon pepper
- 1/2 cup minced fresh parsley
- 1/4 cup lemon juice
- 1 tablespoon minced fresh thyme *or* 1 teaspoon dried thyme
- 1 tablespoon minced fresh rosemary *or* 1 teaspoon dried rosemary, crushed
- 2 teaspoons grated lemon peel
- 2 garlic cloves, minced
- 4-1/2 cups reduced-sodium chicken broth, *divided*
- 1 tablespoon butter
- 1 tablespoon all-purpose flour

Pat turkey dry. Sprinkle with poultry seasoning and pepper. Tuck wings under turkey; tie drumsticks together. Place breast side up on a rack in a roasting pan.

Bake, uncovered, at 325° for 30 minutes. In a large bowl, combine the parsley, lemon juice, thyme, rosemary, lemon peel, garlic and 3 cups broth; pour over turkey. Bake, uncovered, 3 to 3-1/2 hours longer or until a meat thermometer reads 180° in the thigh, basting occasionally with broth mixture. Cover loosely with foil if turkey browns too quickly. Let stand for 20 minutes.

Remove turkey; skim fat from cooking juices. Slice turkey; cool completely and place in resealable freezer bags. Pour cooking juices over turkey. Seal bags and freeze for up to 3 months.

To use frozen turkey: Thaw in refrigerator overnight. Place turkey in a shallow roasting pan; pour remaining broth over turkey. Cover and bake at 350° for 50-60 minutes or until a meat thermometer reads 165°.

Remove turkey to a serving plate and keep warm. In a small saucepan, melt butter. Stir in flour until smooth; gradually add cooking juices. Bring to a boil; cook and stir for 2 minutes or until thickened. Serve with turkey.

Editor's Note: It is best not to use a prebasted turkey for this recipe.

Cranberry Slush

PREP: 10 MIN. + FREEZING
YIELD: 24 SERVINGS (3/4 CUP EACH)

I love to try new recipes. When I find one that is especially well liked, I make a copy, put it in a protective sleeve and place it in a binder. The binders contain my best recipes, and this sweet-tart, bright-red slush is definitely in a binder.

Sharon Delaney-Chronis ★ South Milwaukee, Wisconsin

- 1 package (3 ounces) raspberry gelatin
- 1 cup boiling water
- 4 cups cranberry juice
- 2 cups cold water
- 2 cups rum
- 1 can (12 ounces) frozen lemonade concentrate, thawed
- 1 can (12 ounces) frozen orange juice concentrate, thawed
- 6 cups lemon-lime soda

In a large bowl, dissolve gelatin in boiling water. Stir in the cranberry juice, cold water, rum and concentrates. Transfer to a 3-quart freezer container. Cover and freeze for 12 hours, stirring occasionally. May be frozen for up to 3 months.

To use frozen cranberry mixture: In a punch bowl, combine cranberry mixture and soda. Or for one serving, combine 1/2 cup cranberry mixture and 1/4 cup soda in a glass. Serve immediately.

Potato Puffs

PREP: 35 MIN.   **BAKE:** 10 MIN.   **YIELD:** 2 DOZEN

A crispy coating surrounds a velvety potato filling in these adorable puffs. They make a perfect side for meats and poultry. Best of all, the recipe makes 2 dozen, so you can freeze what you don't need right away.

Eva Tomlinson ★ Bryan, Ohio

- 4 pounds cubed peeled potatoes
- 1/2 cup 2% milk
- 1/4 cup butter, cubed
- 1-1/2 teaspoons salt
- 1/2 cup shredded cheddar cheese
- 1-1/2 cups crushed cornflakes
- 6 tablespoons sesame seeds, toasted

Place potatoes in a large saucepan and cover with water. Bring to a boil. Reduce heat; cover and simmer for 15-20 minutes or until tender. Drain. Mash potatoes with milk, butter and salt. Stir in cheese; chill for 2 hours or until easy to handle.

Combine cornflakes and sesame seeds. Shape potato mixture into 1-1/2-in. balls; roll in cornflake mixture.

Place on baking sheets; cover and freeze until firm. Transfer to a large resealable plastic freezer bag. May be frozen for up to 3 months.

To use frozen potatoes: Place 2 in. apart on greased baking sheets. Bake at 400° for 15-17 minutes or until golden brown.

Carnitas with Orzo and Peppers in Red Mole Sauce

PREP: 1-1/2 HOURS   **BAKE:** 40 MIN.   **YIELD:** 5 SERVINGS

Here's a tasty way to stretch your grocery dollar. Pork shoulder roast is combined with orzo, peppers and mole sauce to make spicy Mexican comfort food.

Kari Wheaton ★ Beloit, Wisconsin

1	boneless pork shoulder butt roast (1-1/2 to 2 pounds), cut into 1/2-inch cubes
1-1/2	teaspoons salt, *divided*
1/2	teaspoon pepper
1	cup uncooked orzo pasta
1	*each* medium green, sweet red and yellow peppers
2	jalapeno peppers, seeded and chopped
1	medium onion, chopped
1	tablespoon olive oil
1	cup chicken broth
1/4	cup red mole sauce
2	tablespoons tomato paste
1	cup (4 ounces) quesadilla *or* Monterey Jack cheese, shredded

Place pork in a 15-in. x 10-in. x 1-in. baking pan, sprinkle with 1 teaspoon salt and 1/2 teaspoon pepper. Bake at 325° for 1-1/2 hours or until pork reaches 160°.

Meanwhile, cook pasta according to package directions; drain and set aside. In a large skillet, saute peppers and onion in oil until crisp-tender. In a greased 13-in. x 9-in. baking pan, combine the orzo, peppers and onion.

In a small saucepan, whisk the chicken broth, mole sauce, tomato paste and remaining salt. Cook and stir until thickened and bubbly. Pour over orzo and vegetables. Stir in pork; sprinkle with cheese. Cool. Cover; may be frozen for up to 3 months.

To use frozen carnitas: Thaw in refrigerator overnight. Remove from the refrigerator 30 minutes before baking. Cover and bake at 350° for 35-40 minutes or until heated through. Uncover; broil 3-4 in. from the heat for 4-5 minutes or until cheese is lightly golden.

Editor's Note: To use immediately, broil as directed. When cutting hot peppers, disposable gloves are recommended.

Ham & Gruyere Mini Quiches

PREP: 30 MIN. + FREEZING   **BAKE:** 20 MIN.
YIELD: 10 MINI QUICHES

By making this in muffin cups, each person gets their own quiche. I have also doubled the recipe and used jumbo muffin cups. Bake the jumbo cups about 10 minutes longer.

Gena Stout ★ Ravenden, Arkansas

4	eggs, lightly beaten
1	cup 2% cottage cheese
1/4	cup 2% milk
2	tablespoons all-purpose flour
1/2	teaspoon baking powder
1/4	teaspoon ground nutmeg
1/4	teaspoon pepper
1-1/2	cups (6 ounces) shredded Gruyere *or* Swiss cheese
3/4	cup finely chopped fully cooked ham
3	tablespoons thinly sliced green onions

In a large bowl, combine the first seven ingredients; fold in the Gruyere cheese, ham and onions. Fill greased muffin cups three-fourths full.

Bake at 375° for 18-22 minutes until a knife inserted near the center comes out clean. Cool for 5 minutes before removing from pans to wire racks.

Transfer quiches to a large resealable plastic freezer bag. May be frozen for up to 3 months.

To use frozen mini quiches: Thaw in the refrigerator overnight. Transfer to a greased baking sheet; bake at 350° for 10-14 minutes or until heated through.

Pork Taquitos

(pictured at left)

PREP: 40 MIN. **BAKE:** 10 MIN. **YIELD:** 1 DOZEN

Taquitos are a popular appetizer, and these homemade bites are so much better than the frozen variety found in the supermarket. If you want the filling to have a little more punch, adjust the seasonings to suit your taste.

- 1 medium onion, finely chopped
- 1 tablespoon canola oil
- 2 garlic cloves, minced
- 2 teaspoons ground cumin
- 1 teaspoon dried oregano
- 1 teaspoon chili powder
- 1/4 teaspoon cayenne pepper
- 2 cups shredded cooked pork
- 1 cup (4 ounces) shredded Mexican cheese blend
- 1/4 cup minced fresh cilantro
- 1/4 cup salsa verde
- 1 tablespoon lime juice
- 12 corn tortillas (6 inches), warmed

Sour cream, guacamole and additional salsa verde

In a large skillet, saute onion in oil until tender. Add the garlic, cumin, oregano, chili powder and cayenne; cook 1 minute longer. Add the pork, cheese, cilantro, salsa and lime juice. Cook and stir until cheese is melted.

Place 2 tablespoons filling over lower third of each tortilla. Roll up tightly. Secure with toothpicks. Repeat with remaining tortillas and filling.

Place taquitos on a greased baking sheet. Bake at 400° for 8 minutes. Cool completely. Discard toothpicks. Place taquitos on a waxed paper-lined 15-in. x 10-in. x 1-in. baking sheet; freeze until firm. Transfer to a resealable plastic freezer bag. May be frozen for up to 3 months.

To use frozen taquitos: Arrange desired number of taquitos in a single layer on a greased baking sheet. Bake at 400° for 12-15 minutes or until golden brown. Serve with sour cream, guacamole and additional salsa verde.

Party Cranberry Meatballs

PREP: 30 MIN. **COOK:** 20 MIN. **YIELD:** 4-1/2 DOZEN

Meatballs make a great party food, and this recipe makes a lot. You can keep them warm in a slow cooker, but they move fast, so plan on refilling it often.

Jessica Hodgson ★ Peach Bottom, Pennsylvania

- 2 eggs, beaten
- 1/3 cup dry bread crumbs
- 1 teaspoon salt
- 1/2 teaspoon onion powder
- 1/2 teaspoon garlic powder
- 1/2 teaspoon dried thyme
- 1/2 teaspoon pepper
- 2 pounds ground turkey
- 1 can (14 ounces) jellied cranberry sauce
- 1 bottle (12 ounces) chili sauce
- 1/4 cup water
- 1/4 cup orange marmalade
- 2 tablespoons red wine vinegar
- 2 tablespoons reduced-sodium soy sauce

In a large bowl, combine the first seven ingredients. Crumble turkey over mixture and mix well. Shape into 1-in. balls.

In a large skillet, cook meatballs in batches until no longer pink; drain.

In a Dutch oven, combine the remaining ingredients. Cook and stir over medium-low heat for 5 minutes. Add meatballs. Bring to a boil. Reduce heat; simmer, uncovered, for 10 minutes or until heated through. Cool. Transfer to freezer containers. Freeze for up to 3 months.

To use frozen meatballs: Thaw in the refrigerator. Heat in a Dutch oven or microwave.

Editor's Note: To use immediately, cook as directed.

Rosemary-Blue Cheese Shortbread

PREP: 20 MIN. **BAKE:** 10 MIN./BATCH
YIELD: ABOUT 4-1/2 DOZEN

The subtle essence of rosemary comes through in these unique, savory blue cheese treats. You'll find that they disappear quickly when you serve them.

- 1 cup (4 ounces) crumbled blue cheese
- 3/4 cup butter, softened
- 1 tablespoon sugar
- 1 tablespoon minced fresh rosemary
- 2 cups all-purpose flour
- 3/4 cup finely chopped walnuts

In a large bowl, beat the blue cheese, butter, sugar and rosemary until well blended. Beat in flour (dough will be crumbly). Shape into two 7-in. rolls; coat with walnuts. Wrap each in plastic wrap. Refrigerate for 4 hours or freeze up to 3 months..

Cut into 1/4-in. slices; place on greased baking sheets. Bake at 375° for 10-12 minutes or until golden brown. Cool on wire racks. Store shortbread in an airtight container in the refrigerator.

To use frozen shortbread: Thaw in the refrigerator. Bake as directed.

Frozen Cranberry Salad

PREP: 20 MIN. + FREEZING **YIELD:** 8 SERVINGS

This recipe is different from most cranberry salads, and it's always delectable. It freezes firm, but it is easy to cut into serving-size pieces.

Suzanne Merrill ★ Nampa, Idaho

- 1 can (14 ounces) jellied cranberry sauce
- 3 tablespoons orange juice
- 1 teaspoon grated orange peel
- 1/2 cup heavy whipping cream
- 2 tablespoons sugar
- 2 tablespoons reduced-fat mayonnaise
- 1/4 cup chopped pecans

Line a 9-in. x 5-in. loaf pan with foil; set aside. Place the cranberry sauce, orange juice and peel in a food processor; cover and process until blended. Transfer to prepared pan.

In a small bowl, beat cream and sugar until it begins to thicken. Stir in mayonnaise. Spread over cranberry mixture; sprinkle with pecans. Cover and freeze for 4 hours or until firm. May be frozen for up to 1 month.

To use frozen salad: Using foil, lift salad out of pan. Cut into pieces.

Chocolate-Filled Cream Puffs

PREP: 40 MIN. + FREEZING **BAKE:** 25 MIN./BATCH
YIELD: 3 DOZEN

I grew up eating cream puffs, and this is my mother's recipe. I make these every year for our school counselor's birthday, and he adores them along with everyone else. I have to triple the batch when I take them to school, but it's worth it!

Diana Voland ★ Martinsville, Indiana

- 1 cup water
- 1/2 cup butter, cubed
- 1 cup all-purpose flour
- 4 eggs

Defrosting Guidelines

Following recipe directions for defrosting. Most items should be defrosted overnight in the refrigerator, not at room temperature. However, some frozen desserts can stand at room temperature for 30 minutes or less to make slicing easier.

CHOCOLATE CREAM FILLING:

- 3/4 cup sugar
- 5 tablespoons baking cocoa
- 3 tablespoons cornstarch
- 1/2 teaspoon salt
- 2 cups 2% milk
- 2 egg yolks, lightly beaten
- 1 tablespoon butter
- 1 teaspoon vanilla extract

Hot fudge ice cream topping and citrus sugar, white chocolate shavings *or* confectioners' sugar, optional

In a large saucepan, bring water and butter to a boil. Add flour all at once and stir until a smooth ball forms. Remove from the heat; let stand for 5 minutes. Add eggs, one at a time, beating well after each addition. Continue beating until mixture is smooth and shiny.

Drop by rounded tablespoonfuls 3 in. apart onto greased baking sheets. Bake at 400° for 20-25 minutes or until golden brown. Remove to wire racks. Immediately split puffs open; remove tops and set aside. Discard soft dough from inside. Cool puffs. Freeze in airtight containers for up to 2 months.

To use frozen cream puffs: Thaw at room temperature for 10 minutes. Place cream puffs on a baking sheet. Bake at 375° for 3-4 minutes or until crisp.

For filling, in a large heavy saucepan, combine the sugar, cocoa, cornstarch and salt. Stir in milk until smooth. Cook and stir over medium-high heat until thickened and bubbly. Reduce heat to low; cook and stir 2 minutes longer.

Remove from the heat. Stir a small amount of hot mixture into egg yolks; return all to the pan, stirring constantly. Bring to a gentle boil; cook and stir 2 minutes longer. Remove from the heat. Gently stir in butter and vanilla. Cover with waxed paper or plastic wrap. Cool for 15 minutes, without stirring.

To serve, spoon chocolate cream filling into cream puffs; replace tops. Top with warmed hot fudge sauce and citrus sugar, white chocolate shavings or confectioners' sugar if desired.

Editor's Note: Citrus sugar can be made by pressing grated citrus peels into sugar to release the oil. Store citrus sugar in an airtight container at room temperature for 2-3 weeks or until the flavor diminishes.

Chocolate-Swirled Peanut Butter Cookies

(pictured at left)

PREP: 25 MIN. + FREEZING **BAKE:** 10 MIN./BATCH
YIELD: ABOUT 6-1/2 DOZEN

Our kids' most requested cookies are peanut butter and chocolate chip, so I came up with this recipe combining those favorite flavors. The two swirled doughs create a lovely pattern on the cookie. Best of all, there's no need for any additional decoration.

Lori Kesinger ★ Baker, Montana

3/4	cup creamy peanut butter
1/2	cup butter, softened
1/2	cup sugar
1/2	cup packed brown sugar
1	egg
1-1/4	cups all-purpose flour
1/2	teaspoon baking powder
1/2	teaspoon baking soda
1/4	teaspoon salt

CHOCOLATE DOUGH:

1/2	cup butter, softened
1/2	cup sugar
1/2	cup packed brown sugar
1	egg
1	teaspoon vanilla extract
1-1/4	cups all-purpose flour
1/4	cup baking cocoa
1/2	teaspoon baking powder
1/2	teaspoon baking soda
1/4	teaspoon salt

In a large bowl, cream the peanut butter, butter and sugars until light and fluffy, about 4 minutes. Beat in egg. Combine the flour, baking powder, baking soda and salt; gradually add to creamed mixture and mix well.

For the chocolate dough, in another large bowl, cream butter and sugars until light and fluffy. Beat in egg and vanilla. Combine the flour, cocoa, baking powder, baking soda and salt; gradually add to creamed mixture and mix well.

Divide each portion in half. Knead one peanut butter and one chocolate portion together 5-10 times or until it just begins to swirl. Shape into a 10-in. log. Wrap in plastic wrap. Repeat with remaining dough. Freeze until ready to use. May be frozen for up to 3 months.

To use frozen cookie dough: Thaw in the refrigerator overnight. Unwrap and cut into 1/4-in. slices. Place 2 in. apart on lightly greased baking sheets. Bake at 350° for 6-8 minutes or until bottoms are lightly browned. Cool for 2 minutes before removing from pans to wire racks.

Five-Cheese Mushroom Ravioli

PREP: 55 MIN. + FREEZING **COOK:** 10 MIN./BATCH
YIELD: 8 SERVINGS

I bet you won't even miss the meat in these scrumptious portobello ravioli. The actual number of raviolis might change, depending on how much filling you use. You can also add cooked meat or sausage to the sauce for a heartier dish.

Karlyn Behnke ★ Litchfield, Minnesota

2	large portobello mushrooms, chopped
1	cup sliced green onions
3	teaspoons olive oil, *divided*
3	garlic cloves, minced
1	cup (4 ounces) shredded part-skim mozzarella cheese
1	cup (4 ounces) shredded provolone cheese
1/2	cup shredded Romano cheese
1/2	cup part-skim ricotta cheese
32	wonton wrappers
4	cups refrigerated Alfredo sauce, warmed
1/4	cup shredded Parmesan cheese
1/4	cup chopped fresh basil

In a large skillet, saute mushrooms and onions in 2 teaspoons oil until tender. Add garlic; saute 1 minute longer. In a large bowl, combine the mozzarella, provolone, Romano and ricotta cheeses. Stir in the mushroom mixture.

Spoon 1 tablespoon mushroom mixture in the center of each wonton wrapper. (Keep wrappers covered with a damp paper towel until ready to use.) With water, moisten all the wonton dough around the mushroom filling. Top with another wonton wrapper; press edges with a fork to seal. Repeat with remaining wrappers and mushroom mixture.

In a large freezer container, place ravioli in a single layer; separate each layer with waxed paper. May be frozen for up to 3 months.

To use frozen ravioli: Bring a large saucepan or Dutch oven of water and remaining oil to a boil. Add the ravioli in batches. Reduce the heat to a gentle simmer; cook for 6-8 minutes or until ravioli are tender. Remove with a slotted spoon and keep warm.

Serve with warmed Alfredo sauce. Sprinkle with Parmesan cheese and basil.

Labeling

Always clearly label packages to be frozen. On the label, include the name of the item and the date. Defrosting and reheating directions are also helpful.

Italian Wedding Soup

PREP: 30 MIN. + FREEZING   **COOK:** 40 MIN.   **YIELD:** 7 CUPS

This soup is so filling and chock-full of veggies. You can substitute chicken sausage, rolled up into little balls, for the meatballs if you'd like.

Amy McGowen ★ Jupiter, Florida

- 1   egg white
- 1/4 cup panko (Japanese) bread crumbs
- 1   teaspoon Italian seasoning
- 1/2 pound ground pork
- 2   medium carrots, chopped
- 2   celery ribs, chopped
- 1   medium parsnip, peeled and chopped
- 1   small onion, finely chopped
- 2   tablespoons olive oil
- 6   cups reduced-sodium chicken broth
- 3   teaspoons herbes de Provence
- 1/2 teaspoon crushed red pepper flakes
- 1/2 teaspoon pepper
- 1   cup uncooked orzo pasta
- 1   package (6 ounces) fresh baby spinach
- 1/4 cup shredded Parmesan cheese
- 1/4 cup minced fresh parsley

In a large bowl, combine the egg white, bread crumbs and Italian seasoning. Crumble pork over mixture and mix well. Shape into 3/4-in. balls.

Place meatballs on a greased rack in a foil-lined 15-in. x 10-in. x 1-in. baking pan. Bake at 350° for 15-18 minutes or until no longer pink.

Meanwhile, in a Dutch oven, saute the carrots, celery, parsnip and onion in oil until tender. Stir in the broth, herbes de Provence, pepper flakes and pepper.

Drain meatballs on paper towels. Bring the soup to a boil; add meatballs. Reduce heat; simmer, uncovered, for

30 minutes. Cool. Transfer to freezer containers. May be frozen for up to 3 months.

To use frozen soup: Thaw in the refrigerator. Transfer to a large saucepan; bring to a boil. Add orzo; cook 8-10 minutes longer or until pasta is tender, stirring occasionally. Add spinach; cook and stir until spinach is wilted. Sprinkle each serving with cheese and parsley.

Eggnog Ladyfinger Dessert

PREP: 20 MIN. + FREEZING   **YIELD:** 12 SERVINGS

My combination of cranberries and eggnog will bring a festive end to any holiday meal.

Carole Resnick ★ Cleveland, Ohio

- 2   packages (3 ounces *each*) ladyfingers, split
- 1   pint raspberry *or* cranberry sorbet
- 3   cups eggnog
- 1   cup evaporated milk
- 1/2 cup sour cream
- 2   packages (3.4 ounces *each*) instant vanilla pudding mix

Fresh raspberries *or* cranberries and fresh mint leaves

Arrange 24 ladyfingers around the edge of an ungreased 9-in. springform pan; arrange 16 ladyfingers over the bottom (save remaining ladyfingers for another use). Spoon sorbet over ladyfingers; cover and freeze for 30 minutes.

In a large bowl, beat the eggnog, evaporated milk, sour cream and pudding mix for 2 minutes or until thickened. Spoon over sorbet. Cover and freeze for 8 hours or overnight.

To use frozen dessert: Remove from the freezer 5-10 minutes before slicing. Garnish with berries and mint.

Christmas DINNERS

Lobster & Steak Dinner

Surf & Turf
pg. 35

**Boston Lettuce Salad with
Green Goddess Dressing**
pg. 36

**Creamy Butternut
Twice-Baked Potatoes**
pg. 37

French Onion Garlic Bread
pg. 38

**Flourless Chocolate Cake
with Rosemary Ganache**
pg. 39

Surf & Turf

PREP: 25 MIN. + CHILLING   **BAKE:** 15 MIN.
YIELD: 4 SERVINGS

For an intimate dinner with close friends, serve this stunning dinner of tenderloin steaks and lobster tail. Your guest will think they are dining at a fine restaurant.

- 2 garlic cloves, minced
- 2 teaspoons plus 2 tablespoons olive oil, *divided*
- 1/4 cup minced fresh parsley
- 3 tablespoons chopped green onions
- 2 tablespoons minced fresh thyme
- 2 teaspoons grated lemon peel
- 1/2 teaspoon salt
- 1/4 teaspoon pepper
- 1/8 teaspoon cayenne pepper
- 1/2 cup butter, softened
- 1 cup soft bread crumbs
- 1/4 cup butter, melted
- 4 lobster tails (8 to 10 ounces *each*)
- 4 beef tenderloin steaks (4 ounces *each*)
- 4 teaspoons coarsely ground pepper

In a small skillet, saute garlic in 2 teaspoons oil until tender; remove from the heat. In a small bowl, combine the parsley, green onions, thyme, lemon peel, salt, pepper, cayenne and sauteed garlic. Set aside 1/2 cup for crumb topping.

Add softened butter to remaining herb mixture; mix well. Shape into a 1-in.-thick log; wrap in plastic wrap. Refrigerate for 30 minutes or until firm.

For crumb topping, combine the bread crumbs, melted butter and reserved herb mixture; set aside.

Split lobster tails in half lengthwise. With cut side up and using scissors, cut along the edge of shell to loosen the cartilage covering the tail meat from the shell; remove and discard cartilage.

Place lobster tails on a baking sheet; top with reserved crumb topping. Bake, uncovered, at 375° for 15-20 minutes or until the meat is firm and opaque and crumbs are golden brown.

Meanwhile, sprinkle steaks with coarse pepper. In a large skillet over medium heat, cook steaks in remaining oil for 4-5 minutes on each side or until meat reaches desired doneness (for medium-rare, a meat thermometer should read 145°; medium, 160°; well-done, 170°).

Unwrap herb butter; cut four 1/4-in.-slices from log. Place one slice on each steak. Serve with lobster. Rewrap remaining butter; refrigerate for 1 week or freeze for up to 3 months.

Butterflying a Lobster Tail

1. With scissors, cut lengthwise through the top shell to the end of the tail, taking care not to cut through the meat. Remove vein, as you would devein a shrimp. Carefully pull the shell away from the meat, leaving meat attached to the tip of the tail.

2. Squeeze the shell together and lay the meat on top of the shell. Make a lengthwise slit down the center of the meat to within 1/2 in. of bottom. Open meat so it lies flat.

3. On each half of meat, make another lengthwise slit down the center to within 1/2 in. of bottom. Fan out tail fins with your fingers.

Boston Lettuce Salad with Green Goddess Dressing

PREP/TOTAL TIME: 30 MIN.
YIELD: 8 SERVINGS (1/2 CUP DRESSING)

Spinach gives this luscious, fresh-tasting salad dressing its green color. The slightly licorice flavor from the tarragon complements the salad greens.

1/3	cup mayonnaise
1/4	cup fresh baby spinach
2	tablespoons sour cream
1	tablespoon chopped green onion (green part only)
1	tablespoon minced fresh parsley
1	tablespoon minced fresh tarragon
1-1/2	teaspoons lemon juice
1-1/2	teaspoons tarragon vinegar *or* white wine vinegar
1	teaspoon anchovy paste
1/4	teaspoon pepper
6	cups Boston lettuce
4	radicchio leaves, torn
1	small cucumber, halved and sliced
1	cup cherry tomatoes, halved

In a blender, combine the first 10 ingredients; cover and process until smooth.

In a large bowl, combine the lettuce, radicchio, cucumber and tomatoes. Serve with dressing.

Festive Tablescape

Giving your table a tourch of Christmas glamour does not need to be expensive. To create a delightful tablescape, look around your home for decorations that would be suitable. Here we feature an assortment of trees and tree toppers. If you collect a special holiday item each year, such as snowmen, Santas, angels, snowflakes, tree toppers, etc, arrange part of your collection in the center of the table or by each place setting.

If you are just starting out and have only a few Christmas decorations, you can still create a magical look. Arrange some of your Christmas ornaments in the center of the table. You can pick one color theme or use an assortment of colors and shapes. Weave some wired ribbon around and through the ornaments, then add a few votives. When you dim the lights and the votives are glowing, the magical scene will delight your guests.

Creamy Butternut Twice-Baked Potatoes

PREP: 1-1/4 HOURS **BAKE:** 10 MIN. **YIELD:** 8 SERVINGS

Here's a new way to make twice-baked potatoes. Smooth mashed potatoes and butternut squash are blended with flavored cream cheese for a festive side.

Sue Schwentke ★ Plainville, Connecticut

  4   large baking potatoes
  3   cups cubed peeled butternut squash
1-1/2   cups water
  4   ounces spreadable garden vegetable cream cheese
  3   tablespoons butter
1/2   teaspoon salt
1/4   teaspoon pepper

Scrub and pierce potatoes. Bake at 375° for 50-55 minutes or until tender.

Meanwhile, in a large saucepan, bring squash and water to a boil. Reduce heat; cover and simmer for 15-20 minutes or until tender. Drain.

Cool baked potatoes for 10 minutes; cut in half lengthwise. Scoop out pulp; leaving thin shells.

In a large bowl, combine potatoes and squash. Mash until smooth. Add the cream cheese, butter, salt and pepper; mix until creamy. Pipe or spoon into potato skins. Bake, uncovered, at 375° for 10-15 minutes or until heated through.

French Onion Garlic Bread

PREP: 40 MIN. **BAKE:** 10 MIN. **YIELD:** 12 SERVINGS

My husband and I love creating new recipes together based on our favorite foods. This is our very first creation as a married couple. The cheesy bread can also be used as an appetizer for a party.

Taryn Camp ★ Oviedo, Florida

- 1 large sweet onion, thinly sliced
- 1 tablespoon olive oil
- 1/2 cup beef broth
- 4 garlic cloves, minced, *divided*
- 1/4 teaspoon dried thyme
- 1/4 cup butter, softened
- 1 loaf (1 pound) French bread, sliced
- 2 tablespoons grated Parmesan cheese
- 2 cups (8 ounces) shredded Gruyere *or* Swiss cheese

In a large saucepan, saute onion in oil for 8-10 minutes or until tender. Add the broth, 1 garlic clove and thyme; bring to a boil. Reduce heat; simmer, uncovered, for 12-15 minutes.

Meanwhile, in a small bowl, combine butter and remaining garlic; stir until creamy. Spread over bread slices. Place on a greased 15-in. x 10-in. baking pan. Bake at 350° for 5-8 minutes or until lightly toasted.

Sprinkle with Parmesan cheese; top with onion mixture and Gruyere cheese. Broil 3-4 in. from the heat for 1-2 minutes or until bubbly.

Flourless Chocolate Cake with Rosemary Ganache

PREP: 40 MIN.   **BAKE:** 30 MIN. + CHILLING
YIELD: 16 SERVINGS

Moist, dense and chocolaty describe this rich cake. A silky chocolate ganache infused with rosemary really takes this dessert over the top.

Kelly Gardner ★ Alton, Illinois

- 1 pound semisweet chocolate, chopped
- 1 cup butter, cubed
- 1/4 cup dry red wine
- 8 eggs
- 1/2 cup sugar
- 1 teaspoon vanilla extract

GANACHE:

- 9 ounces bittersweet chocolate, chopped
- 1 cup heavy whipping cream
- 2 fresh rosemary sprigs

Line the bottom of a greased 9-in. springform pan with parchment paper; grease the paper. Place on a double thickness of heavy-duty foil (about 18 in. square). Securely wrap foil around pan; set aside.

In a large heavy saucepan, heat the chocolate, butter and wine over low heat until chocolate and butter are melted, stirring constantly. Remove from the heat, and cool to room temperature.

Meanwhile, in a large bowl, beat the eggs, sugar and vanilla until frothy and doubled in volume, about 5 minutes. Fold in chocolate mixture. Pour into prepared pan. Place springform pan in a large baking pan; add 1 in. of hot water to larger pan.

Bake at 350° for 28-32 minutes or until outer edges are set (center will jiggle). Remove springform pan from water bath. Cool completely on a wire rack.

Carefully run a knife around edge of pan to loosen; remove sides of pan. Transfer to a serving platter.

For ganache, place chocolate in a small bowl. In a small saucepan, bring cream and rosemary just to a boil. Remove from the heat; discard rosemary. Pour cream over chocolate; whisk until smooth. Cool slightly, stirring occasionally. Pour over cake. Chill until set.

TO MAKE AHEAD: The cake can be made a day in advance. Remove from the refrigerator 1 hour before serving.

Classic Turkey Dinner

Mushroom-Onion Stuffed Turkey
pg. 41

Smoked Gouda & Raspberry Salads
pg. 42

Brown Butter Brussels Sprouts
pg. 42

Holiday Citrus Sweet Potatoes
pg. 43

Whole Wheat Rolls
pg. 45

Apple Brandy Cheesecake
pg. 45

Mushroom-Onion Stuffed Turkey

PREP: 1 HOUR BAKE: 3-1/2 HOURS + STANDING
YIELD: 14 SERVINGS (9 CUPS STUFFING)

I created this superb mushroom and onion stuffing for turkey, and it became a family favorite almost overnight. The blend of fresh mushrooms, onions, wine and whipping cream provides a unique addition to the traditional bread stuffing.

James Hayes ★ Ridgecrest, California

1	loaf (14 ounces) ciabatta bread, cubed
1-1/2	pounds sliced baby portobello mushrooms
4	small onions, finely chopped
2	celery ribs with leaves, finely chopped
6	tablespoons butter
4	garlic cloves, minced
1	cup white wine or reduced-sodium chicken broth
1	cup reduced-sodium chicken broth
1/4	cup minced fresh parsley
1	tablespoon minced fresh thyme *or* 1 teaspoon dried thyme
1/2	teaspoon salt
1/2	teaspoon pepper
1	cup heavy whipping cream
3/4	cup egg substitute
1	turkey (14 to 16 pounds)

Melted butter

Place bread on a baking sheet; bake at 250° for 25-30 minutes or until lightly toasted.

In a large skillet, saute the mushrooms, onions and celery in butter until tender. Add garlic; cook 1 minute longer. Add wine; bring to a boil. Reduce heat; simmer, uncovered, until liquid is evaporated. Stir in the broth, parsley, thyme, salt and pepper; heat through.

In a large bowl, combine toasted bread and mushroom mixture. In a small bowl, whisk the cream and egg substitute; pour over bread mixture and toss to coat.

Just before baking, loosely stuff turkey with 4 cups stuffing. Place remaining stuffing in a greased 8-in. baking dish; refrigerate until ready to bake. Skewer turkey openings; tie drumsticks together. Place breast side up on a rack in a roasting pan. Brush with melted butter.

Bake, uncovered, at 325° for 3-1/2 to 4 hours or until a meat thermometer reads 180° for the turkey thigh and 165° for the stuffing, basting occasionally with pan drippings. Cover loosely with foil if turkey browns too quickly.

Bake additional stuffing, covered, for 20 minutes. Uncover; bake 20 minutes longer or until lightly browned. Cover turkey and let stand for 20 minutes before removing stuffing and carving turkey. If desired, thicken the pan drippings for gravy.

Angel Place Cards

Prepare Iced Holiday Ornament Cookies (page 120), except use a 3-1/2- to 4-in. angel-shaped cookie cutter. If completely icing cookie, prepare icing as recipe directs, or use icing recipe from Cinnamon Snowflake Ornaments (page 126).

After baking, flip cutouts so their flat sides are up. Cut a purchased shortbread cookie in half. Spread the top of shortbread cookie with some icing; attach to body area of cut-out. Repeat with remaining cutouts for the number of place cards you need. Let stand until set.

Flip cutouts right-side up; decorate as desired with icing. Write the names of your guests on half of cookies. Let stand at room temperature for several hours or until firm.

To assemble place cards, pair up a named angel with an unnamed one. Brush shortbread with some icing; press the cutouts together. Gently place angel on its back; let stand at room temperature for several hours or until firm. Repeat for remaining cookies.

Smoked Gouda & Raspberry Salads

PREP/TOTAL TIME: 20 MIN. **YIELD:** 8 SERVINGS

An exceptional homemade raspberry vinaigrette tops this colorful salad. You'll have bursts of flavor and texture from the smoked Gouda, raspberries and crunchy nuts.

Cheryl Perry ★ Hertford, North Carolina

1/4	cup champagne vinegar
4-1/2	teaspoons sugar
1/4	teaspoon kosher salt
1-1/2	cups fresh raspberries, *divided*
1	package (5 ounces) spring mix salad greens
4	ounces Gouda cheese, shaved
1/3	cup Brazil nuts, chopped and toasted
2	shallots, thinly sliced

Place the vinegar, sugar, salt and 1/4 cup raspberries in a food processor; cover and process until pureed.

Divide salad greens among eight salad plates; top with cheese, nuts, shallots and remaining raspberries. Drizzle with dressing.

Brown Butter Brussels Sprouts

PREP: 30 MIN. **BAKE:** 25 MIN. **YIELD:** 8 SERVINGS

Brussels sprouts really get a special treatment in this recipe. The browned butter adds a richness and the panko bread crumbs a nice crunch.

Lori Hiltenbeitel ★ Dayton, Kentucky

1/4	pound sliced pancetta *or* bacon strips, chopped
6	tablespoons butter, *divided*
2	pounds fresh brussels sprouts, quartered
2	shallots, finely chopped
3/4	cup crumbled Gorgonzola cheese
3/4	cup panko (Japanese) bread crumbs

In a large skillet, cook pancetta over medium heat until crisp. Remove to paper towels with a slotted spoon; drain, reserving drippings.

Add 3 tablespoons butter to drippings in skillet; cook over medium heat for 5-7 minutes or until golden brown. Add the brussels sprouts, shallots and pancetta; toss to coat.

Transfer to a greased 11-in. x 7-in. baking dish. Sprinkle with cheese and bread crumbs. Melt remaining butter; drizzle over top. Bake, uncovered, at 375° for 25-30 minutes or until brussels sprouts are tender.

Holiday Citrus Sweet Potatoes

PREP: 1 HOUR   **BAKE:** 35 MIN.   **YIELD:** 8 SERVINGS

Replace your traditional sweet potato recipe with this new version. The fruit sauce provides a bright—but not too sweet—accent to the sweet potatoes. This side is sure to be enjoyed.

Maureen Akins ★ Kent, Washington

6 large sweet potatoes (about 4-1/2 pounds)
1 can (20 ounces) pineapple chunks
1 tablespoon plus 2 teaspoons cornstarch
2 tablespoons dark brown sugar
1 cup orange juice
1 can (11 ounces) mandarin oranges, drained
1 cup dried cranberries

Scrub and pierce sweet potatoes. Bake at 400° for 45-50 minutes or just until tender. Reduce heat to 350°. When cool enough to handle, peel and cut into 1/2-in. slices. Place in a greased 13-in. x 9-in. baking dish.

Drain pineapple, reserving juices. In a small saucepan, combine cornstarch and brown sugar. Gradually stir in orange juice and reserved pineapple juice. Bring to a boil; cook and stir for 2 minutes or until thickened. Add the pineapple, oranges and cranberries; heat through.

Pour sauce over sweet potatoes. Bake, uncovered, at 350° for 35-40 minutes or until bubbly.

Apple Brandy Cheesecake

PREP: 40 MIN. **BAKE:** 1 HOUR + CHILLING
YIELD: 12 SERVINGS

If you like apple pie, you will also enjoy this cheesecake. Bits of apple are scattered throughout the filling, and a cinnamon-brown sugar streusel is a delightful topping to this impressive dessert.

Marian Platt ★ Sequim, Washington

- 1-1/4 cups graham cracker crumbs
- 1/3 cup ground walnuts
- 1/3 cup butter, melted
- 1/2 teaspoon ground cinnamon

FILLING:
- 4 packages (8 ounces *each*) cream cheese, softened
- 1 cup sugar
- 1 cup chunky applesauce
- 1/4 cup heavy whipping cream
- 1/4 cup apple brandy *or* brandy
- 1 teaspoon ground cinnamon
- 1/4 teaspoon ground nutmeg
- 4 eggs, lightly beaten

TOPPING:
- 3/4 cup all-purpose flour
- 3/4 cup packed brown sugar
- 1/3 cup butter, melted
- 1/2 teaspoon ground cinnamon
- 1/4 teaspoon ground nutmeg

In a bowl, combine the cracker crumbs, walnuts, butter and cinnamon. Press onto the bottom and 1-1/2 in. up the sides of a greased 9-in. springform pan. Place pan on a baking sheet. Bake at 350° for 10 minutes. Cool on a wire rack.

In a bowl, beat cream cheese and sugar until smooth. Beat in applesauce, cream, brandy, cinnamon and nutmeg. Add eggs; beat on low speed just until combined. Pour into crust. Return pan to baking sheet. Bake for 35 minutes.

In a small bowl, combine topping ingredients until crumbly. Carefully sprinkle over hot cheesecake. Bake 25-30 minutes longer or until center is just set.

Cool on a wire rack for 10 minutes. Carefully run a knife around edge of pan to loosen; cool 1 hour longer. Refrigerate overnight.

Whole Wheat Rolls

PREP: 40 MIN. + RISING **BAKE:** 10 MIN. **YIELD:** 2 DOZEN

Even though these are whole wheat rolls, they have a light texture and are soft and tender. This recipe reminds me of lots of happy times with my family.

Wilma Orlano ★ Carroll, Iowa

- 1-1/2 cups boiling water
- 1/3 cup wheat bran
- 3 tablespoons ground flaxseed
- 1-1/2 teaspoons salt
- 1 teaspoon ground cinnamon
- 1/3 cup honey
- 1/4 cup canola oil
- 2 packages (1/4 ounce *each*) active dry yeast
- 1/4 cup warm water (110° to 115°)
- 2 teaspoons sugar
- 1-1/2 cups whole wheat flour
- 2-1/2 to 3 cups bread flour

In a small bowl, pour boiling water over the wheat bran, flaxseed, salt and cinnamon. Add the honey and oil. Let stand until mixture cools to 110°-115°, stirring occasionally.

In a large bowl, dissolve yeast in warm water. Add the sugar, whole wheat flour and wheat bran mixture. Beat on medium speed for 3 minutes. Stir in enough bread flour to form a firm dough.

Turn onto a floured surface; knead until smooth and elastic, about 6-8 minutes. Place in a greased bowl, turning once to grease the top. Cover and let rise in a warm place until doubled, about 1 hour. Punch dough down.

Turn onto a lightly floured surface; divide into 24 pieces. Shape each into a roll. Place 2 in. apart on greased baking sheets. Cover and let rise until doubled, about 30 minutes.

Bake at 375° for 10-15 minutes or until golden brown. Remove from pans to wire racks.

Crown Roast Dinner

Crown Roast with
Plum-Apple Stuffing
pg. 47

Artichoke Tomato Bisque
pg. 49

Tra Vigne Green Beans
pg. 47

Green Salad with
Baked Goat Cheese
pg. 48

Peppermint Red Velvet Cake
pg. 51

Crown Roast with Plum-Apple Stuffing

PREP: 30 MIN.   **BAKE:** 3 HOURS + STANDING
YIELD: 14 SERVINGS

All eyes will be on this impressive roast when you place it on your holiday table. The fruit combination of golden raisins, dried plums and apples nicely complements the pork.

Marie Rizzio ★ Interlochen, Michigan

    1   pork crown roast (14 ribs and about 9 pounds)
    2   tablespoons all-purpose flour
  1-1/2 teaspoons kosher salt
   1/4   teaspoon coarsely ground pepper
   1/2   cup chopped pitted dried plums
    1   cup boiling water
  2-1/2 cups cubed whole wheat bread, toasted
    1   cup chopped peeled tart apple
   1/4   cup golden raisins
   1/4   cup unsweetened apple juice
   1/4   cup butter, melted
    2   tablespoons brown sugar
    1   teaspoon grated lemon peel
   1/4   teaspoon paprika
   1/4   teaspoon ground cinnamon

Place roast, rib ends up, in a large shallow roasting pan. Combine the flour, salt and pepper; rub over roast. Cover rib ends with foil. Bake, uncovered, at 350° for 2 hours.

Meanwhile, place plums in a large bowl. Cover with boiling water; let stand for 5 minutes. Drain. Stir in the bread cubes, apple, raisins, apple juice, butter, brown sugar, lemon peel, paprika and cinnamon.

Carefully spoon stuffing into center of roast. Bake 1 to 1-1/2 hours longer or until a meat thermometer reads 160°. Transfer to a warm serving platter. Remove foil. Let roast stand for 10-15 minutes. Cut between ribs to serve.

Tra Vigne Green Beans

PREP: 15 MIN.   **COOK:** 25 MIN.   **YIELD:** 9 SERVINGS

The title of this recipe translates to "among the vines" in Italian. I was inspired by a restaurant in Napa Valley called, yes, you guessed it, Tra Vigne. The flavors in this dish to me represent the essence of its title.

Jenn Tidwell ★ Fair Oaks, California

    2   pounds fresh green beans, trimmed
   12   bacon strips, chopped
    2   shallots, minced
    4   garlic cloves, minced
   1/2   teaspoon salt
   1/2   teaspoon pepper
    2   cups white grape juice
   1/4   cup white wine vinegar
   1/2   cup minced chives

In a large saucepan, bring 4 cups water to a boil. Add green beans; cover and cook for 5 minutes. Drain and immediately place green beans in ice water. Drain and pat dry.

Meanwhile, in a large skillet, cook bacon over medium heat until crisp. Remove to paper towels with a slotted spoon; drain, reserving 1 tablespoon drippings.

In the same skillet saute shallots in bacon drippings until tender. Add garlic, salt and pepper; cook 1 minute longer. Stir in juice and vinegar. Bring to a boil; cook until liquid is reduced by half.

Add green beans and bacon, cook until heated through. Sprinkle with chives.

TO MAKE AHEAD: Boil the green beans, chill in ice water and drain as directed a day in advance. Store in the refrigerator.

Green Salad with Baked Goat Cheese

PREP/TOTAL TIME: **20 MIN.**   YIELD: **8 SERVINGS**

I combined my favorite parts of a variety of salads to create this masterpiece. The warm baked cheese and crunchy croutons are wonderful complements to the tender salad greens.

Deb Morris ★ Wevertown, New York

- 1 log (4 ounces) fresh goat cheese
- 1 tablespoon olive oil
- 1/4 cup seasoned bread crumbs
- 1 package (5 ounces) spring mix salad greens
- 1/2 cup dried cranberries
- 1/2 cup chopped walnuts, toasted
- 4 bacon strips, cooked and crumbled
- 1/2 cup Caesar salad croutons

Salad dressing of your choice

Cut the goat cheese into eight slices; brush both sides with olive oil and coat with bread crumbs. Place cheese on an ungreased baking sheet. Bake at 350° for 5-6 minutes or until cheese is bubbly.

In a large bowl, combine the salad greens, cranberries, walnuts and bacon; transfer to a platter. Top with cheese and croutons. Serve with dressing of your choice.

TO MAKE AHEAD: This salad is quick to throw together, but to save time, coat the cheese ahead of time and bake just before serving.

Goat Cheese

Bright white goat cheese adds a tangy flavor to dishes. Goat cheese can vary in texture from creamy to crumbly. It will dry out if exposed to air, so tightly wrap any leftovers and store for up to 2 weeks in the refrigerator.

Artichoke Tomato Bisque

PREP: 25 MIN. **COOK:** 30 MIN.
YIELD: 12 SERVINGS (3 QUARTS)

Tomatoes and roasted sweet red peppers pair up to create a fabulous base for this herbed cream soup. Serve it as a first course at holiday dinners, and you'll be amazed at the compliments you receive.

Doty Emory ★ Jasper, Georgia

- 1 can (28 ounces) diced tomatoes, undrained
- 1 jar (7-1/2 ounces) roasted sweet red peppers, drained
- 1 medium onion, chopped
- 4 garlic cloves, minced
- 1 teaspoon *each* dried thyme, basil and oregano
- 1 tablespoon butter
- 1 tablespoon olive oil
- 1 can (14-1/2 ounces) vegetable broth
- 1 can (14-1/2 ounces) reduced-sodium chicken broth
- 1 can (14 ounces) water-packed artichoke hearts, rinsed, drained and chopped
- 1 cup heavy whipping cream
- 1 cup whole milk
- 2 tablespoons sherry
- 2 tablespoons minced fresh cilantro *or* 2 teaspoons dried cilantro flakes
- 2 tablespoons cornstarch
- 1/4 cup cold water
- 1/2 teaspoon Creole seasoning
- 1/8 teaspoon pepper

In a blender, cover and process tomatoes and peppers until pureed. In a large saucepan, saute the onion, garlic, thyme, basil and oregano in butter and olive oil until onion is tender.

Add the broths, artichokes, cream, milk, sherry, cilantro and tomato mixture. Bring to a simmer; cook for 10-12 minutes.

In a bowl, whisk cornstarch and water until smooth; gradually add to saucepan. Cook and stir for 3-5 minutes or until thickened; add Creole seasoning and pepper.

Peppermint Red Velvet Cake

PREP: 20 MIN. **BAKE:** 25 MIN. + COOLING
YIELD: 12 SERVINGS

A couple of years ago, I saw a recipe for a peppermint red velvet cake that called for a cake mix. I prefer homemade cakes, so I developed one from scratch. It is a beautiful, elegant dessert. In the summer, I omit the peppermint and use fresh berries, adding them between the layers and on top of the frosting.

Aimee Fortney ★ Fairview, Tennessee

3/4	cup butter, softened
1-1/2	cups sugar
2	eggs
1/2	cup sour cream
1	bottle (1 ounce) food coloring, optional
1	teaspoon white vinegar
2-1/2	cups cake flour
4	teaspoons baking cocoa
1	teaspoon baking powder
1	teaspoon baking soda
1/2	teaspoon salt
1	cup buttermilk

FROSTING:

2	packages (8 ounces *each*) cream cheese, softened
1/2	cup butter, softened
1-1/2	teaspoons peppermint extract
2	cups confectioners' sugar
1	cup crushed peppermint candies
31	peppermint candies

In a large bowl, cream butter and sugar until light and fluffy. Add eggs, one at a time, beating well after each addition. Beat in sour cream, food coloring and vinegar. Combine the flour, baking cocoa, baking powder, baking soda and salt; add to the creamed mixture alternately with the buttermilk, beating well after each addition.

Transfer to two greased and floured 9-in. round baking pans. Bake at 350° for 25-30 minutes or until a toothpick inserted near the center comes out clean.

Cool for 10 minutes before removing from pans to wire racks to cool completely.

For frosting, beat cream cheese and butter until combined. Beat in extract. Gradually add confectioners' sugar; beat until smooth. Spread frosting between layers and over top and sides of cake. Press crushed candies on top and side of cake. Arrange whole candies around bottom of cake.

TO MAKE AHEAD: Wrap cooled cake layers in plastic wrap and place in a freezer bag. The layers can be frozen for up to 1 month. Unwrap cake; thaw on a wire rack. Proceed as directed.

Create a Menu

Use the recipes that follow to tweak one of the previous menus to suit your needs or to create your own holiday menu. For more fabulous dessert options, page through Enchanting Endings, Spices of the Season and Cookies for Santa.

Spiced Apple-Apricot Chutney

PREP: 30 MIN. **COOK:** 1 HOUR + COOLING **YIELD:** 5 CUPS

Your home will be infused with a fabulous aroma while you're making this nicely spiced fruit chutney. Serve it on the side as an accompaniment for your entree. I love to spread leftovers on turkey slices or on a hot roll.

Aysha Schurman ★ Ammon, Idaho

5	cups chopped peeled tart apples
3	cups chopped fresh apricots
1	cup chopped red onion
1	cup golden raisins
1	cup cider vinegar
1/2	cup packed brown sugar
1/2	cup apple cider *or* juice
1	tablespoon minced fresh gingerroot
2	teaspoons ground cinnamon
1/2	teaspoon salt
1/2	teaspoon ground allspice
1/2	teaspoon ground cardamom
1/2	teaspoon grated lemon peel
1/4	teaspoon pepper

In a large saucepan, combine all ingredients. Bring to a boil. Reduce heat; cover and simmer for 20 minutes.

Uncover; simmer 35-45 minutes longer or until mixture reaches desired consistency, stirring occasionally. Transfer to a bowl; cool. Serve at room temperature or chilled. Cover and store in the refrigerator for up to 2 weeks.

Italian Leg of Lamb

PREP: 25 MIN. + MARINATING
BAKE: 2-1/4 HOURS + STANDING
YIELD: 12 SERVINGS (2 CUPS GRAVY)

I wasn't a big fan of lamb until I tried this wonderful recipe. The sauce has bold lemon flavor, which pairs perfectly with the seasoned roast.

Pauline Morelli ★ Riverside, Rhode Island

- 2/3 cup lemon juice
- 1/2 cup canola oil
- 2 tablespoons dried oregano
- 4 teaspoons chopped anchovy fillets
- 3 garlic cloves, minced
- 2 teaspoons ground mustard
- 1 teaspoon salt
One 2-gallon resealable plastic bag
- 1 boneless leg of lamb (5 to 6 pounds), trimmed
- 1/4 cup all-purpose flour
- 1/4 cup cold water

In a small bowl, combine the first seven ingredients. Pour 2/3 cup marinade into the 2-gallon resealable plastic bag. Add the lamb; seal bag and turn to coat. Refrigerate for 8 hours or overnight. Cover and refrigerate remaining marinade.

Drain and discard marinade from lamb. Place leg of lamb on a rack in a roasting pan. Bake, uncovered, at 325° for 2-1/4 to 2-3/4 hours or until meat reaches desired doneness (for medium-rare, a meat thermometer should read 145°; medium, 160°; well-done, 170°).

Remove meat to a serving platter and let stand, covered, for 15 minutes before slicing.

Meanwhile, pour drippings and loosened brown bits into a 2-cup measuring cup. Skim fat; add reserved marinade and enough water to measure 1-3/4 cups.

In a small saucepan, combine flour and cold water until smooth. Gradually stir in drippings. Bring to a boil; cook and stir for 2 minutes or until thickened. Serve with lamb.

Baked Ribs with Cranberry-Chipotle Sauce

PREP: 15 MIN.   **BAKE:** 2 HOURS 10 MIN.
YIELD: 4 SERVINGS

The first time I made these ribs, they were a hit with my children. In fact, they liked them so much that they clamored for me to make them a couple times a month.

Ruth Lee ★ Troy, Ontario

- 3 tablespoons brown sugar
- 4 teaspoons ground cumin
- 4 teaspoons paprika
- 1 teaspoon salt
- 3 pounds pork baby back ribs, cut into serving-size pieces
SAUCE:
- 1 small onion, chopped
- 1 small garlic clove, minced
- 1 tablespoon canola oil
- 1/4 teaspoon ground ginger
- 1/8 teaspoon ground cloves
- 1/8 teaspoon salt
- 1/8 teaspoon pepper
- 3/4 cup fresh *or* frozen cranberries
- 1/3 cup water
- 1/4 cup orange juice
- 2 tablespoons brown sugar
- 1 tablespoon red wine vinegar
- 1 tablespoon molasses
- 1/2 teaspoon chipotle peppers in adobo sauce
- 1/2 teaspoon adobo sauce

In a small bowl, combine the brown sugar, cumin, paprika and salt; rub over ribs. Transfer to a shallow roasting pan. Cover and bake at 350° for 1-3/4 hours. Drain fat from ribs.

Meanwhile, in a large saucepan, saute onion and garlic in oil until tender. Add the ginger, cloves, salt and pepper; cook for 1 minute. Stir in remaining sauce ingredients. Bring to a boil. Reduce heat; cover and simmer for 15-20 minutes or until berries have popped, stirring occasionally. Cool slightly.

Transfer to a blender; cover and process until blended.

Brush 1/2 cup sauce over ribs; bake 25-35 minutes longer or until tender. Serve with remaining sauce.

Colorful Corn Casserole

PREP: 20 MIN. **BAKE:** 35 MIN. **YIELD:** 12 SERVINGS

I gave a makeover to an old family favorite. I added some color with the onion, peppers and chiles. We liked it so well that this version is now a new family favorite.

Jill Cox ★ Lincoln, Nebraska

- 1/2 cup *each* finely chopped sweet red pepper, orange pepper and red onion
- 1/4 cup plus 1/3 cup butter, *divided*
- 4 ounces cream cheese, cubed
- 1/4 cup milk
- 2 eggs, beaten
- 4 cans (15-1/4 ounces *each*) gold and white corn, drained
- 1 can (4 ounces) chopped green chilies
- 1/2 teaspoon salt
- 1/4 teaspoon coarsely ground pepper
- 1 cup (4 ounces) shredded Monterey Jack cheese
- 1 cup seasoned bread crumbs

In large skillet, saute peppers and onion in 1/4 cup butter until tender. Remove from the heat; stir in cream cheese and milk until blended.

In a large bowl, combine the eggs, corn, chilies, salt and pepper. Stir in pepper mixture and Monterey Jack cheese. Transfer to a greased 13-in. x 9-in. baking dish.

Melt remaining butter; add bread crumbs and toss to coat. Sprinkle over corn mixture. Bake, uncovered, at 325° for 35-40 minutes or until a knife inserted near the center comes out clean.

Focaccia Barese

PREP: 30 MIN. + RISING **BAKE:** 30 MIN. **YIELD:** 8 SERVINGS

This focaccia has been in my mom's family for several generations. It is one of my most-requested whenever I am invited to a party. I am not allowed to attend unless I bring my focaccia!

Dora Travaglio ★ Mount Prospect, Illinois

- 1-1/8 teaspoons active dry yeast
- 3/4 cup warm water (110° to 115°), *divided*
- 1/2 teaspoon sugar
- 1/3 cup mashed potato flakes
- 1-1/2 teaspoons olive oil
- 1/4 teaspoon salt
- 1-3/4 cups bread flour
- 1 tablespoon olive oil, *divided*

TOPPING:
- 2 medium tomatoes, thinly sliced
- 1/4 cup pitted Greek olives, halved *or* sliced
- 1-1/2 teaspoons minced fresh *or* dried oregano
- 1/2 teaspoon coarse salt

In a large bowl, dissolve yeast in 1/2 cup warm water. Add sugar; let stand for 5 minutes. Add the potato flakes, oil, salt, 1 cup flour and remaining water. Beat until smooth. Stir in enough remaining flour to form a soft dough.

Turn onto a floured surface; knead until smooth and elastic, about 6-8 minutes. Place in a greased bowl, turning once to grease the top. Cover and let rise in a warm place until doubled, about 1 hour. Punch dough down. Cover and let rest for 10 minutes.

Place 1-1/2 teaspoons olive oil in a 10-in. ovenproof skillet; tilt pan to evenly coat. Add dough; shape dough to fit pan. Cover and let rise until doubled, about 30 minutes.

With fingertips, make several dimples over top of dough. Brush with remaining oil. Blot tomato slices with paper towels. Arrange tomato slices and olives over dough; sprinkle with oregano and salt.

Bake at 375° for 30-35 minutes or until golden brown.

Stuffed Flank Steak with Mushroom Sherry Cream

PREP: 45 MIN.   **BAKE:** 40 MIN. + STANDING
YIELD: 6 SERVINGS (1-1/2 CUPS SAUCE)

The flavor of this stuffed flank steak is just fabulous. It looks impressive, but it's actually easy to do.

Anthony Dolby ★ Howland, Ohio

1	beef flank steak (1-1/2 pounds)
1/3	cup garlic-herb cheese spread
2	tablespoons prepared pesto
3/4	pound whole fresh mushrooms, thinly sliced, *divided*
2	cups fresh baby spinach
1	jar (7 ounces) roasted sweet red peppers, drained and julienned
1	teaspoon coarsely ground pepper
1/2	teaspoon salt
2	tablespoons olive oil, *divided*
1	shallot, sliced
2	cups reduced-sodium beef broth
1	cup sherry
1	cup heavy whipping cream

Split steak horizontally from a long side to within 1/2 in. of opposite side. Turn steak so that a long side is facing you; open steak so it lies flat. Cover with plastic wrap and flatten to 1/4-in. thickness. Remove plastic.

Spread cheese over steak to within 1/2 in. of edges. Layer with pesto, 1-3/4 cups mushrooms, spinach, red peppers, pepper and salt. Roll up jelly-roll style, rolling steak away from you; tie with kitchen string at 1-1/2-in. intervals. Rub with 1 tablespoon oil.

In a large ovenproof skillet, brown steak on all sides. Bake in the skillet at 375° for 40-50 minutes or until meat reaches desired doneness (for medium-rare, a meat thermometer should read 145°; medium, 160°; well-done, 170°). Remove from the pan; cover and keep warm.

In the same skillet, saute shallot and remaining mushrooms in remaining oil until tender. Add broth and sherry to the pan. Bring to a boil; cook until liquid is reduced by half, about 15 minutes. Add cream and bring to a boil; cook until liquid is reduced by half, about 10 minutes. Serve with sliced beef.

Flattening a Flank Steak

1. Using a sharp, long knife, cut steak horizontally from the long side to within 1/2 in. of opposite side.

2. Open steak so it lies flat; cover with plastic wrap. Flatten to 1/4-in. thickness with the flat side of a meat mallet.

Sour Cream & Onion Potato Bake

PREP: 20 MIN. **BAKE:** 45 MIN. **YIELD:** 9 SERVINGS

This might just turn into your go-to recipe for potatoes when you're hosting a dinner party. You can whip it up before the guests arrive, and it can bake while you attend to them.

Susan Marshall ★ Colorado Springs, Colorado

- 5 cups mashed potatoes
- 1/4 cup 2% milk
- 1/4 cup butter, melted
- 4 green onions, thinly sliced
- 1 cup (8 ounces) reduced-fat sour cream
- 4 eggs, *separated*
- 1 teaspoon salt
- 1 teaspoon lemon juice
- 1/4 teaspoon white pepper
- 1/4 teaspoon paprika

In a bowl, combine the potatoes, milk, butter, green onions, sour cream, egg yolks, salt, lemon juice and white pepper.

In a small bowl, beat egg whites until stiff peaks form; fold into potato mixture. Transfer to a greased 11-in. x 7-in. baking dish; sprinkle with paprika.

Bake at 350° for 45-50 minutes or until golden brown.

Holiday Cauliflower Slaw

PREP: 30 MIN. **COOK:** 10 MIN. **YIELD:** 6 SERVINGS

Vividly colored ingredients help keep this salad in step with the holiday season.

Roxanne Chan ★ Albany, California

- 1 cup walnut halves
- 4 tablespoons olive oil, *divided*
- 2 tablespoons sugar
- 1 tablespoon honey
- 1/4 teaspoon *each* ground allspice, cinnamon and cloves
- 2 cups shredded red cabbage
- 2 cups fresh cauliflowerets
- 1 cup watercress
- 1 cup shredded radicchio
- 1/3 cup dried cranberries
- 1/4 cup chopped red onion
- 2 tablespoons pomegranate juice
- 1 tablespoon red wine vinegar
- 1 tablespoon reduced-fat mayonnaise
- 1 garlic clove, minced
- 1/8 teaspoon salt
- 1/8 teaspoon crushed red pepper flakes
- 2 tablespoons minced fresh mint, optional

In a small skillet, cook the walnuts in 2 tablespoons oil over medium heat for 1 minute. Stir in the sugar, honey, allspice, cinnamon and cloves. Cook 3-4 minutes longer or until sugar is melted and nuts are evenly coated. Spread on waxed paper to cool.

In a large bowl, combine the cabbage, cauliflowerets, watercress, radicchio, cranberries and red onion. In a small bowl, whisk the pomegranate juice, vinegar, mayonnaise, garlic, salt, red pepper flakes and remaining oil. Stir in mint if desired. Pour over cabbage mixture; toss to coat.

Place on a serving platter. Garnish with walnuts.

Sparkling Gelatin Salad

PREP: 15 MIN. + CHILLING **YIELD:** 6 SERVINGS

Fruit really shines through this refreshing gelatin salad.

Cassie Alexander ★ Muncie, Indiana

- 2 envelopes unflavored gelatin
- 1-1/2 cups white grape juice, *divided*
- 1-1/2 cups sweet white wine *or* additional white grape juice
- 1/4 cup sugar
- 1 can (15 ounces) mandarin oranges, drained
- 1 cup green grapes, halved
- 3/4 cup fresh raspberries

In a small saucepan, sprinkle gelatin over 1/2 cup juice; let stand for 1 minute. Heat over low heat, stirring until gelatin is completely dissolved. Stir in the wine, sugar and remaining juice. Cook and stir until sugar is dissolved.

Pour into a 1-1/2-qt. serving bowl. Refrigerate until set but not firm, about 1 hour. Fold in the oranges, grapes and raspberries. Refrigerate until firm.

Baked Fontina Orzo

PREP: 20 MIN. **BAKE:** 25 MIN. **YIELD:** 6 SERVINGS

The pasta orzo makes a nice alternative to rice. If you like, replace the peppers with blanched, diced asparagus.

Gilda Lester ★ Millsboro, Delaware

1	tablespoon butter, softened
1-1/2	cups uncooked orzo pasta
1-1/2	cups (6 ounces) shredded fontina cheese
1/2	cup chopped roasted sweet red peppers
1/2	cup sliced ripe olives, drained
2	eggs
1-1/2	cups whole milk
1/8	teaspoon ground nutmeg

Grease six 10-oz. ramekins or custard cups with butter; set aside. Cook orzo according to package directions; drain. In a large bowl, combine the orzo, cheese, peppers and olives. Spoon into prepared ramekins.

In another bowl, whisk the eggs, milk and nutmeg; pour over orzo mixture. Place ramekins on a baking sheet.

Bake at 350° for 25-30 minutes or until a thermometer inserted near the center reads 160°.

Blood Orange Caprese Salad

PREP: 15 MIN. **COOK:** 20 MIN. + COOLING
YIELD: 6 SERVINGS (2/3 CUP DRESSING)

A colorful twist on the classic Caprese Salad of mozzarella, basil and tomato, this one uses blood oranges in place of the tomato and is flavored with pomegranate instead of basil.

1	cup pomegranate juice
2/3	cup sugar
1-1/2	teaspoons lemon juice
1	tablespoon brown sugar
6	lettuce leaves
4	medium blood oranges, peeled and cut into 1/4-inch slices
1	pound fresh mozzarella cheese, cut into 1/4-inch slices
6	teaspoons olive oil
1/4	cup pomegranate seeds
1/4	teaspoon salt

In a saucepan, bring pomegranate juice, sugar and lemon juice to a boil; cook until reduced by half. Remove from the heat. Stir in brown sugar. Cool to room temperature.

Line six salad plates with lettuce; top with orange and cheese slices. Drizzle each with 1 teaspoon oil and 2 teaspoons pomegranate syrup (save remaining syrup for another use). Sprinkle with pomegranate seeds and salt.

Blood Oranges

The sweet, mellow taste and deep red color make blood oranges an eye-catching addition to many dishes. Use the fruit and juice as you would any other orange. Blood oranges get their red color from a pigment called anthocyanin, which is usually found not in oranges, but in cherries, raspberries and blueberries. Look for blood oranges in your supermarket from November through May.

Seasonal
GET-TOGETHERS

Seasonal Get-Togethers

Enjoy the companionship of family and friends throughout the Yuletide season by hosting a casual party. Three are featured here: Winter Solstice, Retro '50s Cocktail Party and St. Lucia's Brunch. The delightful food and decoration ideas will make each festivity a hit. Let's party!

The winter solstice marks the longest night of the year and has been celebrated throughout the ages as the return of the sun. Many of our Christmas traditions—the Yule log, holly, mistletoe, and the colors red and green—originated from the ancient rituals and symbolism surrounding the winter solstice.

In modern times, the winter solstice is an occasion to slow down during the busy holiday season and reconnect with your family and friends. One way to do that is to host a casual meal like the one that follows. While enjoying dinner, light up your home with the soft glow of candles on the table and set around the house (see the directions for the table lights on page 62).

Winter Solstice Cake

PREP: 50 MIN.   **BAKE:** 20 MIN. + COOLING
YIELD: 16 SERVINGS

Bring some rays of sunshine to your table with a gorgeous lemon cake. This dessert will brighten up any winter's night.

- 2 packages (16 ounces *each*) Betty Crocker pound cake mix
- 4 eggs
- 2/3 cup water
- 2/3 cup thawed lemonade concentrate
- 1/2 cup butter, softened
- 2 teaspoons grated lemon peel

CANDY:
- 1 cup light corn syrup
- 2/3 cup sugar
- 1-1/2 teaspoons lemon extract
- 1/8 teaspoon yellow food coloring

LEMON FILLING:
- 2/3 cup heavy whipping cream
- 2 packages (3 ounces *each*) cream cheese, softened
- 2/3 cup confectioners' sugar
- 1/4 cup lemon curd
- 2 teaspoons grated lemon peel

CREAM CHEESE FROSTING:
- 2 packages (8 ounces *each*) cream cheese, softened
- 1/4 cup butter, softened
- 1/4 cup lemon curd
- 2 teaspoons vanilla extract
- 1/4 teaspoon salt
- 6 cups confectioners' sugar
Yellow edible glitter

In a large bowl, beat the first six ingredients. Transfer to three greased and floured 9-in. round baking pans. Bake at 350° for 20-25 minutes or until a toothpick inserted near the center comes out clean. Cool for 10 minutes before removing from pans to wire racks to cool completely.

Meanwhile, line three greased 15-in. x 10-in. x 1-in. baking pans with parchment paper; set aside.

In a large heavy saucepan, combine corn syrup and sugar. Bring to a boil over medium heat, stirring occasionally.

Cover and cook for 3 minutes to dissolve sugar crystals. Uncover and cook, without stirring, until a candy thermometer reads 300° (hard-crack stage).

Remove from the heat; stir in lemon extract and food coloring (keep face away from mixture, as flavoring is very strong). Immediately drizzle into prepared pans, forming small zigzag shapes. Let cool completely.

For filling, beat cream in a bowl until soft peaks form. In another bowl, beat cream cheese until smooth. Beat in the sugar, lemon curd and lemon peel. Fold in whipped cream.

Place one cake layer on a serving plate; spread with 1 cup filling. Repeat. Top with remaining cake layer.

For frosting, in a large bowl, beat cream cheese, butter, lemon curd, vanilla and salt until smooth. Gradually beat in sugar. Frost top and sides of cake. Break candy into shards; insert into frosting, forming rays of sunlight. Sprinkle cake with edible glitter. Refrigerate leftovers.

Editor's Note: We recommend that you test your candy thermometer before each use by bringing water to a boil; the thermometer should read 212°. Adjust your recipe temperature up or down based on your test.

Making Sunrays

Light up the Winter Solstice Cake with lemon-flavored sunrays. These can be made in advance and stored in an airtight container with sheets of waxed paper between layers. On parchment-lined baking sheets, drizzle/pour hot syrup into zigzag patterns. Let stand until completedly cooled. Carefully peel each ray off the parchment paper and store.

Garlic Chicken Sausage Soup with Cannellini Beans

PREP: 15 MIN. **COOK:** 40 MIN.
YIELD: 6 SERVINGS (2-1/2 QUARTS)

Bursting with fabulous Italian flavors, this hearty soup is sure to chase away winter's chills. Serve with some crusty rolls for a satisfying dinner.

Cheryl Ravesi ★ Milford, Massachusetts

- 1 package (12 ounces) fully cooked Italian chicken sausage links, halved lengthwise and sliced
- 1 medium onion, chopped
- 1 tablespoon olive oil
- 3 garlic cloves, minced
- 2 cans (15 ounces *each*) white kidney *or* cannellini beans, rinsed and drained
- 2 cans (14-1/2 ounces *each*) no-salt-added diced tomatoes
- 2 medium zucchini, quartered and sliced
- 1 can (14-1/2 ounces) reduced-sodium chicken broth
- 8 ounces whole fresh mushrooms, quartered
- 1 cup water
- 1/4 cup prepared pesto
- 1/4 cup dry red wine *or* additional reduced-sodium chicken broth
- 1 tablespoon balsamic vinegar
- 1 teaspoon minced fresh oregano
- 1/2 teaspoon pepper
Grated Parmesan cheese

In a Dutch oven, cook chicken sausage and onion in oil until sausage is browned. Add garlic; cook 1 minute longer.

Stir in the beans, tomatoes, zucchini, broth, mushrooms, water, pesto, wine, balsamic vinegar, oregano and pepper. Bring to a boil. Reduce heat; simmer, uncovered, for 25-30 minutes or until vegetables are tender. Sprinkle with cheese.

Seeded Whole Grain Loaf

PREP: 20 MIN. **BAKE:** 4 HOURS **YIELD:** 1 LOAF (1-1/2 POUNDS, 16 SLICES)

My husband and I like whole grain bread, but not the spongy store-bought whole wheat breads. I drastically altered one of my favorite batter bread recipe to create this earthy bread. It is crunchy, chewy and easy. The add-ins are just suggestions. Sometimes I use pepitas, sesame seeds or even 1/4 cup of a multi-grain hot cereal mix.

Amber Rife ★ Columbus, Ohio

1-1/3 cups warm 2% milk (70° to 80°)
3 tablespoons honey
2 tablespoons canola oil
1-1/4 teaspoons salt
2-2/3 cups whole wheat flour
2 tablespoons old-fashioned oats
4 teaspoons vital wheat gluten
1 tablespoon millet
1 tablespoon sunflower kernels
1 tablespoon flaxseed
1 tablespoon cracked wheat *or* additional flaxseed
1 package (1/4 ounce) active dry yeast

In bread machine pan, place all the ingredients in order suggested by manufacturer. Select basic bread setting. Choose crust color and loaf size if available. Bake according to bread machine directions (check dough after 5 minutes of mixing; add 1 to 2 tablespoons of water or flour if needed).

Winter Solstice Table Lights

Wash and dry one 6-in. x 8-in. and two 3-in. x 7-in. clear glass vases. Cut a piece of white tissue paper for each vase that is 1 in. taller and 1/8 in. wider that the vase. Spray each piece with quilter's basting spray. Let white all-purpose thread fall from a spool of thread, making an open looped design on the tissue paper. Allow loops to extend from the sides but not from the top and bottom of the tissue paper piece. Arrange the thread in desired pattern and then lightly pat thread to hold it in place. Repeat with each piece of tissue paper.

Use a 1-in. flat paintbrush to apply matte-finish decoupage medium to outside of one vase. While vase is still wet, wrap the tissue paper around the vase with the top just below the top rim. The thread will be sandwiched in between. Pat smooth, leaving only small wrinkles or creases. Apply decoupage medium to bottom of vase and adhere tissue paper onto bottom of vase. Stand vase upside down until dry. Repeat with each remaining vase.

Use scissors to trim excess thread from edges from each vase. From tissue paper, cut one 7-1/2-in. circle and two 2-1/2-in. circles. Apply decoupage medium to the bottom of vases and place a matching circle centered on bottom of each. In the same way, adhere a white felt circle to the bottom of each vase. Let dry.

Coil white mini lights; place inside large vase. Place a battery-operated tea light in each small vase.

Swiss Souffle Mushrooms

PREP: 20 MIN. + STANDING **BAKE:** 15 MIN.
YIELD: 32 APPETIZERS

Here's a fresh take on stuffed mushrooms. Each one is topped with a delicate Swiss cheese souffle. These will make your appetizer tray look superb.

Karen Sue Garback-Pristera ★ Albany, New York

2	eggs
32	large fresh mushrooms
1/4	cup butter, *divided*
1	cup soft bread crumbs
3/4	cup shredded Swiss cheese
1/2	cup 2% milk
1/4	teaspoon salt
1/8	teaspoon pepper
1/8	teaspoon ground nutmeg, optional

Separate eggs; let stand at room temperature for 30 minutes. Remove stems from mushrooms and finely chop stems to measure 1 cup; set caps aside. Discard or save remaining mushroom stems for another use.

In a large skillet, saute the chopped mushrooms in 2 tablespoons butter until tender; transfer to a large bowl. Add the bread crumbs, cheese, milk, egg yolks, salt, pepper and nutmeg if desired.

In a large bowl, beat egg whites until stiff peaks form. With a spatula, stir a fourth of the egg whites into mushroom mixture until no white streaks remain. Fold in remaining egg whites until combined. Spoon 1 tablespoon filling into each mushroom cap. Place on greased baking sheets. Melt remaining butter; drizzle over mushrooms.

Bake at 400° for 12-15 minutes or until mushrooms are tender and tops are golden brown.

Preparing Mushrooms

Gently remove dirt by rubbing with a mushroom brush or a damp paper towel. Or quickly rinse under cold water, drain and pat dry with paper towels. Do not peel mushrooms. Trim stems. Mushrooms can be eaten raw, marinated, sauteed, stir-fried, baked, broiled or grilled.

Northwoods Wild Rice Soup

PREP: 20 MIN. **COOK:** 20 MIN.
YIELD: 12 SERVINGS (ABOUT 3 QUARTS)

My sister served this to me for the first time, and it was so scrumptious I just had to have the recipe. The cream cheese gives the soup an ultra smooth texture.

Kim Caputo ★ Cannon Falls, Minnesota

  1   pound sliced fresh mushrooms
  1   cup chopped onion
  2   medium carrots, chopped
1/2   cup butter, cubed
1/2   cup all-purpose flour
1/2   teaspoon salt
1/2   teaspoon pepper
  4   cups reduced-sodium chicken broth
  2   cans (12 ounces *each*) evaporated milk
  2   cups cooked wild rice
  2   cups cubed cooked chicken
  1   package (8 ounces) cream cheese, cubed

In a Dutch oven, saute the mushrooms, onion and carrots in butter until vegetables are tender. Stir in the flour, salt and pepper until blended.

Gradually add broth. Bring to a boil; cook and stir for 2 minutes or until thickened. Stir in the milk, rice, chicken and cream cheese; heat through (do not boil).

Cranberry-Chipotle Spinach Salad

(pictured above)

PREP/TOTAL TIME: 20 MIN.   **YIELD:** 8 SERVINGS

My husband doesn't like cooked spinach, but he enjoys it in salads. I created this salad as a way to serve spinach that we both would like, and I have been making it for years.

Lee Bass ★ Magnolia, Texas

1/2   cup raspberry chipotle sauce
1/2   cup orange juice
  1   cup dried cranberries
 10   cups fresh baby spinach
  3   slices red onion, separated into rings
1/2   cup coarsely chopped walnuts, toasted

In a small bowl, whisk chipotle sauce and orange juice. Stir in cranberries. In a large bowl, combine the spinach, onion and walnuts. Drizzle dressing over salad and toss to coat.

Retro '50s party

Be a bad cat and have a big bash at your pad. Can you dig it? So, get on the horn and invite your buds to the scene. In other words, invite your friends over for a '50s party. Set the mood with food and sounds from the likes of Elvis, The Platters, The Everly Brothers and Nat King Cole. Add '50s atmosphere with retro decorations (see the directions for the Aluminum Tree Wall Hanging on page 67.)

Herbed Cheese Canapes

(pictured at left)

PREP: 30 MIN. + CHILLING   **YIELD:** 40 APPETIZERS

Boursin cheese can be expensive to buy. This budget-friendly homemade version of canapes uses cream cheese instead and is absolutely fabulous.

Debra Chylik ★ Valley View, Ohio

2	packages (8 ounces *each*) cream cheese, softened
1/2	cup butter, softened
2	tablespoons minced chives
2	tablespoons minced fresh parsley
4-1/2	teaspoons dried marjoram
1	tablespoon dried basil
1-1/2	teaspoons dried thyme
1	garlic clove, minced
1/2	teaspoon coarsely ground pepper
1/4	teaspoon salt
40	slices snack rye bread
1	small seedless cucumber, cut into 40 very thin slices
1	medium green pepper, finely chopped
1	jar (2 ounces) red caviar

In a large bowl, combine the first 10 ingredients. Cover and refrigerate for at least 1 hour. Just before serving, spread 1 tablespoon on each bread slice. Top with a cucumber slice, 1/2 teaspoon green pepper and about 1/4 teaspoon caviar.

French 75

PREP/TOTAL TIME: 5 MIN.   **YIELD:** 1 SERVING

French 75 was a drink created at Harry's New York Bar in Paris during WWI. The original version of the drink had a powerful kick, like a French 75 mm artillery gun. This version uses less gin.

1	to 1-1/2 cups ice cubes
3/4	ounce gin
1	tablespoon confectioners' sugar
2	teaspoons lemon juice
3	ounces Champagne, chilled

Fill a shaker three-fourths full with ice. Add gin, sugar and lemon juice. Cover and shake for 10-15 seconds or until condensation forms on outside of shaker. Pour into a chilled Champagne flute; top with Champagne.

Pink Christmas Punch

PREP/TOTAL TIME: 10 MIN.
YIELD: 42 SERVINGS (3/4 CUP EACH)

Here is a real family heirloom recipe. Great-Grandma King was the first person in our family to serve this delicious fruit punch. Its pretty pink color is very festive. She used to set out a Christmas Eve spread at her house every year.

Beth Dewese ★ Plano, Texas

1	can (46 ounces) unsweetened pineapple juice, chilled
5-1/4	cups tropical fruit punch, chilled
1	bottle (32 ounces) cranberry juice, chilled
1	bottle (2 liters) ginger ale, chilled
1	pint strawberry ice cream, softened

In a 8-qt. punch bowl, combine the pineapple juice, fruit punch and cranberry juice. Slowly stir in ginger ale and ice cream. Serve immediately.

Steak House Snack Mix

PREP/TOTAL TIME: 15 MIN.   YIELD: 2-1/2 QUARTS

My family prefers steak and potato type meals. One day we thought it would be great to use steak sauce in a Chex Mix snack. So, I came up with this recipe to satisfy their craving for a steak-like treat.

Jennifer Mitchell ★ Altoona, Pennsylvania

- 4 cups Wheat Chex
- 4 cups Rice Chex
- 2 cups cheese crackers
- 1 cup fat-free miniature pretzels
- 6 tablespoons butter, cut up
- 3 tablespoons steak sauce
- 1 tablespoon Worcestershire sauce
- 1 teaspoon cayenne pepper
- 1 cup French-fried onions
- 1 cup salted peanuts
- 3 teaspoons onion powder
- 2 teaspoons garlic powder

In a large microwave-safe bowl, combine the cereals, crackers and pretzels. In a small microwave-safe bowl, melt butter. Stir in the steak sauce, Worcestershire sauce and cayenne; pour over cereal mixture and toss to coat.

Microwave, uncovered, on high, for 4 minutes, stirring every 2 minutes. Add the fried onions, peanuts, onion powder and garlic powder; toss to coat. Spread onto waxed paper to cool. Store in an airtight container.

Olive-Stuffed Celery

PREP/TOTAL TIME: 25 MIN.   YIELD: 2 DOZEN

My grandmother taught both me and my mom how to make this appetizer. We always serve it at Christmas and Thanksgiving. The stuffing is so yummy that even if you don't normally care for the ingredients on their own, you'll love the end result.

Stacy Powell ★ Santa Fe, Texas

- 1 dill pickle spear plus 1 teaspoon juice
- 3 sweet pickles plus 1 teaspoon juice
- 6 pitted ripe olives plus 1 teaspoon juice
- 6 pimiento-stuffed olives plus 1 teaspoon juice
- 1 package (8 ounces) cream cheese, softened
- 1/3 cup Miracle Whip
- 1/4 teaspoon salt
- 1/4 cup finely chopped pecans, toasted
- 6 celery ribs, cut into 2-inch pieces

Finely chop the pickles and olives; set aside. In a small bowl, beat the cream cheese, Miracle Whip, juices and salt until blended. Stir in the pickles, olives and pecans.

Transfer to a small resealable plastic bag. Cut a small hole in the corner of the bag; pipe or stuff into celery sticks. Store in the refrigerator.

Aluminum Tree Wall Hanging

Those old aluminum trees with the brightly colored bulbs are now antiques and hard to come by. To set the scene of the '50s, make one or several of these aluminum trees to hang on the wall.

For each tree, purchase a 12-in.-wide x 18-in.-high x 1-in.-thick sheet of white Styrofoam and two 12-ft. lengths of silver snowflake tinsel garland.

On one of the short edges of the Styrofoam sheet, measure over 6-in. with a ruler and mark the center. Draw a line from the center mark to each corner on the opposite short edge of the Styrofoam sheet to make a triangle shape. See Fig. 1 below. Cut along each marked line with craft or serrated knife to form the base for a tree. Measure and mark 2 in. intervals down both side edges of the tree as in Fig. 2 below.

With wire cutters, cut an 8-in. length of 12-gauge wire. Bend in U-shape. Insert ends through top quarter section of tree. Twist ends together on back and form a loop for hanging.

Starting at top point, use floral or greening pins to attach garland to front of tree, pinning the garland at each mark. When tree shape is covered, wrap and pin a length of garland around the side and bottom edges of the tree shape. Trim away excess. Add small colored ornaments if desired.

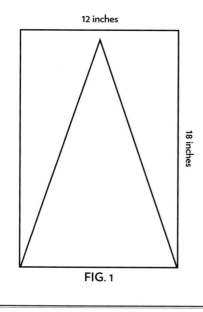

12 inches

18 inches

FIG. 1

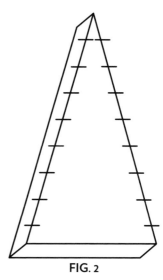

FIG. 2

St. Lucia's Brunch

St. Lucia (or St. Lucy) was a young, wealthy Christian martyr who gave away her dowry to the poor. Her feast, also known as the festival of light, is celebrated in Sweden and other countries and is considered the beginning of the Christmas season. Families celebrate the day by having one daughter dress up in a robe and wreath. She will go around to her family members, offering them coffee and pastries, such as saffron bread (*lussekatter*) and ginger biscuits.

Create a St. Lucia's Centerpiece

A St. Lucia's crown will make a delightful centerpiece when you celebrate the day. Here's how we made the one pictured below.

Insert five evenly spaced candle cups around the top of a 10-in. green Styrofoam floral wreath. Wrap a 48-in. length of artificial wired garland around the sides of wreath and secure as needed with greening or floral pins. With stems all facing in the same direction, add artificial boxwood, bright green and gold glitter berry sprigs as needed to fill in any open spaces. Wrap two 9-ft. lengths of mini star garlands around the wreath. Using a glue gun, glue nine 3/4-in. gold glitter ball ornaments on the wreath. Insert either white tapers or battery-operated tapers into the candle cups.

Tomato & Bacon Brunch Roulade

PREP: 25 MIN.   **BAKE:** 10 MIN.   **YIELD:** 5 SERVINGS

I've served this not only for breakfast and brunch, but even for dinner. If you like, use crispy prosciutto for the bacon.

Beth Klosterboer ★ Miamisburg, Ohio

- 4 eggs
- 6 egg whites
- 2 tablespoons grated Parmesan cheese
- 2 tablespoons heavy whipping cream
- 1/2 teaspoon salt
- Dash pepper
- 1 carton (8 ounces) spreadable sun-dried tomato and basil cream cheese
- 1/4 cup finely chopped oil-packed sun-dried tomatoes
- 6 bacon strips, cooked and crumbled

Line a 15-in. x 10-in. x 1-in. baking pan with parchment paper; grease the paper and set aside.

Place the eggs, egg whites, Parmesan cheese, cream, salt and pepper in a blender; cover and process until frothy. Pour into prepared pan. Bake at 350° for 8-10 minutes or until set.

Remove omelet from oven. Run a knife around edges to loosen; invert onto a kitchen towel. Gently peel off parchment paper.

Spread cream cheese over omelet to within 1 in. of edges. Sprinkle with tomatoes and bacon. Roll up, jelly-roll style, from a long side. Return to baking pan, seam side down.

Bake for 10-15 minutes or until heated through. Cut into slices with a serrated knife.

Braided Orange Wreath

PREP: 40 MIN. + RISING **BAKE:** 25 MIN. + COOLING
YIELD: 12 SERVINGS

All eyes will turn to this gorgeous braid when it is set on the table. This orange-flavored bread will disappear in no time.

Shirley Warren ★ Thiensville, Wisconsin

4	to 4-1/2 cups all-purpose flour
1/2	cup sugar
1	package (1/4 ounce) active dry yeast
1	teaspoon salt
1	cup 2% milk
3	tablespoons butter
3	eggs
3	tablespoons orange juice
1-1/2	teaspoons grated orange peel

GLAZE:

1-1/2	cups confectioners' sugar
2	to 3 tablespoons orange juice
1/2	teaspoon grated orange peel
1/4	cup dried cranberries

In a large bowl, combine 2 cups flour, sugar, yeast and salt. In a small saucepan, heat milk and butter to 120°-130°. Add to dry ingredients; beat just until moistened. Add the eggs, orange juice and peel; beat until blended. Stir in enough remaining flour to form a soft dough.

Turn onto a floured surface; knead until smooth and elastic, about 6-8 minutes. Place in a greased bowl, turning once to grease the top. Cover and let rise in a warm place until doubled, about 1 hour.

Punch dough down. Turn onto a lightly floured surface; divide dough into thirds. Shape each into a 30-in. rope. Braid the ropes; shape into a wreath and pinch ends to seal. Place on a greased baking sheet. Cover and let rise in a warm place until doubled, about 30 minutes.

Bake at 350° for 25-30 minutes or until golden brown. Remove from pan to a wire rack to cool.

In a small bowl, combine the confectioners' sugar, orange juice and peel; drizzle over bread. Sprinkle with cranberries.

Swedish Christmas Rice Pudding

PREP: 10 MIN.   **COOK:** 50 MIN. + CHILLING
YIELD: 9 SERVINGS

Rice pudding is an old-fashioned dessert that is comforting and delicious. The creamy treat has a mild vanilla flavor.

Karla Larson ★ East Moline, Illinois

1	cup water
1/2	cup uncooked long grain rice
Dash salt	
4	cups milk
2/3	cup sugar, *divided*
2	eggs
2	tablespoons butter
1	teaspoon vanilla extract
1/4	teaspoon ground cinnamon

In a heavy saucepan, combine the water, rice and salt; bring to a boil over medium heat. Reduce heat; cover and simmer for 15 minutes or until water is absorbed. Add milk and 1/3 cup sugar; bring to a boil. Reduce heat; simmer, uncovered, for 30-40 minutes or until slightly thickened.

Whisk together the eggs and remaining sugar. Gradually stir 2 cups hot rice mixture into the egg mixture; return all to pan, stirring constantly. Cook and stir over low heat for 3-5 minutes until mixture reaches 160°. Remove from the heat; stir in butter and vanilla. Pour into a serving bowl.

Refrigerate for 2 hours or until chilled. Just before serving, sprinkle with cinnamon.

Hazelnut Coffee

PREP/TOTAL TIME: 15 MIN.   **YIELD:** 4 SERVINGS

The blend of flavors—coffee, hazelnut and a bit of chocolate—make this drink absolutely sensational. It is great for brunch or breakfast, but it's also wonderful for a quiet moment at the end of the day.

Frieda Bliesner ★ McAllen, Texas

4	cups brewed coffee
1/4	cup hazelnut flavoring syrup
1	tablespoon sugar
1/8	teaspoon ground cinnamon
1/4	cup heavy whipping cream
1	tablespoon chocolate hazelnut spread

In a large saucepan, combine the coffee, flavoring syrup, sugar and cinnamon; heat through. Divide coffee mixture among four mugs.

In a small bowl, beat cream and hazelnut spread until thickened. Gently spoon onto tops of drinks. Serve immediately.

Editor's Note: This recipe was tested with Torani brand flavoring syrup. Look for it in the coffee section. Look for chocolate hazelnut spread in the peanut butter section.

Fireside Glogg

PREP: 45 MIN.   **COOK:** 20 MIN.
YIELD: 8 SERVINGS (3/4 CUP EACH)

This traditional Scandinavian recipe is served during the holidays. An aromatic blend of spices flavor this superb wine-based beverage. It is served warmed and its sweet, fruity taste will warm you to your toes.

Sue Brown ★ West Bend, Wisconsin

4	cups port wine *or* apple cider, *divided*
3	cups fresh *or* frozen cranberries, thawed
1/4	cup packed brown sugar
4	orange peel strips (3 inches)
3	cinnamon sticks (3 inches)
5	slices fresh peeled gingerroot
5	cardamom pods
5	whole cloves
4	cups apple cider *or* juice
1/2	cup blanched almonds
1/2	cup raisins

In a large saucepan, combine 3 cups wine, cranberries, brown sugar, orange peel, cinnamon, ginger, cardamom and cloves. Cook over medium heat until berries pop, about 15 minutes. Mash slightly and cook 10 minutes longer.

Strain and discard pulp, orange peel and spices. Return mixture to pan; stir in the cider, almonds, raisins and remaining wine. Bring to a boil. Reduce heat; simmer, uncovered, for 15 minutes.

Fresh Fruit Salad with Pomegranate

(pictured below)

PREP/TOTAL TIME: 25 MIN.   **YIELD:** 8 SERVINGS

The brightly colored fruits in this salad will perk up your morning. This is such a wonderful and easy dish to make.

Laura Brodine ★ Colorado Springs, Colorado

1/3	cup pomegranate juice
1/4	cup sugar
1	teaspoon grated tangerine peel
4	tangerines, peeled and sectioned
2	medium kiwifruit, peeled, halved and sliced
1	medium apple, peeled and cut into 1/2-inch slices
1	large ripe banana, sliced
1	large pear, cut into 1/2-inch slices
1-1/2	cups cubed fresh pineapple
1/2	cup pomegranate seeds

In a small saucepan, combine pomegranate juice and sugar. Bring to a boil; cook until liquid is reduced by half. Stir in tangerine peel; cool to room temperature.

In a large bowl, combine the remaining ingredients. Pour pomegranate mixture over fruit; toss gently to coat. Serve immediately with a slotted spoon.

Light CHRISTMAS

This season is a time for parties, gatherings and indulgent food. With all the delights you're offered, it's easy to gain a few pounds. If you're watching calories, turn to the recipes in this chapter. They are lower in calories and fat than traditional holiday fare but special enough to ring in the holidays deliciously!

Hoisin Pork Chops with Fennel Slaw

PREP: 25 MIN. **GRILL:** 15 MIN. **YIELD:** 4 SERVINGS

My Asian-inspired pork chops are coated with a spicy glaze that gives them a rich, reddish-brown color. The unique fennel slaw goes so well with these chops.

Gilda Lester ★ Millsboro, Delaware

- 1 large fennel bulb, halved and thinly sliced
- 1 cup thinly sliced radicchio
- 1/2 cup julienned green pepper
- 1/4 cup dried currants
- 1 tablespoon capers, drained
- 3 tablespoons lemon juice
- 1 teaspoon honey
- 2 tablespoons olive oil
- 1/4 teaspoon salt
- 1/4 teaspoon hot pepper sauce
- 2 tablespoons chopped fennel fronds
- 1/4 cup ketchup
- 1/4 cup hoisin sauce
- 2 chipotle peppers in adobo sauce, finely chopped
- 1 tablespoon balsamic vinegar
- 1 tablespoon molasses
- 4 bone-in pork loin chops (7 ounces *each*)

In a large bowl, combine the first five ingredients. In a small bowl, whisk the lemon juice, honey, oil, salt and pepper sauce. Pour over slaw mixture and toss to coat. Sprinkle with fennel fronds. Chill until serving.

In a small bowl, combine the ketchup, hoisin sauce, chipotle peppers, balsamic vinegar and molasses. Moisten a paper towel with cooking oil; using long-handled tongs, lightly coat the grill rack.

Grill pork, covered, over medium heat or broil 4 in. from the heat for 4-5 minutes on each side or until a meat thermometer reads 160°, basting occasionally with glaze mixture. Serve with slaw.

NUTRITION FACTS: 1 pork chop with 1 cup fennel slaw equals 395 calories, 16 g fat (4 g saturated fat), 87 mg cholesterol, 813 mg sodium, 31 g carbohydrate, 4 g fiber, 32 g protein. **DIABETIC EXCHANGES:** 4 lean meat, 1-1/2 starch, 1-1/2 fat, 1 vegetable.

Orange Sorbet

PREP: 20 MIN. + FREEZING **YIELD:** 1-1/4 QUARTS

Add a splash of color to the dinner table with this sorbet. The refreshing orange flavor of this frozen delight makes it a great dessert or palate cleanser between courses.

- 1 cup sugar
- 1 cup water
- 12 orange peel strips (1 to 3 inches)

3   cups orange juice
3   tablespoons lemon juice
2   tablespoons orange liqueur *or* vodka

In a small saucepan, bring the sugar, water and orange peel to a boil. Cook and stir until sugar is dissolved; discard orange peel. Set aside to cool.

In a large bowl, combine the orange juice, lemon juice, orange liqueur and reserved sugar mixture. Fill the cylinder of the ice cream freezer; freeze according to the manufacturer's directions.

Transfer to a freezer container; freeze the sorbet for 8 hours or overnight.

TO MAKE AHEAD: This sorbet can be made 2 weeks before serving.

NUTRITION FACTS: 1/2 cup equals 123 calories, 0 fat (0 saturated fat), 0 cholesterol, trace sodium, 29 g carbohydrate, trace fiber, trace protein. **DIABETIC EXCHANGE:** 1-1/2 starch.

Frozen Citrus Bowls

PREP: 25 MIN. + FREEZING   **YIELD:** 12 SERVINGS

Impress your company with these easy-to-make bowls. The thin citrus slices add a magical feel to a special dessert.

1/2   cup sugar
1/2   cup water
2   medium oranges, thinly sliced
2   large lemons, thinly sliced
2   large limes, thinly sliced
Lemon sorbet, orange sorbet and reduced-fat vanilla ice cream

In a small saucepan, bring sugar and water to a boil over medium heat. Reduce heat; simmer, uncovered, for 3-5 minutes or until sugar is dissolved, stirring occasionally. Cool to room temperature.

Line twelve 10-oz. ramekins or custard cups with plastic wrap. Dip fruit slices in sugar mixture; allow excess to drip off. Place alternating slices in bowls, overlapping slightly; cover and freeze for 8 hours or overnight.

Scoop 1/2 cup sorbet or ice cream into each citrus bowl. Cover and freeze until serving.

Gently remove citrus bowls from ramekins. Serve immediately.

NUTRITION FACTS: 1/2 cup ice cream or sorbet equals 131 calories, 1 g fat (1 g saturated fat), 7 mg cholesterol, 22 mg sodium, 30 g carbohydrate, trace fiber, 1 g protein. **DIABETIC EXCHANGE:** 2 starch.

Making a Citrus Bowl

It's easy to make these fun serving bowls. Thinly slice citrus fruit. Here we used oranges, lemons and limes. Line 10-oz. ramekins with plastic wrap. Dip each citrus slice in sugar syrup, then place in the ramekin. Overlap slices, making sure that there is no hole in the bottom of the citrus bowl. Freeze at least 8 hours. Before serving, gently peel plastic wrap from citrus bowls.

Flank Steak with Cranberry Chimichurri

PREP: 25 MIN. + MARINATING **GRILL:** 15 MIN.
YIELD: 8 SERVINGS (1 CUP CHIMICHURRI)

Chimichurri is an Argentinean herb sauce that's served with grilled meats. The addition of cranberries makes this version not only festive, but delectable. It's a wonderful accompaniment to the tender flank steak.

Cheryl Perry ★ Hertford, North Carolina

- 1   medium papaya
- 1   cup chopped sweet onion
- 1   tablespoon ground cumin
- 1/2 teaspoon pepper
- 1   beef flank steak (2 pounds)

CHIMICHURRI:
- 1   cup fresh cilantro sprigs
- 1   cup fresh parsley sprigs
- 1   cup dried cranberries
- 1   shallot, finely chopped
- 2   tablespoons white wine vinegar
- 1   tablespoon smoked paprika
- 3   garlic cloves, minced
- 2   teaspoons minced fresh oregano
      or 3/4 teaspoon dried oregano
- 2   teaspoons grated lime peel
- 1   teaspoon brown sugar
- 1/2 teaspoon salt
- 1/8 teaspoon crushed red pepper flakes
- 1/4 cup olive oil
- 1/4 cup water

Peel and cube papaya, reserving seeds; place papaya and seeds in a food processor. Add the onion, cumin and pepper; cover and process until smooth. Pour into a large resealable plastic bag. Add the beef; seal bag and turn to coat. Refrigerate for 8 hours or overnight.

For chimichurri, place the cilantro, parsley, cranberries, shallot, vinegar, paprika, garlic, oregano, lime peel, brown sugar, salt and pepper flakes in a clean food processor. While processing, gradually add oil and water in a steady stream. Refrigerate until serving.

Drain beef and discard marinade. If grilling, moisten a paper towel with cooking oil; using long-handled tongs, lightly coat the grill rack. Grill beef, covered, over medium heat or broil 4 in. from the heat for 6-8 minutes on each side or until meat reaches desired doneness (for medium-rare, a meat thermometer should read 145°; medium, 160°; well-done, 170°).

Let stand for 5 minutes before cutting steak thinly across the grain. Serve with chimichurri.

NUTRITION FACTS: 3 ounces cooked beef with 2 tablespoons chimichurri equals 293 calories, 15 g fat (4 g saturated fat), 54 mg cholesterol, 222 mg sodium, 17 g carbohydrate, 2 g fiber, 23 g protein.
DIABETIC EXCHANGES: 3 lean meat, 1 starch, 1 fat.

Sweet & Creamy Tomato Soup

PREP: 20 MIN. **COOK:** 25 MIN.
YIELD: 10 SERVINGS (2-1/2 QUARTS)

I live in a remote area of Alaska and have learned to cook from what I have in my pantry. After many years of trial and error, I believe I've perfected this soup. It freezes well and goes great with sourdough bread.

Virgie Scarbro ★ Lgiugig, Alaska

2	large onions, chopped
2	tablespoons butter
4	garlic cloves, minced
4	cans (14-1/2 ounces *each*) diced tomatoes, undrained
1/2	cup water
4	teaspoons brown sugar
2	bay leaves
2	tablespoons minced fresh basil
	or 2 teaspoons dried basil
1/4	teaspoon salt
1/4	teaspoon pepper
2	tablespoons all-purpose flour
3	tablespoons cold water
2	cans (12 ounces *each*) fat-free evaporated milk

Thinly sliced fresh basil leaves, optional

In a Dutch oven, saute onions in butter until tender. Add garlic; cook 2 minutes longer. Stir in the tomatoes, water, brown sugar, bay leaves, basil, salt and pepper. Bring to a boil. Reduce heat; simmer, uncovered, for 10 minutes.

Combine flour and water until smooth. Stir into tomato mixture. Cook and stir for 2 minutes or until thickened. Stir in evaporated milk; heat through (do not boil). Discard bay leaves. Garnish with fresh basil if desired.

NUTRITION FACTS: 1 cup equals 133 calories, 2 g fat (2 g saturated fat), 9 mg cholesterol, 364 mg sodium, 22 g carbohydrate, 3 g fiber, 7 g protein. **DIABETIC EXCHANGES:** 2 vegetable, 1 fat-free milk, 1/2 fat.

Black Forest Cannoli Parfaits

PREP: 25 MIN. + CHILLING **YIELD:** 8 SERVINGS

My family loves cannoli, but I don't love making the shells. These parfaits are an easy way to enjoy the flavor without spending time baking the shells.

Anna Ginsberg ★ Austin, Texas

1	package (16 ounces) frozen pitted tart cherries, thawed
2	tablespoons sugar
1	tablespoon cornstarch
2	teaspoons lemon juice

PARFAIT:

1	carton (15 ounces) reduced-fat ricotta cheese
1	package (8 ounces) fat-free cream cheese
1/4	cup sugar
2	tablespoons maple syrup
2	teaspoons lemon juice
2	teaspoons vanilla extract
2	cups reduced-fat whipped topping
1/3	cup miniature semisweet chocolate chips
20	chocolate wafers, crushed

Drain cherries, reserving liquid in a 1-cup measuring cup. Add enough water to measure 1/3 cup; set aside.

In a small saucepan, combine sugar and cornstarch; stir in reserved cherry juice mixture until smooth. Bring to a boil; cook and stir for 2 minutes or until thickened. Remove from the heat; stir in cherries and lemon juice. Cool.

Place the ricotta, cream cheese and sugar in a food processor; cover and process until smooth. Add the syrup, lemon juice and vanilla; process until combined. Gently fold in whipped topping and chocolate chips.

Place 1 tablespoon crushed wafers in each of eight parfait glasses. Top with 1/3 cup cheese mixture and a heaping tablespoonful of cherry sauce. Repeat layers. Refrigerate for at least 2 hours before serving.

NUTRITION FACTS: 1 parfait equals 300 calories, 9 g fat (6 g saturated fat), 15 mg cholesterol, 291 mg sodium, 46 g carbohydrate, 2 g fiber, 10 g protein.

Lauren's Bouillabaisse

(pictured at left)

PREP: 30 MIN. **COOK:** 20 MIN. **YIELD:** 12 SERVINGS

This golden-colored soup is brimming with an assortment of seafood and is topped with savory sourdough croutons.

Lauren Covas ★ New Brunswick, New Jersey

2/3	cup chopped roasted sweet red pepper, drained
1/4	cup reduced-fat mayonnaise

CROUTONS:
6	slices sourdough bread
1	garlic clove, halved

BOUILLABAISSE:
1	medium onion, chopped
1	tablespoon olive oil
2	garlic cloves, minced
2	plum tomatoes, chopped
1/2	teaspoon saffron threads *or* 2 teaspoons ground turmeric
3-1/2	cups cubed red potatoes
2-1/2	cups thinly sliced fennel bulb
1	carton (32 ounces) reduced-sodium chicken broth
3	cups clam juice
2	teaspoons dried tarragon
24	fresh littleneck clams
24	fresh mussels, scrubbed and beards removed
1	pound red snapper fillet, cut into 2-inch pieces
3/4	pound uncooked large shrimp, peeled and deveined
1/4	cup minced fresh parsley

Place red pepper and mayonnaise in a food processor; cover and process until smooth. Refrigerate until serving.

For croutons, rub one side of each bread slice with garlic; discard garlic. Cut bread slices in half; place on an ungreased baking sheet. Bake at 400° for 4-5 minutes on each side or until lightly browned.

In a stockpot, saute onion in oil until tender. Add garlic; cook 1 minute longer. Reduce heat; stir in tomatoes and saffron. Add the potatoes, fennel, broth, clam juice and tarragon. Bring to a boil. Reduce heat; simmer, uncovered, for 10-12 minutes or until potatoes are almost tender.

Add the clams, mussels, snapper and shrimp. Cook, stirring occasionally, for 10-15 minutes or until clams and mussels open and fish flakes easily with a fork. Discard any unopened clams or mussels. Spoon into bowls; sprinkle with parsley. Spread pepper mayo over croutons; serve with bouillabaisse.

NUTRITION FACTS: 1-2/3 cups with 2 teaspoons spread on 1/2 slice of bread equals 239 calories, 5 g fat (1 g saturated fat), 70 mg cholesterol, 684 mg sodium, 23 g carbohydrate, 2 g fiber, 24 g protein. **DIABETIC EXCHANGES:** 3 lean meat, 1-1/2 starch, 1/2 fat.

Tomato Shrimp Fettuccine

PREP/TOTAL TIME: 30 MIN. **YIELD:** 4 SERVINGS

Easy-to-prepare shrimp get a spicy twist with the addition of crushed red pepper flakes. Adjust the pepper flakes if you'd prefer it milder.

Julie Berger ★ Chandler, Arizona

6	ounces uncooked fettuccine
1	medium onion, chopped
1	tablespoon olive oil
3	garlic cloves, minced
1/2	cup reduced-sodium chicken broth
1/2	cup white wine *or* additional reduced-sodium chicken broth
3	tablespoons lemon juice
1	pound uncooked medium shrimp, peeled and deveined
3	plum tomatoes, seeded and chopped
1/2	teaspoon salt
1/4	teaspoon crushed red pepper flakes
1/4	cup minced fresh basil

Cook fettuccine according to package directions.

Meanwhile, in a large skillet, saute onion in oil until tender. Add garlic; cook 1 minute longer. Stir in the broth, wine and lemon juice. Bring to a boil; cook until liquid is reduced by half.

Add the shrimp, tomatoes, salt and pepper flakes. Cook, uncovered, over medium heat for 5-6 minutes or until shrimp turn pink. Stir in basil. Drain pasta; toss with shrimp mixture.

NUTRITION FACTS: 1-1/4 cups equals 315 calories, 6 g fat (1 g saturated fat), 138 mg cholesterol, 519 mg sodium, 38 g carbohydrate, 3 g fiber, 26 g protein. **DIABETIC EXCHANGES:** 3 lean meat, 2 starch, 1 vegetable.

In a small skillet, saute garlic in remaining oil for 1 minute. Add vinegar and pepper flakes; bring to a boil. Pour over salad and toss to coat. Sprinkle with sesame seeds. Serve immediately.

NUTRITION FACTS: 1 cup equals 141 calories, 8 g fat (1 g saturated fat), 0 cholesterol, 255 mg sodium, 13 g carbohydrate, 4 g fiber, 6 g protein. **DIABETIC EXCHANGES:** 1-1/2 fat, 1 vegetable, 1/2 starch.

Sesame Broccoli Florets

PREP/TOTAL TIME: 20 MIN.   **YIELD:** 4 SERVINGS

This side is so easy to jazz up! If you like, add some strips of sweet yellow or red pepper, or toss in some chopped cilantro for a tangy kick.

Kathryn White ★ Pinehurst, North Carolina

- 3 garlic cloves, minced
- 1 tablespoon minced fresh gingerroot
- 1 tablespoon olive oil
- 4-1/2 cups fresh broccoli florets
- 2 tablespoons reduced-sodium soy sauce
- 1 teaspoon sesame seeds, toasted
- 1 teaspoon sesame oil
- 1/4 teaspoon crushed red pepper flakes

In a large skillet or wok, stir-fry garlic and ginger in olive oil until tender. Add the broccoli, soy sauce, sesame seeds, sesame oil and pepper flakes; stir-fry 4 minutes longer. Cover and cook for 3-4 minutes or until broccoli is tender.

NUTRITION FACTS: 3/4 cup equals 76 calories, 5 g fat (1 g saturated fat), 0 cholesterol, 329 mg sodium, 6 g carbohydrate, 3 g fiber, 3 g protein. **DIABETIC EXCHANGES:** 1 vegetable, 1 fat.

Wilted Shiitake Spinach Salad

PREP: 40 MIN.   **YIELD:** 8 SERVINGS

Spinach salad takes on an Asian flair with shiitake mushrooms, baby corn, sesame oil and edamame. A warm rice vinegar dressing and a sprinkling of sesame seeds complete the taste experience.

Roxanne Chan ★ Albany, California

- 1 pound sliced fresh shiitake mushrooms
- 1/2 teaspoon salt
- 1/4 teaspoon pepper
- 2 tablespoons sesame oil, *divided*
- 1 cup frozen shelled edamame
- 6 cups fresh baby spinach
- 1 medium mango, peeled and sliced
- 1 cup canned baby corn (cobs cut in half)
- 1/4 cup sliced radishes
- 1/4 cup thinly sliced seeded cucumber
- 1/4 cup minced fresh cilantro
- 1/4 cup salted roasted almonds, chopped
- 1 green onion, thinly sliced
- 1 garlic clove, minced
- 3 tablespoons rice vinegar
- 1/4 teaspoon crushed red pepper flakes
- 3 tablespoons sesame seeds, toasted

In a large skillet, saute mushrooms with salt and pepper in 1 tablespoon oil until tender. Meanwhile, cook edamame according to package directions. Set aside.

In a salad bowl, combine the spinach, mango, corn, radishes, cucumber, cilantro, almonds, onion, mushrooms and edamame.

What is Edamame?

Edamame is the Japanese name for fresh soybeans. You can buy these green gems fresh from late spring to early fall, or frozen shelled or unshelled year-round. Edamame is a nutrient-packed food. It's a complete protein, which means it contains all the essential amino acids. It's also rich in fiber, vitamin K, many of the B vitamins, iron, magnesium and isoflavones. You can use edamame in salads, soups and vegetable dishes, or enjoy it for a healthy snack.

Roasted Pork Loin with Fig Sauce

PREP: 1 HOUR **BAKE:** 1-1/2 HOURS
YIELD: 16 SERVINGS (6-1/4 CUPS SAUCE)

Pairing pork roast with fruit is a classic preparation, but this recipe gives it an superb twist, pairing it with figs. Family and friends with be thrilled with the wonderful combination. If you have any figs left over, try the Spiced Figs Poached in Wine, page 82, for dessert.

Rian Macdonald ★ Powder Springs, Georgia

- 1 pound dried figs, quartered
- 1 cup sherry *or* reduced-sodium chicken broth
- 1 medium lemon, sliced
- 1 cinnamon stick (3 inches)
- 2 whole cloves
- 1 boneless rolled pork loin roast (4 to 5 pounds)
- 1 teaspoon salt
- 1/4 teaspoon ground cinnamon
- 1/4 teaspoon pepper
- 1/2 cup orange juice
- 1/4 cup honey
- 2 tablespoons cornstarch
- 2 cups reduced-sodium chicken broth

In a large saucepan, combine the first five ingredients. Bring to a boil. Reduce heat; simmer, uncovered, for 10 minutes. Remove from the heat. Cover and steep for 1 hour. Strain figs, discarding the lemon, cinnamon stick and cloves. Reserve liquid and set aside.

Sprinkle roast with salt, ground cinnamon and pepper. Place roast on a rack in a shallow roasting pan. Bake, uncovered, at 350° for 1 hour. In a small bowl, combine the orange juice, honey and reserved liquid; brush over pork. Bake 30-60 minutes longer or until a meat thermometer reads 160°, basting occasionally.

Remove meat to a serving platter; keep warm. Skim fat from cooking juices; transfer to a large saucepan. Add figs. Combine cornstarch and broth until smooth. Gradually stir into the pan. Bring to a boil; cook and stir for 2 minutes or until thickened. Serve with pork.

NUTRITION FACTS: 3 ounces cooked pork with 1/3 cup sauce equals 249 calories, 5 g fat (2 g saturated fat), 56 mg cholesterol, 256 mg sodium, 25 g carbohydrate, 4 g fiber, 23 g protein. **DIABETIC EXCHANGES:** 3 lean meat, 1 fruit, 1/2 starch.

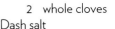

　　2　whole cloves
Dash salt
　　10　ounces dried figs, halved
Reduced-fat vanilla ice cream *or* plain Greek yogurt, optional

In a large saucepan, combine the first eight ingredients. Stir in figs. Bring to a boil. Reduce heat; cover and simmer for 35-45 minutes or until the figs are tender. Remove figs and set aside.

　　Bring poaching liquid to a boil; cook until liquid is reduced to about 1/2 cup. Strain into a small bowl; add figs. Cool. Serve with ice cream or yogurt if desired.

TO MAKE AHEAD: The spiced figs can be made several days before serving. Cover and refrigerate until using.

NUTRITION FACTS: 1/4 cup (calculated without ice cream or yogurt) equals 142 calories, trace fat (0 saturated fat), 0 cholesterol, 25 mg sodium, 31 g carbohydrate, 4 g fiber, 1 g protein. **DIABETIC EXCHANGE:** 1-1/2 starch.

Spiced Figs Poached in Wine

PREP: 15 MIN.　**COOK:** 50 MIN.　**YIELD:** 8 SERVINGS

If you haven't had figs before, this is a delicious way to introduce yourself to them. The flavors from the spices and the wine blend together to nicely complement the figs in this change-of-pace dessert.

　　2　cups dry red wine
　1/4　cup sugar
　1/4　cup balsamic vinegar
　　1　tablespoon lemon juice
　　1　cinnamon stick (3 inches)
　　1　lemon peel strip

Dried Figs

There are hundreds of varieties of figs, but Calimyrna, Mission and Kalamata are the dried figs most readily available in the supermarket. Look for them in the dried fruit aisle or produce section.

We used dried Calimyrna figs in this recipe. They have a golden color and a sweet, nutty, delicate, almost floral flavor. Mission or Black Mission figs have purplish black skins and have an intense, chewy sweetness. Kalamata dried figs are from the Kalamata region of Greece and have a golden color and a sweet flavor.

Any leftover figs can be eaten as a snack, or chopped and sprinkled on salads, hot breakfast cereal, rice and couscous. Also try chopped figs as a replacement for raisins or dried cranberries in baked goods.

Figs are also a good source of calcium, potassium, magnesium, iron, copper, manganese and fiber.

Cran-Apple Wild Rice

PREP: 10 MIN. **COOK:** 25 MIN. **YIELD:** 6 SERVINGS

If you'd like an alterative to stuffing, try my delightful wild rice side. It has flecks of red and touch of sweetness from dried cranberries. The rice goes great with a variety of meats and poultry, and your guests will love it.

Debra Keil ★ Owasso, Oklahoma

- 1 cup dried cranberries
- 1 cup orange juice
- 1 package (6 ounces) long grain and wild rice mix
- 2 medium onions, coarsely chopped
- 2 teaspoons brown sugar
- 2 tablespoons butter
- 1 medium tart apple, diced
- 1/2 teaspoon ground cinnamon
- 1 tablespoon grated orange peel

In a 2-qt. microwave-safe dish, combine cranberries and orange juice. Cover and cook on high for 2 minutes; set aside. Meanwhile, prepare rice mix according to package directions.

In a large skillet, saute onions and brown sugar in butter for 5-6 minutes. Stir in apple and cinnamon. Reduce heat to medium-low; cook for 25-30 minutes or until onions are caramel in color, stirring occasionally.

Drain cranberries; discard juice. Stir in the rice, onion mixture and orange peel.

NUTRITION FACTS: 3/4 cup equals 250 calories, 6 g fat (4 g saturated fat), 15 mg cholesterol, 423 mg sodium, 48 g carbohydrate, 3 g fiber, 4 g protein.

Roasted Sweet Potato Salad

PREP: 20 MIN. **BAKE:** 30 MIN. **YIELD:** 6 SERVINGS

Tender sweet potatoes are tossed with crunchy nuts and chewy dried cherries for a colorful burst of flavors and delightful textures.

Fran Fehling ★ Staten Island, New York

    4   cups cubed peeled sweet potatoes
    1   tablespoon olive oil
  1/2   cup chopped walnuts, toasted
  1/3   cup dried cherries, chopped
  1/4   cup minced fresh parsley
    2   tablespoons reduced-fat mayonnaise
4-1/2   teaspoons white vinegar
    1   tablespoon honey
  1/2   teaspoon grated lime peel
  1/4   teaspoon salt

Place potatoes in a 15-in. x 10-in. x 1-in. baking pan coated with cooking spray. Drizzle with oil; toss to coat. Bake at 400° for 30-45 minutes or until tender. Cool to room temperature.

In a large bowl, combine the walnuts, cherries, parsley and potatoes. In a small bowl, combine the mayonnaise, vinegar, honey, lime peel and salt. Pour over potato mixture and toss to coat. Serve warm or cold.

TO MAKE AHEAD: Roast the sweet potatoes the day before. Cover and refrigerate overnight. To serve warm, reheat in the microwave.

NUTRITION FACTS: 1/2 cup equals 211 calories, 10 g fat (1 g saturated fat), 2 mg cholesterol, 189 mg sodium, 28 g carbohydrate, 4 g fiber, 3 g protein. **DIABETIC EXCHANGES:** 2 starch, 1 fat.

Garlic-Parmesan Mashed Cauliflower

PREP: 30 MIN. **BAKE:** 25 MIN. **YIELD:** 4 SERVINGS

Here's an alternative to mashed potatoes. With the addition of sour cream and Parmesan cheese, it's simply delicious.

Amy Green ★ Carrollton, Texas

    1   medium head cauliflower, broken into florets
    2   garlic cloves, peeled
  1/4   cup 2% milk
  1/4   cup sour cream
  1/4   cup grated Parmesan cheese
  1/4   teaspoon salt
  1/4   teaspoon pepper

Place 1 in. of water in a large saucepan; add cauliflower and garlic. Bring to a boil. Reduce heat; cover and simmer for 10-12 minutes or until crisp-tender. Drain and cool slightly. Transfer to a blender; add the remaining ingredients. Cover and process until smooth.

Spoon into a 1-qt. baking dish coated with cooking spray. Bake, uncovered, at 350° for 25-30 minutes or until heated through and top is lightly browned.

NUTRITION FACTS: 3/4 cup equals 98 calories, 4 g fat (3 g saturated fat), 16 mg cholesterol, 280 mg sodium, 10 g carbohydrate, 4 g fiber, 6 g protein. **DIABETIC EXCHANGES:** 1 vegetable, 1 fat.

Jeweled Holiday Salads

PREP/TOTAL TIME: 30 MIN. **YIELD:** 6 SERVINGS

Pomegranate seeds add a holiday touch to a red and green salad. The seeds look like glistening jewels.

Hollyan Battiste ★ Barrington, New Jersey

    1   cup fresh raspberries
  1/4   cup white balsamic vinegar
    1   tablespoon lime juice
    1   tablespoon honey
  1/4   cup canola oil
SALAD:
    1   bunch romaine, torn
    1   cup seedless red grapes, halved
    1   cup fresh raspberries
  1/2   small red onion, thinly sliced
  1/2   cup pomegranate seeds
  1/3   cup chopped walnuts, toasted

Combine the first four ingredients in a blender; cover and process until smooth. While processing, gradually add oil in a steady stream. Chill until serving.

Divide romaine among six serving plates; top with grapes, raspberries, onion, pomegranate seeds and walnuts. Drizzle with dressing.

TO MAKE AHEAD: Prepare salad dressing a day in advance; mix well before serving.

NUTRITION FACTS: 1 serving equals 202 calories, 14 g fat (1 g saturated fat), 0 cholesterol, 9 mg sodium, 19 g carbohydrate, 5 g fiber, 3 g protein.

Citrus Ginger-Carrot Soup

PREP: 25 MIN.　**COOK:** 30 MIN.　**YIELD:** 5 SERVINGS

The bright orange color of my cream soup gives a festive start to a holiday meal. The carrot, ginger and orange juice blend together to deliver a wonderfully flavored soup.

Jenn Tidwell ★ Fair Oaks, California

- 1　medium onion, chopped
- 1　tablespoon canola oil
- 3　garlic cloves, minced
- 1　pound medium carrots, thinly sliced
- 1　tablespoon minced fresh gingerroot
- 1/4　teaspoon pepper
- 2　cans (14-1/2 ounces *each*) reduced-sodium chicken broth
- 1/2　cup orange juice
- 1　bay leaf
- 1/4　cup reduced-fat sour cream
- 2　tablespoons minced fresh cilantro

In a large saucepan, saute onion in oil until tender. Add garlic; cook 2 minutes longer. Add the carrots, ginger and pepper; cook for 2 minutes.

Stir in the broth, orange juice and bay leaf. Bring to a boil. Reduce heat; cover and simmer for 20-25 minutes or until carrots are tender. Discard bay leaf. Cool slightly.

In a blender, process soup in batches until smooth. Return all to pan and heat through. Garnish with sour cream and cilantro.

NUTRITION FACTS: 1 cup equals 117 calories, 4 g fat (1 g saturated fat), 4 mg cholesterol, 546 mg sodium, 17 g carbohydrate, 3 g fiber, 5 g protein.
DIABETIC EXCHANGES: 1 starch, 1 vegetable, 1/2 fat.

Turkey in Cognac Cream Sauce

PREP: 20 MIN.   **COOK:** 20 MIN.   **YIELD:** 4 SERVINGS

I found this recipe in a magazine and over the years have adjusted it to suit my family's taste. It is special enough for company and easy enough for a weeknight meal.

Virginia Anthony ★ Jacksonville, Florida

1	package (17.6 ounces) turkey breast cutlets
1/4	teaspoon plus 1/8 teaspoon salt, *divided*
1/4	teaspoon coarsely ground pepper
2	tablespoons mustard seeds, crushed
4-1/2	teaspoons olive oil, *divided*
1-1/2	cups sliced fresh mushrooms
1	shallot, finely chopped
1	garlic clove, minced
1/3	cup reduced-sodium chicken broth
3	tablespoons Cognac *or* 3 tablespoons brandy
1	plum tomato, seeded and chopped
1/4	cup half-and-half cream
4-1/2	teaspoons minced fresh basil

Sprinkle turkey with 1/4 teaspoon salt and pepper; press on mustard seeds. In a large nonstick skillet over medium heat, cook turkey in 3 teaspoons oil in batches for 2-3 minutes on each side or until no longer pink. Remove and keep warm.

In the same skillet, saute mushrooms and shallot in remaining oil until tender. Add garlic; cook 1 minute longer. Remove from the heat; stir in broth and Cognac, stirring to loosen browned bits from pan. Add tomato and cream. Bring to a boil; cook until liquid is reduced by half. Stir in basil and remaining salt. Serve with turkey.

NUTRITION FACTS: 4 ounces cooked turkey with 1/3 cup sauce equals 260 calories, 9 g fat (2 g saturated fat), 85 mg cholesterol, 341 mg sodium, 6 g carbohydrate, 1 g fiber, 34 g protein. **DIABETIC EXCHANGES:** 4 lean meat, 1 fat, 1/2 starch.

Thyme Butternut Squash

PREP: 1-1/4 HOURS   **BAKE:** 35 MIN.   **YIELD:** 9 SERVINGS

This comforting and savory side is spiced with a pleasant combination of cinnamon, nutmeg and mace.

Eleanor Davis ★ Sun Lakes, Arizona

- 1 large butternut squash (5 to 6 pounds)
- 1 tablespoon brown sugar
- 1 tablespoon 2% milk
- 1 tablespoon orange juice concentrate
- 1 tablespoon butter
- 1 tablespoon maple syrup
- 1 tablespoon honey
- 1 teaspoon grated orange peel
- 1 teaspoon dried thyme
- 1 teaspoon ground cinnamon
- 1/2 teaspoon salt
- 1/4 teaspoon ground nutmeg
- 1/4 teaspoon ground mace
- 1/4 teaspoon pepper

Cut squash in half; discard seeds. Place squash cut side down in a 13-in. x 9-in. baking pan; add 1/2 in. of hot water. Cover and bake at 350° for 55-65 minutes or until squash is tender. Cool to room temperature.

Meanwhile, in a large bowl, combine the remaining ingredients. Remove squash from shell and add to bowl; mash until smooth.

Transfer to an 8-in. square baking dish coated with cooking spray. Bake at 350° for 35-45 minutes or until heated through.

NUTRITION FACTS: 3/4 cup equals 141 calories, 2 g fat (1 g saturated fat), 3 mg cholesterol, 151 mg sodium, 33 g carbohydrate, 8 g fiber, 2 g protein. **DIABETIC EXCHANGE:** 1-1/2 starch.

Fresh Pear Cake

PREP: 25 MIN.   **BAKE:** 45 MIN. + COOLING
YIELD: 16 SERVINGS

Old-fashioned pear spice cake is a wonderful ending to a meal. It's not too heavy or rich, and the moist treat is brimming with flavor.

Audrey Golden ★ Cary, North Carolina

- 1-1/2 cups sugar
- 3/4 cup (6 ounces) fat-free plain yogurt
- 1/2 cup canola oil
- 4 egg whites
- 1 egg
- 3 cups all-purpose flour
- 1-1/2 teaspoons baking soda
- 1-1/2 teaspoons ground cinnamon
- 1 teaspoon salt
- 1/2 teaspoon ground nutmeg
- 1/2 teaspoon ground cloves
- 2 cups chopped peeled fresh pears
- 1/3 cup chopped pecans
- 1 teaspoon confectioners' sugar

Coat a 10-in. fluted tube pan with cooking spray and sprinkle with flour. In a large bowl, beat the sugar, yogurt, oil, egg whites and egg until well blended. Combine the flour, baking soda, cinnamon, salt, nutmeg and cloves; gradually beat into yogurt mixture until blended. Stir in pears and pecans.

Transfer to prepared pan. Bake at 350° for 45-55 minutes or until a toothpick inserted near the center comes out clean. Cool the cake for 10 minutes before removing from pan to a wire rack to cool completely. Dust with confectioner's sugar.

NUTRITION FACTS: 1 slice equals 264 calories, 9 g fat (1 g saturated fat), 13 mg cholesterol, 291 mg sodium, 42 g carbohydrate, 2 g fiber, 5 g protein.

Almond Blondies

PREP: 15 MIN.   **BAKE:** 25 MIN. + COOLING
YIELD: 16 SERVINGS

These make a nice change from typical chocolate brownies. When I bake up a batch, they never last long at my house.

Cindy Pruitt ★ Grove, Oklahoma

- 2 eggs
- 1/2 cup sugar
- 1/2 cup packed brown sugar
- 1/3 cup butter, melted
- 1 teaspoon vanilla extract
- 1/4 teaspoon almond extract
- 1-1/3 cups all-purpose flour
- 1/2 teaspoon baking powder
- 1/4 teaspoon salt
- 1/4 cup chopped almonds

In a large bowl, beat the eggs, sugar and brown sugar for 3 minutes. Add butter and extracts; mix well. Combine the flour, baking powder and salt. Gradually add to the creamed mixture beating just until blended. Fold in almonds.

Pour into an 8-in. square baking pan coated with cooking spray. Bake at 350° for 25-30 minutes or until a toothpick inserted near the center comes out clean. Cool on a wire rack. Cut into squares.

NUTRITION FACTS: 1 bar equals 143 calories, 6 g fat (3 g saturated fat), 36 mg cholesterol, 88 mg sodium, 21 g carbohydrate, 1 g fiber, 2 g protein. **DIABETIC EXCHANGES:** 1-1/2 starch, 1 fat.

Chocolate Espresso Cake

(pictured at left)

PREP: 30 MIN.   **BAKE:** 15 MIN. + COOLING
YIELD: 14 SERVINGS

You can have your cake and eat it, too, with this lower-in-calorie but rich-tasting treat. This single-layer chocolate cake is draped with a fantastic cherry sauce.

- 2 eggs
- 2 egg whites
- 1/2 cup buttermilk
- 1/3 cup strong brewed coffee
- 3 tablespoons canola oil
- 1 teaspoon vanilla extract
- 1 cup all-purpose flour
- 2/3 cup baking cocoa
- 1/2 cup packed brown sugar
- 1-1/2 teaspoons baking powder
- 1/4 teaspoon baking soda
- 1/4 teaspoon salt

CHERRY TOPPING:

- 1/2 cup cherry juice blend
- 1/2 cup port wine *or* additional cherry juice blend
- 2/3 cup dried tart cherries
- 2 tablespoons honey

Dash salt

- 1 package (12 ounces) frozen pitted dark sweet cherries, thawed and halved
- 1 tablespoon cornstarch
- 2 tablespoons water
- 1/2 teaspoon almond extract
- 1 cup sweetened whipped cream

Coat a 9-in. round baking pan with cooking spray and sprinkle with flour. In a large bowl, beat the eggs, egg whites, buttermilk, coffee, oil and vanilla until well blended. Combine the flour, cocoa, brown sugar, baking powder, baking soda and salt; gradually beat into egg mixture until blended.

Transfer to prepared pan. Bake at 350° for 15-20 minutes or until a toothpick inserted near the center comes out clean. Cool for 10 minutes before removing from pan to a wire rack. Cool completely.

In a saucepan, combine the cherry juice, wine, dried cherries, honey and salt. Bring to a boil. Reduce heat; simmer, uncovered, for 8-11 minutes or until liquid is reduced by half. Stir in dark cherries; cook and stir for 2 minutes.

Combine cornstarch and water; whisk into cherry mixture. Cook and stir for 1-2 minutes or until thickened. Remove from the heat; stir in extract. Cool.

Serve cake with cherry topping; garnish with whipped cream.

NUTRITION FACTS: 1 slice with 2 tablespoons topping and 1 tablespoon whipped cream equals 213 calories, 8 g fat (3 g saturated fat), 42 mg cholesterol, 153 mg sodium, 31 g carbohydrate, 2 g fiber, 4 g protein. **DIABETIC EXCHANGES:** 2 starch, 1-1/2 fat.

Skinny Eggplant Parmesan

PREP: 45 MIN.   **BAKE:** 30 MIN. + STANDING
YIELD: 4 SERVINGS

You save a lot of calories by baking eggplant patties. I like to add some strips of sweet red pepper while sauteing the mushrooms for a pop of color.

Mary Bannister ★ Albion, New York

- 1/2 cup fat-free milk
- 1 cup dry bread crumbs
- 2 teaspoons Italian seasoning, *divided*
- 1 large eggplant, peeled and cut into 1/2-inch slices
- 1/2 pound sliced fresh mushrooms
- 1 cup chopped sweet onion
- 2 teaspoons olive oil
- 2 garlic cloves, minced
- 8 fresh basil leaves, thinly sliced
- 1 jar (24 ounces) marinara sauce
- 1/4 cup dry red wine *or* vegetable broth
- 3/4 cup shredded part-skim mozzarella cheese
- 3/4 cup part-skim ricotta cheese
- 1/4 cup shredded Parmesan cheese

Place milk in a shallow bowl. In another shallow bowl, combine bread crumbs and 1 teaspoon Italian seasoning. Dip eggplant in milk, then bread crumb mixture. Place on a baking sheet coated with cooking spray. Bake at 350° for 30-40 minutes or until tender.

Meanwhile, in a large skillet, saute mushrooms and onion in oil until tender. Add garlic; cook 1 minute longer. Remove from the heat. Stir in basil and remaining Italian seasoning.

Spread 1/2 cup marinara sauce into a 2-qt. baking dish coated with cooking spray. In a small bowl, combine wine and remaining marinara sauce. Layer with half of the eggplant, mushroom mixture, mozzarella cheese, ricotta cheese and 3/4 cup sauce mixture. Repeat layers. Top with remaining sauce; sprinkle with Parmesan cheese.

Bake, uncovered, at 350° for 30-35 minutes or until heated through and cheese is melted. Let stand for 10 minutes before cutting.

NUTRITION FACTS: 1 serving equals 342 calories, 11 g fat (6 g saturated fat), 31 mg cholesterol, 560 mg sodium, 42 g carbohydrate, 10 g fiber, 20 g protein. **DIABETIC EXCHANGES:** 2 lean meat, 2 vegetable, 1-1/2 starch, 1/2 fat.

Selecting an Eggplant

Select eggplants that are firm and feel heavy for their size The skin should be smooth, glossy and taut. Avoid eggplants with blemishes and rust spots. The green cap should be intact and the stem should not show signs of mold.

Swirled Pumpkin Cheesecake Bars

PREP: 30 MIN.   **BAKE:** 20 MIN. + CHILLING
YIELD: 16 SERVINGS

Enjoy this holiday dessert without worrying about calories. Plus, it is so luscious that no one will think that it is light!

Jean Ecos ★ Hartland, Wisconsin

  1 cup graham cracker crumbs
  2 tablespoons sugar
  2 tablespoons reduced-fat butter, melted
FILLING:
  11 ounces reduced-fat cream cheese
  1/3 cup reduced-fat sour cream
  1/3 cup sugar
  2 teaspoons all-purpose flour
  1/2 teaspoon vanilla extract
  1 egg, lightly beaten
  1/2 cup canned pumpkin
  1 tablespoon brown sugar

In a small bowl, combine cracker crumbs and sugar; stir in butter. Press onto the bottom of a 9-in. square baking dish coated with cooking spray. Bake at 325° for 7-10 minutes or until set. Cool on a wire rack.

For filling, in a large bowl, beat the cream cheese, sour cream, sugar, flour and vanilla until smooth. Add egg; beat on low just until combined. Remove 3/4 cup batter to a small bowl; stir in pumpkin and brown sugar until well blended.

Pour plain batter over crust. Drop pumpkin batter by tablespoons over plain batter. Cut through batter with a knife to swirl. Bake at 325° for 20-25 minutes or until center is almost set. Cool on a wire rack for 1 hour. Cover and refrigerate for at least 2 hours. Refrigerate leftovers.

NUTRITION FACTS: 1 bar equals 117 calories, 6 g fat (4 g saturated fat), 31 mg cholesterol, 135 mg sodium, 13 g carbohydrate, trace fiber, 3 g protein. **DIABETIC EXCHANGES:** 1 starch, 1 fat.

Swedish Turkey Meatballs with Noodles

PREP: 30 MIN.   **BAKE:** 15 MIN.   **YIELD:** 5 SERVINGS

A classic is made lighter by using lean ground turkey instead of ground beef. When you serve company this flavorful dish, they won't even guess it is turkey.

Rita Lemons ★ Macomb, Michigan

  1 egg
  1/4 cup 2% milk
  2-1/2 teaspoons Worcestershire sauce, *divided*
  1/2 cup seasoned bread crumbs
  1/2 cup finely chopped onion
  1 tablespoon minced fresh parsley
  1 garlic clove, minced
  3/4 teaspoon salt, *divided*
  1/2 teaspoon pepper, *divided*
  1/4 teaspoon ground allspice
  1 package (20 ounces) lean ground turkey
  6 cups uncooked yolk-free noodles
  2 tablespoons cornstarch
  2 cups reduced-sodium beef broth
  2/3 cup reduced-fat sour cream
  2 teaspoons snipped fresh dill *or* 3/4 teaspoon dill weed

In a large bowl, combine the egg, milk, 1/2 teaspoon Worcestershire sauce, bread crumbs, onion, parsley, garlic, 1/2 teaspoon salt, 1/4 teaspoon pepper and allspice. Crumble turkey over mixture and mix well. Shape into 1-1/2-in. balls. Place meatballs in a 15-in. x 10-in. baking pan coated with cooking spray. Bake at 375° for 15-20 minutes or until no longer pink.

Meanwhile, cook noodles according to package directions. In a large saucepan, combine cornstarch and broth until smooth. Bring to a boil; cook and stir for 2 minutes or until thickened. Remove from the heat.

Stir in the sour cream, dill and remaining Worcestershire sauce, salt and pepper. Drain noodles; stir into sauce. Serve with meatballs.

TO MAKE AHEAD: Make the meatballs up to 2 days ahead. Reheat in the microwave. Proceed as directed.

NUTRITION FACTS: 2/3 cup meatballs with 1-1/4 cups noodles equals 473 calories, 14 g fat (5 g saturated fat), 145 mg cholesterol, 903 mg sodium, 49 g carbohydrate, 3 g fiber, 33 g protein.

Carefree ENTERTAINING

Cook fettuccine according to package directions.

Meanwhile, in a large skillet coated with cooking spray, cook chicken over medium heat until no longer pink. Add garlic; cook 1 minute longer. Remove from the pan and keep warm.

Add the milk, cream cheese and salt to skillet; cook and stir until smooth. Stir in the artichoke hearts, red pepper and Parmesan cheese.

Drain fettuccine. Stir in sauce and chicken; heat through. Sprinkle with basil.

Tomato Vinaigrette Salad

PREP/TOTAL TIME: 25 MIN. **YIELD:** 10 SERVINGS

A few years ago, I found a recipe in our local newspaper for this tart vinaigrette. Since then I have used it often, and I frequently add it to tomato-artichoke salad.

Janelle Moore ★ Federal Way, Washington

- 10 cups torn romaine
- 2 large tomatoes, seeded and chopped
- 1 jar (7-1/2 ounces) marinated quartered artichoke hearts, drained and cut into 1/2-inch pieces
- 1 can (2-1/4 ounces) sliced ripe olives, drained
- 1 small red onion, thinly sliced
- 1/4 cup shredded Parmesan cheese

VINAIGRETTE:
- 1 large tomato, seeded and chopped
- 3 tablespoons red wine vinegar
- 1 tablespoon balsamic vinegar
- 1 tablespoon honey
- 2 small garlic cloves, minced
- 1-1/2 teaspoons Dijon mustard
- 3/4 teaspoon salt
- 1/2 teaspoon pepper
- 1/3 cup olive oil

In a serving bowl, combine romaine, tomatoes, artichoke hearts, olives, onion and cheese.

In a blender, combine the tomato, vinegars, honey, garlic, mustard, salt and pepper; cover and process until blended. While processing, gradually add oil in a steady stream. Pour over salad; toss to coat. Serve immediately.

Chicken and Artichoke Fettuccine Alfredo

PREP/TOTAL TIME: 30 MIN. **YIELD:** 4 SERVINGS

The artichokes make a nice addition to this velvety chicken Alfredo. It goes together in a half hour, so it's great for weeknights or entertaining.

Priscilla Yee ★ Concord, California

- 1/2 pound uncooked fettuccine
- 1 pound boneless skinless chicken breasts, cut into strips
- 1 garlic clove, minced
- 3/4 cup 2% milk
- 4 ounces cream cheese, cubed
- 1/2 teaspoon salt
- 1 can (14 ounces) water-packed artichoke hearts, rinsed, drained and halved
- 1 medium sweet red pepper, chopped
- 1/2 cup shredded Parmesan cheese
- 1/4 cup thinly sliced fresh basil

Slow Cooker Apple Pudding Cake

PREP: 15 MIN.   **COOK:** 2 HOURS   **YIELD:** 10 SERVINGS

A comforting dessert like this is a superb treat on a chilly night. Since it's made in a slow cooker, it does not require any attention from you, so it's great when entertaining. It separates into three layers.

Ellen Schroeder ★ Reedsburg, Wisconsin

2	cups all-purpose flour
2/3	cup plus 1/4 cup sugar, *divided*
3	teaspoons baking powder
1	teaspoon salt
1/2	cup cold butter
1	cup 2% milk
2	medium tart apples, peeled and chopped
1-1/2	cups orange juice
1/2	cup honey
2	tablespoons butter, melted
1	teaspoon ground cinnamon
1-1/3	cups sour cream
1/4	cup confectioners' sugar

In a small bowl, combine the flour, 2/3 cup sugar, baking powder and salt. Cut in butter until mixture resembles coarse crumbs. Stir in milk just until moistened. Spread into the bottom of a greased 4- or 5-qt. slow cooker; sprinkle apples over batter.

In a small bowl, combine the orange juice, honey, melted butter, cinnamon and remaining sugar; pour over apples. Cover and cook on high for 2-3 hours or until apples are tender.

In a small bowl, combine sour cream and confectioners' sugar. Serve with warm pudding cake.

Hearty Beef & Bean Chili

(pictured at left)

PREP: 25 MIN.　**COOK:** 6 HOURS
YIELD: 14 SERVINGS (3-1/2 QUARTS)

*The slow cooker makes my chili ideal for entertaining.
After a few minutes of prep, it cooks on its own. Your guests
will really enjoy this nicely seasoned, hearty dish.*

Jan Wagner-Cuda ★ Deer Park, Washington

　2　pounds ground beef
　6　cans (16 ounces *each*) hot chili beans, undrained
　1　can (10 ounces) diced tomatoes and green
　　　chilies, undrained
　1　can (8 ounces) tomato sauce
1/4　cup chopped onion
　2　tablespoons molasses
　1　teaspoon salt-free Southwest chipotle seasoning blend
　1　teaspoon Worcestershire sauce
1/2　teaspoon salt
1/2　teaspoon ground cumin
1/2　teaspoon chili powder

In a large skillet, cook beef over medium heat until no
longer pink; drain. Transfer to a 6-qt. slow cooker.

Stir in the remaining ingredients. Cover and cook
on low for 6-8 hours or until heated through.

Spicy Salsa Muffins

PREP: 20 MIN.　**BAKE:** 15 MIN. + COOLING
YIELD: 1 DOZEN

*At a farmers market in Coweta, Oklahoma, the Grenter
brothers sell these wonderful, slightly spicy muffins every
Saturday. If you buy some, you can request a copy of the recipe.*

Ginger Sullivan ★ Cutler Bay, Florida

　1　cup all-purpose flour
　1　cup cornmeal
　3　tablespoons sugar
　3　teaspoons baking powder
1/4　teaspoon salt
3/4　cup chunky salsa
1/2　cup half-and-half cream
　6　tablespoons butter, melted
　1　egg, lightly beaten

In a bowl, combine flour, cornmeal, sugar, baking powder
and salt. In another bowl, combine salsa, cream, butter and
egg. Stir into dry ingredients just until moistened.

Fill greased muffin cups three-fourths full. Bake at
400° for 15-18 minutes or until a toothpick inserted near
the center comes out clean. Cool for 5 minutes before
removing from pan to a wire rack. Serve warm.

Pocketed Place Mats

These quick and easy place mats are great
for buffet-style entertaining. They practically
set the table for you! Your guests can grab a
place mat at the buffet line, and they'll have
their flatware and napkin, too.

To make them, topstitch a 4- x 5-in. pocket
to the lower left corner of a purchased place
mat. Insert silverware in pockets. Roll place
mats with the pocket on the outside. Tie a
napkin around each place mat to secure.

Avocado Tangerine Salad

(pictured at left)

PREP/TOTAL TIME: 25 MIN.   YIELD: 8 SERVINGS

This perky orange and green salad is drizzled with a tangy mustard dressing. It's quick, easy and delicious, making it great for a weeknight dinner or a company meal.

Francis Garland ★ Anniston, Alabama

1/2	cup olive oil
2	tablespoons plus 1-1/2 teaspoons white wine vinegar
4-1/2	teaspoons white balsamic vinegar
1	tablespoon Dijon mustard
3	small garlic cloves, minced
1	teaspoon grated lemon peel
1/2	teaspoon sugar
1/4	teaspoon salt
1/4	teaspoon coarsely ground pepper
8	cups torn mixed salad greens
2	medium ripe avocados, peeled
4	tangerines, peeled and sectioned
1/2	cup shredded Parmesan cheese
4	bacon strips, cooked and crumbled

For dressing, in a small bowl, combine the first nine ingredients. Divide salad greens among eight plates. Slice avocados; arrange avocados and tangerines over greens. Drizzle with dressing; sprinkle with cheese and bacon.

Smoked Salmon Cheese Spread

PREP/TOTAL TIME: 15 MIN.   YIELD: 2-1/2 CUPS

Here's a wonderfully creamy mixture of smoked salmon, Creole seasoning and cream cheese that can be used as a spread for crackers or a dip for pretzels, chips or veggies.

Jill Campbell ★ Huntsville, Texas

2	packages (8 ounces *each*) cream cheese, softened
1	package (4 ounces) smoked salmon *or* lox
3	tablespoons horseradish sauce
1	tablespoon lemon juice
1	tablespoon Worcestershire sauce
1/4	teaspoon coarsely ground pepper
1/4	teaspoon Creole seasoning

Chopped walnuts and snipped fresh dill
Assorted crackers

In a food processor, combine the first seven ingredients; cover and process until blended. Spoon into a serving dish; garnish with walnuts and dill. Chill until serving. Serve with crackers.

Spicy Apricot Sangria

PREP: 25 MIN. + CHILLING   YIELD: 7 SERVINGS

Scented with cinnamon, allspice and cloves, this sweet-tart punch makes a fantastic beverage for winter and fall. If you like, use one medium red-skinned apple and one medium green-skinned apple for even more color.

3	cinnamon sticks (3 inches)
10	whole allspice
10	whole cloves
6	cups apricot nectar
1	cup water
1/2	cup lemon juice
2	cups ginger beer, chilled
1	large apple, cubed
1	large pear, cubed
1	medium orange, sliced
1	medium lemon, sliced

Place the cinnamon, allspice and cloves on a double thickness of cheesecloth; bring up corners of cloth and tie with string to form a bag.

Place the apricot nectar, water, lemon juice and spice bag in a large saucepan. Bring to a boil. Remove from the heat; cover and steep for 5 minutes. Transfer to a pitcher. Cover and refrigerate at least 3 hours. Discard spice bag.

Just before serving, add the ginger beer and fruits.

Caramelized Onion & Fig Pizza

PREP: 45 MIN.   **BAKE:** 10 MIN.   **YIELD:** 20 SERVINGS

Here's a sensational variation on traditional pizza. It is creamy, sweet and a little salty. The buttery crunch of the pine nuts make a wonderful flavor accent. I like to serve it with a mixed baby greens salad and a vinaigrette.

Connie Balbach ★ Bemidji, Minnesota

1	large onion, chopped
2	tablespoons olive oil, *divided*
3	garlic cloves, minced
1/4	teaspoon pepper
1	tube (13.8 ounces) refrigerated pizza crust
1	package (8 ounces) cream cheese, softened
1	teaspoon minced fresh thyme *or* 1/4 teaspoon dried thyme
6	ounces dried figs, chopped
6	thin slices prosciutto *or* deli ham, chopped
1/3	cup pine nuts
1	cup (4 ounces) shredded provolone cheese

In a large skillet, saute onion in 1 tablespoon oil until softened. Reduce heat to medium-low; cook, stirring occasionally, for 30-35 minutes or until deep golden brown. Add garlic and pepper; cook 1 minute longer.

Unroll crust into a greased 15-in. x 10-in. x 1-in. baking pan; flatten dough and build up edges slightly. Bake at 425° for 7-10 minutes or until golden brown.

In a small bowl, beat the cream cheese, thyme and remaining oil until blended. Spread over crust. Top with onion mixture, figs, prosciutto and nuts; sprinkle with cheese. Bake 6-10 minutes longer or until cheese is melted.

TO MAKE AHEAD: This recipe takes minutes to put together when you caramelize the onions the day before. Cover and refrigerate the onions until ready to use.

Mushroom Caponata

PREP: 40 MIN.   **COOK:** 10 MIN.   **YIELD:** 6 CUPS

This is a lovely appetizer when served with crostini, pita bread, bagel chips or crackers. I've also used it as a topping over a salad of mixed greens. This mushroom version of a caponata is a unique change from the eggplant variety.

Julia Cotton ★ Pacific Palisades, California

- 2 large green peppers, chopped
- 1 large onion, chopped
- 2 tablespoons butter, *divided*
- 2 tablespoons olive oil, *divided*
- 2 pounds fresh mushrooms, coarsely chopped
- 1/2 cup pitted Greek olives, chopped
- 1/4 cup balsamic vinegar
- 1/4 cup tomato paste
- 1 tablespoon sugar
- 1 teaspoon dried oregano
- 1/2 teaspoon salt
- 1/4 teaspoon coarsely ground pepper

Bagel chips *or* lightly toasted French bread baguette slices

In a large skillet, saute green peppers and onion in 1 tablespoon butter and 1 tablespoon oil for 10 minutes or until golden brown.

Add half of the mushrooms and remaining butter and oil; saute until tender. Remove onion mixture and set aside. Saute remaining mushrooms until tender. Return all to the pan. Cover and simmer over medium-high heat for 2 minutes.

Add the olives, vinegar, tomato paste, sugar, oregano, salt and pepper. Reduce heat; simmer, uncovered, for 10 minutes or until thickened.

Serve warm or at room temperature with bagel chips or baguette slices.

TO MAKE AHEAD: The caponata can be made 2 days in advance; cover and refrigerate. Reheat over low heat when ready to serve.

Light Seafood Tartlets

PREP/TOTAL TIME: 30 MIN.   **YIELD:** 2-1/2 DOZEN

These are delightful little nibbles to add to a buffet. The warm tarts have a rich crab flavor and are easy to pick up and eat.

Lisa Heine ★ Hamburg, New York

- 1 package (8 ounces) reduced-fat cream cheese
- 2 cans (4 ounces *each*) small shrimp, rinsed and drained
- 1 can (6 ounces) crabmeat, drained, flaked and cartilage removed
- 1/2 cup shredded part-skim mozzarella cheese
- 2 green onions, chopped
- 1 tablespoon Dijon mustard
- 2 packages (1.9 ounces *each*) frozen miniature phyllo tart shells

In a large bowl, combine the first six ingredients. Drop filling by rounded tablespoonfuls into each tart shell; place on an ungreased baking sheet. Bake at 350° for 12-14 minutes or until filling is set. Serve immediately.

TO MAKE AHEAD: The filling can be made a day ahead; cover and refrigerate until ready to use.

Amaretto-Peach Cheese Spread

PREP/TOTAL TIME: 10 MIN.   **YIELD:** 16 SERVINGS

During the Christmas season we have an appetizer dinner with two other couples. This super-simple treat is one of the items we've served, and it's very popular. It makes a delightful dessert, too.

Judy Wilson ★ Sun City West, Arizona

- 2 packages (8 ounces *each*) cream cheese, softened
- 1 jar (18 ounces) peach preserves
- 1 cup finely chopped pecans
- 2 tablespoons Amaretto

Gingersnap cookies

Place cream cheese on a serving plate. In a small bowl, combine the preserves, pecans and Amaretto; spoon over cream cheese. Serve with gingersnap cookies.

Filets with Mushroom & Brandy Cream Sauce

(pictured at left)

PREP: 45 MIN. **GRILL:** 15 MIN.
YIELD: 4 SERVINGS (2 CUPS CREAM SAUCE)

This silky sauce, brimming with a quartet of mushrooms and flavored with a splash of brandy, will turn any steak into a special dinner.

Tina Eliopoulos ★ Tucson, Arizona

    3/4   cup sliced fresh mushrooms
    3/4   cup sliced baby portobello mushrooms
    3/4   cup sliced fresh shiitake mushrooms
    3/4   cup fresh oyster mushrooms
    1-1/2 teaspoons chopped shallot
      2   tablespoons butter
      2   garlic cloves, minced
    1/2   cup brandy
      1   cup beef broth
    1/2   cup heavy whipping cream
    4-1/2 teaspoons cornstarch
    4-1/2 teaspoons water
    1/4   teaspoon salt
      4   beef tenderloin steaks (6 ounces *each*)

In a large skillet, saute mushrooms and shallot in butter until tender. Add garlic; cook 1 minute longer. Remove from the heat. Add brandy; cook over medium heat until liquid is evaporated.

Add broth and cream; bring to a boil. Reduce heat; simmer, uncovered, for 10 minutes. Combine cornstarch and water until smooth; stir into skillet. Return to a boil; cook and stir for 1-2 minutes or until thickened. Stir in salt.

Meanwhile, grill steaks, covered, over medium heat for 6-7 minutes on each side or until meat reaches desired doneness (for medium-rare, a meat thermometer should read 145°; medium, 160°; well-done, 170°). Serve with sauce.

Faux Profiteroles with Warm Caramel Sauce

PREP/TOTAL TIME: 25 MIN.
YIELD: 6 SERVINGS (1-1/2 CUPS SAUCE)

Croissants are a super quick stand-in for cream puffs in this luscious treat. The from-scratch caramel sauce couldn't be easier to make, and it's irresistible with butter pecan ice cream.

      6   miniature croissants
      1   cup sugar
    1/4   cup water
      1   cup heavy whipping cream
      2   tablespoons butter
      3   cups butter pecan ice cream

Place croissants on a baking sheet; bake at 350° for 5 minutes or until warmed.

In a small saucepan, combine sugar and water. Bring to a boil. Cook and stir over medium heat until sugar is dissolved. Increase heat to medium-high. Cook without stirring until mixture turns an amber color and a candy thermometer reads 330°. Remove from the heat; gradually stir in cream and butter until smooth.

Split croissants horizontally. Place a scoop of ice cream on the bottom half of each croissant; replace tops. Drizzle each with 2 tablespoons caramel sauce (save remaining sauce for another use).

Editor's Note: We recommend that you test your candy thermometer before each use by bringing water to a boil; the thermometer should read 212°. Adjust your recipe temperature up or down based on your test.

South-of-the-Border Chicken Salad with Tequila Lime Dressing

PREP/TOTAL TIME: 30 MIN.   **YIELD:** 4 SERVINGS

Add a burst of color to your table with a main-dish salad that tastes like a fiesta. For a simple garnish, sprinkle the salad with lightly crushed tortilla chips.

Annette Hottenstein ★ Cockeysville, Maryland

2 romaine hearts, cut into 1/2-inch strips
2 cups shredded cooked chicken breast
3 plum tomatoes, seeded and chopped
1 medium ripe avocado, peeled and cubed
1/2 cup frozen corn, thawed
1/2 cup black beans, rinsed and drained
1/4 cup crumbled queso fresco
1/4 cup minced fresh cilantro
3 green onions, thinly sliced

DRESSING:
3 tablespoons olive oil
3 tablespoons lime juice
2 tablespoons tequila
4-1/2 teaspoons honey
1 garlic clove, minced
1/4 teaspoon salt
1/4 teaspoon coarsely ground pepper

In a large salad bowl, combine the first nine ingredients. In a small bowl, whisk the dressing ingredients. Pour over salad; toss to coat.

Strawberries with Vanilla Mascarpone and Balsamic Drizzle

PREP/TOTAL TIME: 20 MIN.   **YIELD:** 4 SERVINGS

Fresh strawberries shine in my simple but sophisticated delicacy. The balsamic vinegar syrup adds an interesting sweet-savory quality to the dessert.

Cathy McInnes ★ Randolph, New Jersey

- 1/4 cup sugar
- 1/4 cup balsamic vinegar
- 1 cup Mascarpone cheese
- 2 tablespoons confectioners' sugar
- 1 teaspoon vanilla extract
- 1 pound fresh strawberries, sliced

In a small saucepan, bring sugar and vinegar to a boil; cook until liquid is reduced to 1/4 cup, about 2 minutes.

In a small bowl, combine the cheese, confectioners' sugar and vanilla. Divide strawberries among four dessert plates. Top with cheese mixture; drizzle with balsamic mixture.

Candy Cane Martini

PREP/TOTAL TIME: 5 MIN.   **YIELD:** 1 SERVING

Here's a drink that showcases mint, a popular seasonal flavor. Plus, it's a festive translucent pink color.

Ice cubes
- 1-1/2 ounces vodka
- 1 ounce clear creme de cacao
- 1/4 ounce peppermint schnapps liqueur
- 1/4 teaspoon grenadine syrup

Miniature candy cane

Fill a mixing glass or tumbler three-fourths full with ice. Add the vodka, creme de cacao, peppermint schnapps and grenadine syrup; stir until condensation forms on outside of glass. Strain into a chilled cocktail glass. Garnish with a candy cane.

Horseradish Mashed Potatoes

PREP: 20 MIN.   **COOK:** 15 MIN.   **YIELD:** 6 SERVINGS

The mild horseradish flavor in these mashed potatoes makes them a sensational accompaniment for a savory beef roast.

Margaret Hanson-Maddox ★ Montpelier, Indiana

- 2-1/2 pounds potatoes (about 8 medium), peeled and cubed
- 4 garlic cloves, minced
- 1-1/2 teaspoons salt, *divided*
- 1/4 cup mayonnaise
- 3 tablespoons prepared horseradish
- 2 tablespoons butter
- 1/2 teaspoon pepper

Place potatoes in a Dutch oven and cover with water. Add garlic and 1/2 teaspoon salt. Bring to a boil. Reduce heat; cover and cook for 10-15 minutes or until tender. Drain, reserving 2/3 cup cooking liquid; set aside.

Mash potatoes with the reserved cooking liquid, mayonnaise, horseradish, butter, pepper and remaining salt.

Yogurt Fruit Parfaits

PREP/TOTAL TIME: 20 MIN.   **YIELD:** 4 SERVINGS

These parfaits are a fun and delectable way to get a serving of fruit into your diet. If you like, set the ingredients out and let each person build their own parfait.

Fran Fehling ★ Staten Island, New York

- 1 can (8 ounces) unsweetened pineapple chunks, drained
- 3/4 cup sliced fresh strawberries
- 3 tablespoons honey
- 2 cups plain Greek yogurt
- 3 ounces white baking chocolate, finely chopped
- 1/3 cup flaked coconut
- 1/4 cup pineapple preserves
- 4 gingersnap cookies, crushed
- 1/4 cup pistachios

In a small bowl, combine the pineapple, strawberries and honey. In another small bowl, combine the yogurt, chocolate, coconut and pineapple preserves.

Divide half of yogurt mixture among four parfait glasses. Layer with half of the cookies and fruit mixture. Repeat layers. Sprinkle with pistachios.

Chocolate Cherry Martini

PREP/TOTAL TIME: 5 MIN.   **YIELD:** 1 SERVING

Don't be fooled by the innocent, creamy look of this layered drink. It has a chocolate-cherry flavor that can pack a punch.

- 1-1/2 to 2 cups ice cubes
- 1-1/2 ounces chocolate-flavored vodka
- 1/2 ounce cherry brandy
- 4 ounces half-and-half cream
- 1/2 teaspoon maraschino cherry juice
- 1 tablespoon chocolate syrup
- 2 maraschino cherries

Fill a shaker three-fourths full with ice. Add the vodka, brandy, cream and cherry juice.

Cover and shake for 10-15 seconds or until condensation forms on outside of shaker. Place syrup in the bottom of a chilled cocktail glass; strain vodka mixture on top. Serve with cherries.

Editor's Note: For a more festive look, serve this martini in a sugar-rimmed glass. Moisten the rim of the glass with water. Sprinkle coarse sugar on a plate; hold the glass upside down and dip the rim in sugar.

Maple Ricotta Mousse with Candied Pecans

PREP/TOTAL TIME: 25 MIN.   **YIELD:** 4 SERVINGS

Ricotta gives a bit of texture to this heavenly mousse, which is flavored with maple syrup. Sweet, toasted pecans add a delightful crunch.

Kathleen Gill ★ Pahrump, Nevada

- 2/3 cup maple syrup
- 1/4 cup chopped pecans
- 1-1/4 cups ricotta cheese
- 1/2 cup Mascarpone cheese
- 1/2 cup heavy whipping cream

Place syrup in a small saucepan; bring to a boil. Reduce heat; simmer, uncovered, for 5 minutes. Remove from the heat and set aside.

In a small heavy skillet, cook pecans over medium heat until toasted, about 3 minutes. Drizzle with 1 tablespoon syrup. Cook and stir 1 minute longer. Spread on foil to cool.

In a large bowl, beat ricotta and mascarpone cheeses until light and fluffy. Gradually beat in 1/3 cup syrup.

In a small bowl, beat cream until stiff peaks form. Gently fold into cheese mixture. Spoon into dessert dishes. Drizzle with remaining syrup and sprinkle with pecans.

Cookies
FOR SANTA

Orange Poppy Seed Cookies

PREP: 25 MIN. + CHILLING   **BAKE:** 10 MIN./BATCH
YIELD: ABOUT 6 DOZEN

My friend Sandy and I have gotten together for years to bake Christmas cookies. One year we made 16 different kinds in a day. I like this cookie because the orange flavor makes a nice change of pace from all the classic holiday cookies.

Kathy Jessen ★ Sarasota, Florida

1/2	cup butter, softened
3/4	cup sugar
1	egg
1/4	cup poppy seeds
4-1/2	teaspoons grated orange peel
2	cups all-purpose flour
1-1/2	teaspoons baking powder
1/2	teaspoon salt

Colored sugar

In a large bowl, cream butter and sugar until light and fluffy. Beat in the egg, poppy seeds and orange peel. Combine the flour, baking powder and salt; gradually add to creamed mixture and mix well.

Shape into two 10-in. rolls; roll each in colored sugar and wrap in plastic wrap. Refrigerate for 4 hours or until firm.

Cut into 1/4-in. slices. Place 1 in. apart on ungreased baking sheets. Bake at 350° for 9-11 minutes or until set and edges are lightly browned. Cool for 3 minutes before removing to wire racks. Store in airtight containers.

Santa Plate

Santa will exclaim a jolly "Ho, Ho, Ho" when he sees cookies set out for him on a special platter. To do this quick and easy craft, use a clear glass plate with a smooth back (pictured here is an 8-in. plate).

Remove any stickers from back of plate and wash plate to remove smudges or fingerprints. Cut a 10-in. square of 100% cotton or cotton-blend fabric.

Using a flat paintbrush, apply satin finish decoupage medium evenly to back of plate. With right side of fabric facing back of plate, place fabric on back of plate. Smooth out wrinkles and remove any air bubbles. Let dry for about 15 minutes. Use paintbrush to apply decoupage medium to the fabric on the back of the plate. Let dry. Trim any excess fabric even with edge of plate.

Lightly sand the back of the plate with finishing sandpaper to remove any ridges. Apply another thin layer of decoupage medium. Let dry and sand lightly. Paint back of plate with acrylic craft paint to match background of fabric. Let dry.

Plate can be wiped with a damp cloth to clean. Do not submerge plate in water.

Pretzel Cookies

PREP: 45 MIN. + CHILLING   **BAKE:** 10 MIN./BATCH
YIELD: 4 DOZEN

Here's a different look from all the round and cutout cookies. It's easy to shape this shortbread-like dough into pretzels. You can sprinkle them with colored sugar or sprinkles if you desire.

Johnna Johnson ★ Scottsdale, Arizona

1	cup butter, softened
1-1/4	cups confectioners' sugar
1	egg
1/2	cup sour cream
1/2	teaspoon almond extract
1/2	teaspoon vanilla extract
3	cups all-purpose flour
1/2	teaspoon baking soda
1/4	cup sliced almonds, chopped
1/4	cup coarse sugar

EGG WASH:

1	egg
1	tablespoon water

In a large bowl, cream butter and confectioners' sugar until light and fluffy. Beat in the egg, sour cream and extracts. Combine flour and baking soda; gradually add to creamed mixture and mix well. Cover and refrigerate for 2 hours or until firm.

Divide dough into fourths; shape each portion into a 6-in. roll. Cut the rolls into 1/2-in. slices; roll each into a 10-in. rope. Shape into pretzels; place 2 in. apart on greased baking sheets.

In a small bowl, combine almonds and sugar. In another bowl, whisk egg and water. Brush each cookie with egg wash: sprinkle with almond mixture. Bake at 400° for 8-10 minutes or until firm. Cool for 1 minute before removing to wire racks.

TO MAKE AHEAD: Dough can be made 2 days in advance. Wrap in plastic wrap and place in a resealable bag. Store in the refrigerator.

Shaping Cookie Dough Into Pretzels

1. Take a 10-in. cookie dough rope and make a circle with about 2 inches of each end overlapping.
2. Taper ends and twist where they overlap.
3. Flip the twisted ends over the circle; place ends on edge of circle.

Master Cookie Mix

PREP/TOTAL TIME: 15 MIN.   **YIELD:** 6 CUPS

Simplify your cookie baking with this master mix. It's ideal for this busy time of year. The mix can be made and refrigerated, then over the course of a week, with a few additional ingredients, you can make four delectable cookies.

- 2   cups butter, softened
- 2   cups sugar
- 2   eggs
- 2   egg yolks
- 2   teaspoons vanilla extract
- 5   cups all-purpose flour
- 1   teaspoon salt

In a large bowl, cream butter and sugar until light and fluffy. Beat in the eggs, egg yolks and vanilla. Combine flour and salt; gradually add to creamed mixture and mix well.

Store in an airtight container in the refrigerator for up to 1 week.

Master Cookie Mix may be used to prepare the following recipes: Almond Bars, page 109; Chocolate-Hazelnut Pinwheels, page 109; Thumbprint Cookies, page 110; and Peppermint Twists, page 110.

Almond Bars

PREP: 10 MIN. **BAKE:** 20 MIN. + COOLING
YIELD: 4 DOZEN

For a last-minute sweet treat for a potluck or classroom party, you can't beat these delicate bars. Using the master cookie mix and four other ingredients, you can have bars ready to pop in the oven in minutes.

<pre>
1-1/2 cups Master Cookie Mix (page 108), softened
    1 egg white
  1/2 cup sliced almonds
    1 tablespoon sugar
  1/4 teaspoon ground cinnamon
</pre>

Press cookie mix into a greased 13-in. x 9-in. baking pan. Beat egg white until foamy; brush over dough. Top with almonds. Combine sugar and cinnamon; sprinkle over top.

Bake at 350° for 18-22 minutes or until lightly browned. Cool on a wire rack for 10 minutes. Cut into diamonds. Cool completely.

Chocolate-Hazelnut Pinwheels

PREP: 10 MIN. + CHILLING **BAKE:** 10 MIN./BATCH
YIELD: 4-1/2 DOZEN

The shortbread-like flavor of the cookie is married with a delicious hazelnut-chocolate filling to make a delightful treat.

<pre>
1-1/2 cups Master Cookie Mix (page 108), softened
  1/3 cup chocolate hazelnut spread
  1/4 cup finely chopped hazelnuts
</pre>

On a lightly floured surface, roll cookie mix into a 14-in. x 9-in. rectangle. Spread hazelnut spread to within 1/2 in. of edges; sprinkle with hazelnuts. Roll up tightly, jelly-roll style, starting with the long side; wrap in plastic wrap. Refrigerate for 2 hours or until firm.

Unwrap and cut into 1/4-in. slices. Place 2 in. apart on ungreased baking sheets. Bake at 375° for 8-10 minutes or until edges are lightly browned. Remove the cookies to wire racks to cool.

Editor's Note: Look for chocolate hazelnut spread in the peanut butter section. This recipe was tested with Nutella.

Peppermint Twists

PREP: 15 MIN. **BAKE:** 10 MIN./BATCH + COOLING
YIELD: 2-1/2 DOZEN

Serve your family and friend these delicate twists that showcase one of the most popular flavors of the season, peppermint! These cookies will perk up any dessert tray.

1-1/2	cups Master Cookie Mix (page 108), softened
1	cup confectioners' sugar
2	tablespoons 2% milk
1/4	to 1/2 teaspoon peppermint extract

Red colored sugar

Shape cookie mix into 3/4-in. balls. Roll each ball into a 6-in. rope. Bend the rope in half and twist twice. Place 2 in. apart on ungreased baking sheets.

Bake at 350° for 8-10 minutes or until bottoms are lightly browned. Remove to wire racks to cool completely. Combine the confectioners' sugar, milk and extract; drizzle over cookies. Sprinkle with colored sugar.

Thumbprint Cookies

PREP: 10 MIN. **BAKE:** 15 MIN./BATCH **YIELD:** 2 DOZEN

Speckled with chopped nuts and topped with a candied cherry, these tender cookies will disappear fast.

1-1/2	cups Master Cookie Mix (page 108), softened
1	egg white, beaten
3/4	cup finely chopped pecans
12	red *or* green candied cherries, halved

Shape cookie mix into 1-in. balls. Roll in egg white, then in pecans. Using the end of a wooden spoon handle, make an indentation in the center of each ball. Fill with a candied cherry half. Place 2 in. apart on greased baking sheets.

Bake at 350° for 12-15 minutes or until set. Remove to wire racks to cool.

Scalloped Mocha Cookies

PREP: 30 MIN. + CHILLING **BAKE:** 10 MIN./BATCH
YIELD: 5 DOZEN

I tore this recipe out of a magazine many years ago, and they are one of my most-requested cookies. They contain the four Cs: coffee, chocolate, cinnamon and crunch. Sprinkling them with coarse sugar adds a little glitz to the cookies.

Loraine Meyer ★ Bend, Oregon

2/3 cup butter, softened
1 cup sugar
1 egg
2 ounces unsweetened chocolate, melted and cooled
1/2 teaspoon vanilla extract
1-3/4 cups all-purpose flour
1 tablespoon instant coffee granules
1/4 teaspoon ground cinnamon
1/8 teaspoon salt
Coarse sugar *or* edible glitter

In a small bowl, cream butter and sugar until light and fluffy. Beat in the egg, chocolate and vanilla. Combine the flour, coffee granules, cinnamon and salt; gradually add to creamed mixture.

Shape dough into a disk; wrap in plastic wrap. Refrigerate for 1 hour or until easy to handle.

On a floured surface, roll out dough to 1/4-in. thickness. Cut with a floured 2-1/4-in. scalloped cookie cutter. Place 2 in. apart on ungreased baking sheets. Sprinkle with coarse sugar or edible glitter.

Bake at 350° for 8-9 minutes or until set. Remove to wire racks.

Christmas Wreath Cookies

PREP: 1 HOUR + CHILLING
BAKE: 10 MIN./BATCH + COOLING   **YIELD:** 7 DOZEN

The maple frosting gives these festive Christmas wreath sugar cookie cutouts an unexpected and wonderful flavor. Won't Santa be surprised!

Kate Stierman ★ Dubuque, Iowa

    2   cups butter, softened
    3   cups confectioners' sugar
    2   eggs
    2   teaspoons vanilla extract
    5   cups all-purpose flour
    2   teaspoons baking soda
    2   teaspoons cream of tartar
FROSTING:
    8   cups confectioners' sugar
    1   cup shortening
    2   teaspoons maple flavoring
  1/2   to 2/3 cup 2% milk
  1/4   to 1/2 teaspoon red food coloring
  1/2   teaspoon green food coloring

In a large bowl, cream butter and confectioners' sugar until light and fluffy. Beat in eggs and vanilla. Combine the flour, baking soda and cream of tartar; gradually add to creamed mixture and mix well. Divide into four portions. Cover and refrigerate for 1-2 hours or until easy to handle.

On a lightly floured surface, roll out one portion to 1/4-in. thickness. Cut with a floured 2-1/2-in. round cookie cutter. Place 1 in. apart on parchment paper-lined baking sheets; cut out centers using a floured 1-in. round cookie cutter.

Bake at 375° for 8-10 minutes or until lightly browned. Cool for 2 minutes before removing to wire racks to cool completely. Repeat with remaining dough.

For frosting, in a large bowl, combine the confectioners' sugar, shortening, maple flavoring and enough milk to achieve piping consistency.

Place 3/4 cup frosting in a small bowl; tint with red food coloring. Tint remaining frosting green. Using a #13 star tip, pipe green frosting over cookies. With a #2 round tip and red frosting, pipe bows onto wreaths.

TO MAKE AHEAD: The dough can be made 2 days in advance. Let stand at room temperature for 30 minutes before rolling out. Cookies can be baked 1 week ahead of time and stored in an airtight container or frozen, unfrosted, for up to 1 month.

Cherry Pecan Chews

PREP: 30 MIN.   **BAKE:** 25 MIN. + CHILLING   **YIELD:** 3 DOZEN

This oldie but goodie was given to me by my sister many, many years ago. She obtained the recipe when she worked in the kitchen of a country club. The cake-like cookie, brimming with candied fruit and pecans, is reminiscent of fruitcake.

Margaret Reinhardt ★ Muskego, Wisconsin

- 3/4 cup cake flour
- 1/2 cup butter, melted
- 1 teaspoon vanilla extract
- 3/4 cup finely chopped pecans
- 6 tablespoons finely chopped red candied cherries
- 6 tablespoons finely chopped candied pineapple
- 3 egg whites
- 1/2 teaspoon salt
- 3/4 cup sugar
- 1/2 cup confectioners' sugar

In a large bowl, whisk the flour, butter and vanilla until combined. Stir in pecans and fruits. In another large bowl, beat egg whites and salt on medium speed until soft peaks form. Gradually add sugar, beating on high until stiff, glossy peaks form and sugar is dissolved. Fold into the flour mixture.

Spread into a greased 9-in. square baking pan. Bake at 350° for 25-30 minutes or until golden brown. Cool on a wire rack. Cover and refrigerate overnight.

Cut into squares and roll in confectioners' sugar. Store in an airtight container.

No-Bake Chocolate Cookie Triangles

PREP: 15 MIN. + CHILLING   **YIELD:** 32 COOKIES

When you need a special treat but time is short, try these no-bake bars. They take only a few minutes to make. They are rich, chocolaty and so good.

Linda Stemen ★ Monroeville, Indiana

- 3/4 cup butter, cubed
- 8 ounces semisweet chocolate, chopped
- 20 vanilla wafers, coarsely crushed
- 1/2 cup chopped pecans

In a microwave, melt butter and chocolate; stir until smooth. Cool slightly. Stir in wafer crumbs and pecans. Transfer to a greased foil-lined 8-in. square pan. Cover and refrigerate for 2 hours or until firm.

Using foil, lift cookies out of pan. Discard foil; cut into triangles. Refrigerate leftovers.

Raspberry & Pink Peppercorn Meringues

PREP: 15 MIN. **BAKE:** 20 MIN. + COOLING
YIELD: 4 DOZEN

A classic meringue has been updated with the subtle flavor of raspberry, a drizzle of chocolate and a sprinkling of pink peppercorns to create a delightful treat.

3	egg whites
1/4	teaspoon cream of tartar
Dash salt	
3/4	cup sugar
1	teaspoon raspberry extract
5	to 8 drops food coloring, optional
1/4	cup semisweet chocolate chips
1	teaspoon shortening
2	tablespoons whole pink peppercorns, crushed

Place egg whites in a large bowl; let stand at room temperature for 30 minutes. Add cream of tartar and salt; beat on medium speed until soft peaks form. Gradually add sugar, 1 tablespoon at a time, beating on high until stiff glossy peaks form and sugar is dissolved. Beat in extract and food coloring if desired.

Cut a small hole in the corner of a pastry or plastic bag; insert a large star tip. Fill bag with egg white mixture. Pipe 1-1/4-in.-diameter cookies onto parchment paper-lined baking sheets. Bake at 300° for 20-25 minutes or until set and dry. (Turn oven off; leave meringues in oven for 1 hour.) Remove to wire racks.

In a microwave, melt chocolate chips and shortening; stir until smooth. Drizzle over cookies; sprinkle with peppercorns. Store in an airtight container.

Cappuccino Cookies

PREP: 30 MIN. + CHILLING
BAKE: 10 MIN./BATCH + COOLING   **YIELD:** 2-1/2 DOZEN

Coffee lovers will really enjoy these tender bites. There are hits of coffee flavor in both the cookie and the glaze.

Heather Rotunda ★ St. Cloud, Minnesota

1	teaspoon instant espresso powder
1	teaspoon vanilla extract
1	cup butter, softened
1/2	cup confectioners' sugar
2-1/4	cups all-purpose flour
1	tablespoon baking cocoa
1/4	teaspoon salt
1/4	teaspoon ground cinnamon
GLAZE:	
2	cups confectioners' sugar
1/4	cup cold brewed coffee
4	teaspoons butter, melted
1/4	teaspoon ground cinnamon
30	chocolate-covered coffee beans

In a small bowl, dissolve espresso powder in vanilla.

In a large bowl, cream butter and confectioners' sugar until light and fluffy. Beat in vanilla mixture. Combine the flour, cocoa, salt and cinnamon; gradually add to creamed mixture and mix well. Cover and refrigerate for 30 minutes or until easy to handle.

Shape into 1-in. balls. Place 2 in. apart on ungreased baking sheets; flatten slightly. Bake at 400° for 7-9 minutes or until set. Remove to wire racks to cool completely.

In a small bowl, combine the confectioners' sugar, coffee, butter and cinnamon. Dip each cookie in coffee mixture; allow excess to drip off. Place on a waxed paper-lined baking sheet and top with a coffee bean. Chill until set.

Spread bottoms of cookies with melted chocolate. Place chocolate side up on waxed paper-lined baking sheets. Refrigerate until set.

For glaze, in a small saucepan, bring brown sugar and butter to a boil. Cook and stir for 30 seconds. Remove from the heat; cool for 5 minutes. Whisk in milk until smooth. Stir in confectioners' sugar. Immediately drizzle over top of cookies. Let stand until set.

TO MAKE AHEAD: The dough can be made 2 days in advance. Iced cookies can be stored for 1 week in an airtight container at room temperature or frozen for up to 1 month.

Panforte Cookie Cups

PREP: 25 MIN. + CHILLING
BAKE: 20 MIN. + COOLING   **YIELD:** 2 DOZEN

A tassie-like treat takes on an Italian flair in these Panforte Cookie Cups. The filling of nuts, dried and candied fruits, and spices make it reminscent of Panforte bread.

Roxanne Chan ★ Albany, California

1/2	cup butter, softened
1	package (3 ounces) cream cheese, softened
2	tablespoons sugar
1	cup all-purpose flour
1/2	teaspoon ground allspice

FILLING:

3/4	cup confectioners' sugar
1	egg
3	tablespoons chopped pecans
3	tablespoons chopped dates
3	tablespoons dried cranberries
3	tablespoons grated semisweet chocolate
2	tablespoons chopped candied orange peel
2	tablespoons chopped crystallized ginger

Additional confectioners' sugar, optional

In a large bowl, cream the butter, cream cheese and sugar until light and fluffy. Combine flour and allspice; stir into creamed mixture just until combined. Cover and refrigerate for 1 hour or until easy to handle.

Meanwhile, in a small bowl, combine the confectioners' sugar, egg, pecans, dates, cranberries, chocolate, orange peel and ginger. Roll dough into 1-in. balls; press onto the bottoms and up the sides of greased miniature muffin cups. Place 1 teaspoon filling in each cup.

Bake at 350° for 18-22 minutes or until edges are golden brown. Cool for 10 minutes before removing from pans to wire racks. Dust with additional confectioners' sugar if desired.

TO MAKE AHEAD: The dough can be made 2 days in advance. Wrap in plastic wrap and place in a resealable bag. Store in the refrigerator.

Caramel-Walnut Star Cookies

PREP: 30 MIN.   **BAKE:** 15 MIN./BATCH + CHILLING
YIELD: 2 DOZEN

These cookies will shine brightly on any dessert tray. In fact, the first time I sampled these crisp, buttery stars was at a potluck. I spent the evening tracking down the person who brought them so I could obtain the recipe. I have made them every Christmas since then.

Sandy Topalof ★ North Royalton, Ohio

1-1/2	cups all-purpose flour
1/3	cup sugar
1/2	cup cold butter
2	tablespoons 2% milk
1/2	teaspoon vanilla extract
1/2	cup chopped walnuts, toasted
24	walnut halves
2/3	cup semisweet chocolate chips, melted

GLAZE:

1/4	cup packed brown sugar
2	tablespoons butter, cubed
1	tablespoon 2% milk
1/3	cup confectioners' sugar

In a small bowl, combine flour and sugar. Cut in butter until mixture resembles coarse crumbs. Stir in milk and vanilla, then walnuts.

On a lightly floured surface, roll out dough to 1/4-in. thickness. Cut with a 3-in. star-shaped cookie cutter dipped in flour. Place 2 in. apart on greased baking sheets. Press a walnut half in the center of each. Bake at 350° for 12-15 minutes or until edges are lightly browned. Remove to wire racks to cool.

Cashew Baklava

PREP: 50 MIN. **BAKE:** 20 MIN. + STANDING
YIELD: 2 DOZEN

I always wanted to make Baklava, but it seemed like so much work. The son of my neighbor's friend showed us both how. It's really quite easy and so delicious. I like to mix up the nuts in the filling and use cashews, walnuts or pecans.

Lorraine Caland ★ Thunder Bay, Ontario

- 1-1/2 cups salted cashews
- 1-1/2 cups chopped walnuts
-   1/2 cup sugar
-     1 teaspoon ground cardamom
-   1/2 teaspoon ground cinnamon
-   1/4 teaspoon ground allspice
-   2/3 cup butter, melted
-    16 sheets phyllo dough (14 inches x 9 inches)

SYRUP:
- 1-1/3 cups sugar
-   2/3 cup water
-   2/3 cup honey
-     3 lemon slices
-     2 whole cloves
-   1/2 teaspoon ground cinnamon

For filling, in a food processor, combine the cashews, walnuts, sugar, cardamom, cinnamon and allspice. Cover and pulse until nuts are finely chopped. Brush a 13-in. x 9-in. baking pan with some of the butter. Unroll phyllo dough; trim to fit into pan.

Layer four sheets of phyllo dough in prepared pan, brushing each with butter. (Keep remaining dough covered with plastic wrap and a damp towel to prevent it from drying out.) Sprinkle with a third of the nut mixture. Repeat layers twice. Top with remaining phyllo dough, brushing each sheet with butter.

Using a sharp knife, cut into 24 triangles. Bake at 350° for 20-25 minutes or until golden brown.

Meanwhile, in a large saucepan, combine the syrup ingredients. Bring to a boil. Reduce heat; simmer, uncovered, for 10 minutes, stirring occasionally. Discard lemon slices and cloves. Pour over warm baklava. Cool completely in pan on a wire rack. Cover and let stand overnight.

Anise Spritz Cookies

PREP: 15 MIN. **BAKE:** 10 MIN./BATCH **YIELD:** 8 DOZEN

Buttery and delicate spritz cookies just melt in your mouth. The flavor of licorice from the anise extract makes them special.

Genise Krause ★ Sturgeon Bay, Wisconsin

-     1 cup butter, softened
-   2/3 cup sugar
-     1 egg
-     1 teaspoon anise extract
-   1/2 teaspoon vanilla extract
- 2-1/4 cups all-purpose flour
-     1 teaspoon baking powder

Red and green sprinkles

In a large bowl, cream butter and sugar until light and fluffy. Beat in egg and extracts. Combine flour and baking powder; gradually add to the creamed mixture.

Using a cookie press fitted with disk of your choice, press dough 1 in. apart onto ungreased baking sheets. Decorate with sprinkles. Bake at 375° for 7-8 minutes or until set. Remove to wire racks.

Neapolitan Bars

PREP: 30 MIN. **BAKE:** 30 MIN. + CHILLING
YIELD: 4 DOZEN

The colors of the season are featured in this moist bars, which are layered with cherry and apricot preserves.

Nancy Foust ★ Stoneboro, Pennsylvania

1	cup butter, softened
1	cup sugar
1	egg
1	teaspoon vanilla extract
2-1/2	cups all-purpose flour
1-1/2	teaspoons baking powder
1/2	teaspoon salt
1	to 2 drops green food coloring
1	to 2 drops red food coloring
1/3	cup miniature semisweet chocolate chips
1/4	cup finely chopped maraschino cherries, patted dry
1/3	cup flaked coconut
1/2	teaspoon rum extract
1/4	cup cherry preserves
1/4	cup apricot preserves

Line a greased 13-in. x 9-in. baking pan with waxed paper; grease the paper and set aside.

In a large bowl, cream butter and sugar until light and fluffy. Beat in egg and vanilla. Combine the flour, baking powder and salt; gradually add to creamed mixture and mix well.

Divide dough in thirds. Tint one portion green and one portion red; leave the remaining portion white. Add chocolate chips to green portion, cherries to red portion, and coconut and rum extract to white portion. Spread one portion into prepared pan. Bake at 350° for 7-9 minutes or until edges are golden brown.

Immediately invert onto a wire rack and remove waxed paper. Place another wire rack on top and turn over. Cool completely. Repeat with remaining portions, preparing pan each time.

Place pink layer on a large piece of plastic wrap, about 30 in. long. Spread with cherry preserves. Top with white layer and spread with apricot preserves. Top with green layer. Bring plastic over layers. Slide onto a baking sheet and set a cutting board on top to compress layers. Refrigerate overnight.

With a sharp knife, trim 1/4 in. from each edge. Cut into bars. Store in an airtight container.

Forming Neapolitan Bars

Weighing down Neapolitan Bars overnight with a cutting board helps the jam sink into the layers so they will hold together when they are cut. Be sure to use a cutting board that is large enough to cover the entire cookie layer.

Hot Chocolate Linzer Cookies

PREP: 30 MIN. + CHILLING
BAKE: 10 MIN./BATCH + COOLING   **YIELD:** 20 COOKIES

This is like having hot chocolate in a cookie. These adorable cookies are filled with marshmallow creme to make them taste even more authentic.

1	cup butter, softened
1	cup sugar
1/2	cup packed brown sugar
1	egg
1	teaspoon vanilla extract
2	cups all-purpose flour
3/4	cup ground almonds
1/2	cup baking cocoa
1	teaspoon baking soda
1-1/4	cups marshmallow creme

In a large bowl, cream butter and sugars until light and fluffy. Beat in egg and vanilla. Combine the flour, ground almonds, cocoa and baking soda; gradually add to creamed mixture and mix well. Cover and refrigerate for 2 hours or until easy to handle.

On a lightly floured surface, roll out dough to 1/16-in. thickness. Cut with a floured 3-in. gingerbread man cookie cutter. Using a floured 3/4-in. heart-shaped cookie cutter, cut a heart from half of the cookies.

Place cookies on greased baking sheets. Bake at 375° for 7-9 minutes or until set. Remove the cookies to wire racks to cool completely.

Spread the bottom of each solid cookie with 1 tablespoon marshmallow creme; gently place cutout cookies over creme. Store in an airtight container.

TO MAKE AHEAD: The dough can be made 2 days in advance. Let stand at room temperature for 30 minutes before rolling out. Cookies can be baked 1 week ahead of time and stored in an airtight container or frozen, without the filling, for up to 1 month.

the flour, baking powder and salt; gradually add to sugar mixture and mix well. Stir in the figs, 3/4 cup chips and walnuts. Cover and refrigerate for at least 2 hours.

Drop by rounded tablespoonfuls 2 in. apart onto parchment paper-lined baking sheets. Bake at 350° for 8-10 minutes or until bottoms are lightly browned. Remove to wire racks to cool completely.

In a microwave, melt remaining chips; stir until smooth. Drizzle over cookies; let stand until set. Store the cookies in an airtight container.

Mint Sandwich Cookies

PREP: 45 MIN. + CHILLING
BAKE: 10 MIN./BATCH + COOLING   **YIELD:** 46 COOKIES

These minty sandwich cookies were a tradition in my husband's family. When we married, I found the recipe and have continued to make them for the holidays.

Janet White ★ New Glarus, Wisconsin

2/3	cup butter-flavored shortening
1/2	cup sugar
1	egg
1	cup mint chocolate chips
1/4	cup light corn syrup
1-3/4	cups all-purpose flour
2	teaspoons baking soda
1/2	teaspoon salt

Additional sugar

FILLING:

1	cup (6 ounces) semisweet chocolate chips
1/2	cup butter, cubed
1	teaspoon peppermint extract

In a large bowl, cream shortening and sugar until light and fluffy. Beat in egg. In a microwave-safe bowl, melt mint chips and corn syrup; stir until smooth. Add to creamed mixture. Combine the flour, baking soda and salt; gradually add to chocolate mixture and mix well. Refrigerate for at least 2 hours.

Shape teaspoonfuls of dough into balls; roll in additional sugar. Place 2 in. apart on ungreased baking sheets. Bake at 350° for 6-8 minutes or until tops are cracked. Remove to wire racks to cool completely.

In a microwave, melt chocolate chips and butter; stir until smooth. Stir in extract. Refrigerate for 30 minutes or until it reaches spreading consistency. Spread on the bottoms of half of the cookies; top with remaining cookies.

TO MAKE AHEAD: The dough can be made 2 days in advance. Wrap in plastic wrap and place in a resealable bag. Store in the refrigerator.

Fig, Walnut & White Chip Cookies

PREP: 20 MIN. + CHILLING
BAKE: 10 MIN./BATCH + COOLING   **YIELD:** 3 DOZEN

I use figs from my own tree to make these cookies. The white chips add a touch of sweetness.

Michaela Rosenthal ★ Woodland Hills, California

3/4	cup packed brown sugar
1/2	cup sugar
1/2	cup unsalted butter, melted
2	eggs
2	tablespoons heavy whipping cream
1	teaspoon grated lemon peel
1	teaspoon vanilla extract
1-1/4	cups all-purpose flour
3/4	teaspoon baking powder
1/2	teaspoon salt
1	cup dried figs, finely chopped
1	cup white baking chips, *divided*
3/4	cup chopped walnuts

In a large bowl, beat sugars and butter until blended. Beat in the eggs, cream, lemon peel and vanilla. Combine

Iced Holiday Ornament Cookies

PREP: 1 HOUR + CHILLING
BAKE: 10 MIN./BATCH + STANDING   **YIELD:** 4 DOZEN

*It wouldn't be Christmas for my family without these sugar
cookies. Best of all, you can bake and decorate them up to a
week ahead of time and store them in an airtight container.*

Lea Reiter ★ Thousand Oaks, California

1/2	cup butter, softened
2/3	cup sugar
1	egg
3	tablespoons orange liqueur *or* orange juice
2-1/4	cups all-purpose flour
1	teaspoon baking powder
1/2	teaspoon salt

ICING:

3-3/4	cups confectioners' sugar
1/4	cup water
1/4	cup orange liqueur *or* additional water
4	teaspoons meringue powder

Food coloring of your choice
Ribbon, optional

In a bowl, cream butter and sugar until light and fluffy. Beat
in egg and liqueur. Combine flour, baking powder and salt.
Gradually add to creamed mixture; mix well. Shape dough into
a ball; flatten into a disk. Wrap in plastic wrap; chill for 1 hour.

On a lightly floured surface, roll dough to 1/8-in.
thickness. Cut with floured 2-1/2-in. ornament-shaped
cookie cutters. Place 2 in. apart on greased baking sheets.
If hanging cookies, make a hole with a plastic straw about
1/2 in. from the top of each cookie.

Bake at 350° for 6-8 minutes or until lightly browned.
Remove to wire racks to cool completely. Use plastic straw
to reopen holes in cookies.

For icing, in a large bowl, combine the confectioners'
sugar, water, liqueur and meringue powder; beat on low
speed just until combined. Beat on high for 4-5 minutes or
until stiff peaks form. Tint with food coloring as desired.
(Keep unused icing covered at all times with a damp cloth.
If necessary, beat again on high speed to restore texture.)

Using pastry bags and small round tips, decorate cookies
as desired. Let dry at room temperature for several hours
or until firm. Thread ribbon through the holes. Store in an
airtight container.

Editor's Note: Meringue powder is available from Wilton Industries.
Call 1-800/794-5866 or visit wilton.com.

Piping Frosting on Cookies

Pipe a bead of icing around the
edge of cookies. Thin remaining
icing if necessary, so that it will flow
smoothly. Fill in the cookies with
icing, letting the icing flow up to the
outline. Let cookies dry overnight.

Making a Heart Chain Design

Place a dot of icing equally spaced
around a cookie. Starting in the center
of one of the dots, drag a toothpick
through the center, forming a heart.
Repeat with each dot while icing is
still wet to form a chain of hearts.

Tabletop Cookie Ornament Tree

Add a festive flair to a buffet or tabletop with this stunning cookie tree centerpiece. Prepare the Iced Holiday Ornament Cookies on page 120, using a straw to create a hole as recipe directs. Ice and decorate one side of the cookies and let dry. Turn dry cookies over, ice and decorate other side, then let dry. Thread a narrow ribbon through the hole in the cookie and hang on ornament tree. When your guests are ready to leave, have them select a cookie from the tree to take with them as a party favor.

Cranberry Port Cookies

PREP: 40 MIN. + COOLING
BAKE: 15 MIN./BATCH + COOLING   **YIELD:** 3-1/2 DOZEN

This is my version of a recipe that I tasted years ago, and my family loves it. The flaky cookies are filled with a scrumptious combination of dried cranberries, cinnamon, lemon and a hint of port.

Leslie Forte ★ Oakhill, Virginia

  1 package (6 ounces) dried cranberries
1/2 cup sugar
1/2 cup port wine *or* unsweetened apple juice
1/4 cup water
  1 tablespoon lemon juice
  1 teaspoon grated lemon peel
1/2 teaspoon ground cinnamon
  2 packages (15 ounces *each*) refrigerated pie pastry
GLAZE:
  2 cups confectioners' sugar
  3 tablespoons water
  2 tablespoons light corn syrup

In a large saucepan, combine the first seven ingredients. Bring to a boil. Cook and stir for 1-2 minutes or until sugar is dissolved. Remove from the heat; cool slightly. Transfer to a food processor; cover and process until cranberries are finely chopped. Cool completely.

Roll out each pastry on a lightly floured surface to 1/16-in. thickness. Using a 2-1/2-in. round cookie cutter, cut out 21 circles from each pastry. Place a heaping teaspoonful of filling in the center of half of the circles; top with remaining circles. Press edges with a fork to seal.

Place on ungreased baking sheets. Bake at 375° for 12-15 minutes or until edges begin to brown. Remove to wire racks to cool.

In a small bowl, combine glaze ingredients; drizzle over cookies.

Cranberry Lime Macaroons

(pictured above)

PREP: 15 MIN.   **BAKE:** 10 MIN./BATCH   **YIELD:** 3 DOZEN

It won't be the holidays for my family and friends if I didn't make my chewy, lime-flavored macaroons. I usually make several batches a week during the season.

Alisa Costa ★ Chatham, New York

        2   egg whites
      2/3   cup sugar
        2   teaspoons vanilla extract
    1-1/2   teaspoons grated lime peel
      1/2   teaspoon salt
        3   cups finely shredded unsweetened coconut
      1/2   cup dried cranberries, chopped

In a small bowl, whisk egg whites for 1 minute. Whisk in the sugar, vanilla, lime peel and salt. Stir in coconut and cranberries.

Drop by rounded tablespoonfuls 2 in. apart onto parchment paper-lined baking sheets. Bake at 350° for 8-10 minutes or until golden brown. Cool for 5 minutes before removing from pans to wire racks.

Snowball Cookies

PREP: 25 MIN.   **BAKE:** 10 MIN./BATCH   **YIELD:** 4-1/2 DOZEN

The dusting of confectioners' sugar on these buttery coconut balls makes them look like little snowballs.

Sonya Labbe ★ Los Angeles, California

        1   cup unsalted butter, softened
      1/2   cup confectioners' sugar
        2   cups all-purpose flour
      1/4   teaspoon salt
        2   cups flaked coconut, chopped
    Additional confectioners' sugar

In a large bowl, cream butter and confectioners' sugar until light and fluffy. Combine flour and salt; gradually add to creamed mixture and mix well. Stir in coconut.

Shape into 1-in. balls; place 2 in. apart on ungreased baking sheets. Bake at 350° for 10-13 minutes or until lightly browned

Cool on pans for 3 minutes before removing to wire racks. Roll warm cookies in additional confectioners' sugar.

Spices
OF THE SEASON

Spices of the Season

Wonderful aromas drift through your house as breads, cakes, cookies and other desserts bake during the Christmas season. So many of the scents, flavors and memories associated with the holidays come from this fragrant collection of spices: cinnamon, nutmeg, cloves, ginger, cardamom, allspice, mace and aniseed. The recipes featured in this chapter showcase those marvelous spices.

Cherry Spice Cake

PREP: 30 MIN. **BAKE:** 25 MIN. + COOLING
YIELD: 16 SERVINGS

At least four generations of women in my family have baked Cherry Spice Cake. It's always my mom's pick for her birthday. I like to use cream cheese frosting on the cake, but when my mother was growing up, my grandma used buttercream frosting.

Laurie Sanders ★ Manchester, Michigan

1/2	cup butter, softened
1-1/2	cups sugar
2	eggs
2	cups all-purpose flour
1	teaspoon ground cinnamon
1	teaspoon ground cloves
1/2	teaspoon baking soda
1/4	teaspoon baking powder
1/4	teaspoon salt
1	cup buttermilk
1	can (14-1/2 ounces) pitted tart cherries, drained
1/2	cup chopped pecans *or* walnuts

FROSTING:

1	package (8 ounces) cream cheese, softened
3-3/4	cups confectioners' sugar
1	to 2 teaspoons water
2	to 3 drops red food coloring, optional

Additional chopped pecans, optional

Line two 9-in. round baking pans with waxed paper. Grease and flour the pans and paper; set aside.

In a large bowl, cream butter and sugar until light and fluffy. Add eggs, one at a time, beating well after each addition. Combine the flour, cinnamon, cloves, baking soda, baking powder and salt. Add to the creamed mixture alternately with buttermilk, beating well after each addition. Fold in cherries and pecans.

Transfer batter to prepared pans. Bake at 350° for 25-30 minutes or until a toothpick inserted near the center comes out clean. Cool for 10 minutes before removing from pans to wire racks to cool completely.

For frosting, in a large bowl, beat cream cheese until fluffy. Add confectioners' sugar and enough water to achieve spreading consistency. Tint with food coloring if desired. Spread frosting between layers and over top and sides of cake. Garnish with additional pecans. Store in the refrigerator.

Storing Cakes

Cakes with fillings or frosting that contain perishable ingredients (such as cream cheese, yogurt, whipping cream, sour cream and eggs) should be stored in the refrigerator. Place the cake in the refrigerator for 20 or 30 minutes to allow the frosting to firm up. If the cake has been cut, place a piece of plastic wrap over the cut surface and another piece over the entire cake. When the cake is removed from the refrigerator for serving, immediately remove the plastic wrap. Otherwise, as the cake warms up, the plastic wrap will stick to the frosting.

Seasonal Spices

Here are the spices that are traditionally used to create those special holiday treats. They are all available ground; some are also sold in other forms.

To keep the spices at peak flavor and fragrance, store them in a tightly closed glass or heavy-duty plastic container in a cool, dry place. Don't store them by the range or in direct sunlight. Ground spices lose their intensity after 6 months. Whole spices can be kept 1 to 2 years.

1. Candied Ginger
2. Whole Cloves
3. Star Anise
4. Anise Seed
5. Whole Nutmeg & Grated Nutmeg
6. Whole Allspice
7. Cinnamon Sticks
8. Gingerroot
9. Caradmon Pods
10. Ground Mace

Bake at 200° for 20-30 minutes. Remove to paper towels to dry thoroughly. When completely dry and cool, string a ribbon strip through each hole; tie the ends together to form a loop. Decorate ornaments as desired with royal icing and glitter.

ROYAL ICING: In a large bowl, combine 1-3/4 cups confectioners' sugar, 4-1/2 teaspoons meringue powder and 2 to 3 tablespoons warm water. Beat on high speed with a portable mixer for 7-10 minutes or on low speed with a stand mixer for 4-5 minutes or until stiff peaks form. Tint with food coloring if desired. Place a damp paper towel over bowl to prevent frosting from drying out while using. Yield: about 1-1/2 cups.

Cinnamon Snowflake Ornaments

PREP: 40 MIN. **BAKE:** 20 MIN. + DRYING
YIELD: ABOUT 10 (4-INCH ORNAMENTS)

Fill your home with the scent of Christmas with these lovely nonedible spice ornaments. Thread a narrow ribbon through each and hang them on your tree, in the window, from the chandelier or by the fireplace.

   1 cup applesauce
Approximately 3/4 cup ground cinnamon
   2 tablespoons ground cloves
   1 tablespoon ground nutmeg
   1 tablespoon ground allspice
Plastic straw
Ribbon
Royal icing and edible glitter

In a large bowl, combine the applesauce and spices; mix well until a stiff dough forms, adding additional cinnamon if needed. Divide dough in fourths.

On a board dusted with additional cinnamon, roll out each portion of dough to 1/4-inch thickness. Cut into shapes using 4-in. snowflake-shaped cookie cutters dipped in cinnamon. Reroll scraps. Place cutouts on parchment paper-lined baking sheets. Make a hole with a plastic straw about 1/2 in. from the top of each ornament.

Granny's Gingerbread Cake with Caramel Sauce

PREP: 25 MIN. **BAKE:** 35 MIN. **YIELD:** 9 SERVINGS

The rich molasses and spice flavor of this old-time dessert is complemented by a buttery caramel sauce.

Joy Sparks ★ Muskegon, Michigan

   9 tablespoons butter, softened
1/3 cup sugar
   1 cup molasses
   1 egg

2-1/4 cups all-purpose flour
   1 teaspoon baking soda
   1 teaspoon ground ginger
   1 teaspoon ground cinnamon
 1/4 teaspoon salt
 3/4 cup water
CARAMEL SAUCE:
   1 cup packed brown sugar
   1 tablespoon cornstarch
   1 cup cold water
 1/4 cup butter, cubed
   1 teaspoon vanilla extract
Whipped cream, optional

In a large bowl, cream butter and sugar until light and fluffy. Beat in molasses and egg until well blended. Combine the flour, baking soda, ginger, cinnamon and salt; add to creamed mixture alternately with water.

Transfer to a greased 9-in. square baking pan. Bake at 325° for 35-40 minutes or until a toothpick inserted near the center comes out clean. Place on a wire rack.

For caramel sauce, in a small saucepan, combine brown sugar and cornstarch. Stir in water until smooth. Bring to a boil; cook and stir for 2 minutes or until thickened. Remove from the heat; stir in butter and vanilla until smooth. Serve with warm cake. Top with whipped cream if desired.

Russian Holiday Bread

PREP: 40 MIN. + RISING **BAKE:** 40 MIN. + COOLING
YIELD: 2 LOAVES (12 SLICES EACH)

I modified a recipe I found in a cookbook to create this yeast bread chock-full of raisins and candied fruit. The cardamom gives it marvelous aroma and a delectable flavor. I give loaves of this bread as gifts during the holidays, and the recipients are always pleased.

Loraine Meyer ★ Bend, Oregon

   2 packages (1/4 ounce *each*) active dry yeast
 1/2 cup warm water (110° to 115°)
   2 eggs
 3/4 cup 2% milk
 1/2 cup sugar
 1/4 cup butter, softened
   2 teaspoons salt
   2 teaspoons grated lemon peel
   1 teaspoon ground cardamom
   4 to 5 cups all-purpose flour
 1/2 cup chopped blanched almonds
 1/4 cup *each* chopped candied citron, orange peel
     and red cherries
 1/4 cup raisins

In a large bowl, dissolve yeast in warm water. Add the eggs, milk, sugar, butter, salt, lemon peel, cardamom and 2 cups flour. Beat until smooth. Beat in the almonds, citron, orange peel, cherries and raisins. Stir in enough remaining flour to form a soft dough (dough will be sticky).

Turn onto a floured surface; knead until smooth and elastic, about 6-8 minutes. Place in a greased bowl, turning once to grease the top. Cover and let rise in a warm place until doubled, about 1 hour.

Punch dough down. Shape into two loaves. Place in two greased 8-in. x 4-in. loaf pans. Cover and let rise until nearly doubled, about 30 minutes.

Bake at 350° for 40-45 minutes or until golden brown. Remove from pans to wire racks to cool.

Cinnamon Sticky-Bun Ice Cream

PREP: 1 HOUR + FREEZING   **YIELD:** 2-1/4 QUARTS

This creamy homemade cinnamon ice cream has a rich caramel swirl and chunks of cinnamon buns. Serve the extra caramel sauce over this or other ice cream or pound cake.

1-3/4	cups whole milk
2/3	cup plus 2 cups sugar, *divided*
2	eggs, beaten
3	cups heavy whipping cream, *divided*
2	teaspoons ground cinnamon
1	teaspoon vanilla extract
1	cup butter, cubed
1/2	cup water
1	tablespoon corn syrup
2	baked cinnamon buns, cubed
9	tablespoons chopped pecans, toasted

In a large heavy saucepan, heat milk and 2/3 cup sugar until bubbles form around sides of pan. Whisk a small amount of hot mixture into eggs; return all to the pan, whisking constantly. Cook and stir over low heat until mixture reaches at least 160° and coats the back of a spoon.

Remove from the heat. Quickly transfer to a bowl; place in ice water and stir for 2 minutes. Stir in 2 cups cream, cinnamon and vanilla. Press waxed paper onto surface of custard. Refrigerate for several hours or overnight.

For caramel, combine the butter, water and corn syrup in a heavy saucepan. Cook and stir over medium-low heat until butter is melted. Add the remaining sugar; cook and stir until sugar is dissolved.

Bring to a boil over medium heat without stirring. Boil for 4 minutes, without stirring. Continue to boil for 12-15 minutes, stirring constantly, or until mixture is caramel-colored. Remove from the heat. Carefully stir in remaining cream until smooth; set aside to cool.

Fill cylinder of ice cream freezer two-thirds full; freeze according to the manufacturer's directions. Refrigerate remaining mixture until ready to freeze.

In a large freezer container, layer a third of the ice cream, 1/2 cup caramel, 2/3 cup cinnamon buns and 3 tablespoons pecans. Repeat two times. Swirl mixture; freeze until firm. Serve with remaining caramel.

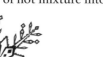

Cranberry-Apple Pie

PREP: 30 MIN. + STANDING
BAKE: 1 HOUR + COOLING   **YIELD:** 8 SERVINGS

Dried cranberries add flecks of festive red color to my tender apple pie. Your kitchen will be filled with a spicy aroma as the pie bakes.

Suzanne Earl ★ Spring, Texas

    2   cups all-purpose flour
    2   tablespoons sugar
    1   teaspoon salt
  3/4   teaspoon ground cardamom
  1/2   cup cold butter
  1/4   cup butter-flavored shortening
    5   to 7 tablespoons cold water
    1   egg white
    1   teaspoon water
FILLING:
    2   cups ice water
  1/2   cup lemon juice
    7   medium apple, peeled and sliced (about 8 cups)
  1/2   cup plus 1 teaspoon sugar, *divided*
  1/3   cup plus 1 tablespoon brown sugar, *divided*
  1/4   cup cornstarch
    2   tablespoons quick-cooking tapioca
    1   teaspoon ground cinnamon
  1/4   teaspoon ground nutmeg
    1   cup dried cranberries
    2   tablespoons butter, cut up
    1   egg yolk
    1   teaspoon water

In a large bowl, combine the flour, sugar, salt and cardamom; cut in butter and shortening until crumbly. Gradually add water, tossing with a fork until dough forms a ball. Divide dough in half so that one portion is slightly larger than the other; wrap each in plastic wrap. Refrigerate for 2 hours or until easy to handle.

Roll out larger portion to fit a 9-in. deep-dish pie plate. Transfer pastry to pie plate. Trim pastry even with edge. Beat egg white and water; brush over pastry.

For filling, in a large bowl, combine ice water and lemon juice. Add apples; let stand for 20 minutes. Combine 1/2 cup sugar, 1/3 cup brown sugar, cornstarch, tapioca, cinnamon and nutmeg.

Drain apples; pat dry. Combine apples and cranberries. Add sugar mixture; toss to coat. Let stand for 15 minutes. Spoon filling into crust; sprinkle with remaining brown sugar and dot with butter.

Roll out remaining pastry to fit top of pie. Place over filling. Trim, seal and flute edges. Cut slits in pastry. Beat egg yolk and water; brush over pastry. Sprinkle with remaining sugar.

Bake at 425° for 20 minutes. Reduce heat to 350° bake 40-45 minutes longer or until crust is golden brown and the filling is bubbly. Cover with foil during the last 20-30 minutes to prevent overbrowning if necessary. Cool on a wire rack.

Honey Roasted Pears

PREP: 10 MIN.   **BAKE:** 45 MIN.   **YIELD:** 4 SERVINGS

My family has passed down this recipe for generations. The elegant pears are simple to make and require only a few minutes of prep, but the results are sensational.

Jan Sokol ★ Overland Park, Kansas

    4   medium pears, peeled
    2   cardamom pods, crushed
    1   teaspoon sugar
  1/4   teaspoon ground cinnamon
  1/8   teaspoon ground cloves
  2/3   cup water
  1/4   cup honey
Whipped cream

Core pears from bottom, leaving stems intact. Place in a greased 11-in. x 7-in. baking dish. Sprinkle with cardamom, sugar, cinnamon and cloves. In a small saucepan, combine water and honey; bring to a boil for 3 minutes. Pour over pears.

Bake, uncovered, at 400° for 45-55 minutes or until tender, basting every 15 minutes. Serve warm with whipped cream.

Chai Cupcakes

PREP: 25 MIN. **BAKE:** 25 MIN. + COOLING
YIELD: 1 DOZEN

You'll get a double dose of the spicy blend that's frequently used to flavor tea in these moist cupcakes. Both the batter and frosting use chai, which combines some of the best flavors of the season.

- 1/2 teaspoon *each* ground ginger, cinnamon, cardamom and cloves
- 1/8 teaspoon pepper
- 1/2 cup butter, softened
-   1 cup sugar
-   1 egg
- 1/2 teaspoon vanilla extract
- 1-1/2 cups cake flour
- 1-1/2 teaspoons baking powder
- 1/4 teaspoon salt
- 2/3 cup 2% milk

FROSTING:
-   6 tablespoons butter, softened
-   3 cups confectioners' sugar
- 3/4 teaspoon vanilla extract
-   3 to 4 tablespoons 2% milk

Ground cinnamon

In a small combine the ginger, cinnamon, cardamom, cloves and pepper; set aside.

In a large bowl, cream butter and sugar until light and fluffy. Beat in egg and vanilla. Combine the flour, baking powder, salt and 1-1/2 teaspoons spice mixture. Gradually add to creamed mixture alternately with milk, beating well after each addition.

Fill paper-lined muffin cups two-thirds full. Bake at 350° for 24-28 minutes or until a toothpick inserted near the center comes out clean. Cool for 10 minutes before removing from pans to wire racks to cool completely.

In a bowl, beat butter until fluffy; beat in the sugar, vanilla and remaining spice mixture until smooth. Add enough milk to achieve desired consistency. Pipe frosting over cupcakes; sprinkle with cinnamon.

Lancaster Spiced Ice Cream Dessert

PREP: 25 MIN. + FREEZING **YIELD:** 8 SERVINGS

Plain vanilla ice cream gets a Christmas makeover with this recipe. Many people can't identify the spices, but they all recognize the flavor as one of warmth and the holidays.

Donna Noel ★ Gray, Maine

1	quart French vanilla ice cream, softened
1/3	cup chopped dried apricots
1/3	cup dried cranberries, chopped
1/3	cup raisins, chopped
2	cups heavy whipping cream, *divided*
1/2	teaspoon ground ginger
1/4	teaspoon ground mace
1/4	teaspoon ground cardamom
1	tablespoon sugar

Additional chopped dried apricots, dried cranberries and raisins
Honey and additional ground mace

In a large bowl, combine the ice cream, apricots, cranberries and raisins. In a small bowl, beat 1 cup cream until it begins to thicken. Add the ginger, mace and cardamom; beat until stiff peaks form. Fold into ice cream. Spoon into a 1-1/2-qt. gelatin mold. Freeze for 4 hours or overnight.

To unmold, wrap bottom of frozen mold in a warm towel until loosened, or dip mold in a pan of warm water. Invert onto a serving plate.

In a small bowl, beat the remaining cream until it begins to thicken. Add sugar; beat until soft peaks form. Spread over top and sides of dessert; sprinkle with additional apricots, cranberries and raisins. Freeze until serving. Let stand for 10 minutes before slicing. Drizzle with honey and sprinkle with additional mace.

Arabian Spiced Nuts

PREP/TOTAL TIME: 25 MIN. **YIELD:** 4 CUPS

Baharat is a North African spice blend that usually consists of peppercorns, cinnamon, nutmeg and other spices. The blend varies by region and even individual cooks. This blend gives the nuts a sweet, then spicy, peppery flavor.

Veronica Gantley ★ Norfolk, Virginia

BAHARAT:

2	tablespoons whole peppercorns
2	tablespoons whole allspice
1	teaspoon ground cinnamon
1/2	teaspoon ground nutmeg

SPICED NUTS:

1/4	cup honey
4	cups lightly salted mixed nuts (1-1/4 pounds)
1/4	cup sugar

In a spice grinder or with a mortar and pestle, combine peppercorns and allspice; grind until mixture becomes a fine powder. Add cinnamon and nutmeg; grind until blended. Store in an airtight container for up to 6 months.

For the spiced nuts, in a 2-qt. microwave-safe dish, microwave honey for 30-45 seconds or until bubbly. Stir in nuts. Transfer to a foil-lined 15-in. x 10-in. x 1-in. baking pan. Bake at 325° for 10 minutes, stirring once. Cool for 5 minutes.

In a small bowl, combine sugar and 1 tablespoon Baharat spice mix. Sprinkle over nuts and toss to coat.

TO MAKE AHEAD: This recipe can be made up to a week in advance.

Caramel Potato Rolls

(pictured at left)

PREP: 20 MIN. + RISING **BAKE:** 25 MIN. **YIELD:** 1 DOZEN

There is a burst of cinnamon in every bite of these ooey-gooey tender rolls. They are good to have on hand when someone drops in for a cup of coffee. Maybe that's why we have so many people dropping in for coffee at our house.

Florence Jerome ★ Helena, Montana

2-1/2	to 3 cups all-purpose flour
1/2	cup sugar
1/4	cup mashed potato flakes
1/4	cup nonfat dry milk powder
1	package (1/4 ounce) active dry yeast
1	teaspoon salt
1	cup hot water
1/4	cup canola oil
1	egg, beaten

TOPPING:

1	cup packed brown sugar
1/4	cup light corn syrup
3	tablespoons butter
36	pecan halves

FILLING:

1/3	cup sugar
2	tablespoons ground cinnamon
3	tablespoons butter, melted

In a large bowl, combine 1 cup flour, sugar, potato flakes, milk powder, yeast and salt. In a small saucepan, heat water and oil to 120°-130°. Add to dry ingredients; beat just until moistened. Add egg; beat until smooth. Stir in enough remaining flour to form a soft dough (dough will be sticky).

Turn onto a floured surface; knead until smooth and elastic, about 6-8 minutes. Place in a greased bowl, turning once to grease the top. Cover and let rise in a warm place until doubled, about 1 hour. Punch dough down.

In a small saucepan, combine the brown sugar, corn syrup and butter; cook and stir over medium heat until sugar is dissolved. Pour into a well greased 13-in. x 9-in. baking dish; sprinkle with pecans.

Turn dough onto a lightly floured surface. Roll into a 12-in. x 15-in. rectangle. Combine sugar and cinnamon. Brush melted butter to within 1/2 in. of edges; sprinkle with sugar mixture. Roll up jelly-roll style, starting with a long side; pinch seam to seal. Cut into 12 rolls.

Place rolls, cut side up, in dish. Cover and let rise in a warm place until doubled, about 15-20 minutes. Bake at 375° for 25-30 minutes. Immediately invert onto a serving platter.

Cardamom-Walnut Pound Cake

PREP: 25 MIN. **BAKE:** 1 HOUR + COOLING
YIELD: 12 SERVINGS

A number of years ago I ordered a slice of walnut cake at a local restaurant that was known for its homemade desserts. The cake was wonderful, and I searched for a recipe to match its great taste. I found this one, and I think it is just as scrumptious.

Rita Glieden ★ Hutchinson, Minnesota

1	cup butter, softened
2	cups sugar
7	eggs
3	teaspoons vanilla extract
2	cups all-purpose flour
3	teaspoons ground cardamom
1/2	teaspoon salt
1/2	cup 2% milk
2	cups finely chopped walnuts

ICING:

3/4	cup confectioners' sugar
3	to 4 teaspoons 2% milk

In a large bowl, cream butter and sugar until light and fluffy, about 5 minutes. Add eggs, one at a time, beating well after each addition. Beat in vanilla. Combine the flour, cardamom and salt; add to the creamed mixture alternately with milk. Beat just until combined. Fold in walnuts.

Transfer batter to a greased and floured 10-in. fluted tube pan. Bake at 325° for 1 to 1-1/4 hours or until a toothpick inserted near the center comes out clean. Cool for 10 minutes before removing from pan to a wire rack to cool completely.

For icing, combine confectioners' sugar and enough milk to achieve desired consistency. Drizzle over cake.

Pumpkin-Cranberry Cake Doughnuts

PREP: 40 MIN. **COOK:** 5 MIN. **YIELD:** 1-1/2 DOZEN

Pumpkin and cranberry really say holiday in my moist, spiced doughnuts. They are so good, you may be tempted to eat them all in one sitting.

Carolyn Cope ★ Allston, Maryland

      3   tablespoons butter, softened
      1   cup sugar
      2   eggs
      1   teaspoon vanilla extract
  3-1/2   cups all-purpose flour
      2   teaspoons baking powder
      1   teaspoon salt
      1   teaspoon ground cinnamon
    1/2   teaspoon baking soda
    1/2   teaspoon ground ginger
    1/4   teaspoon ground cloves
    1/8   teaspoon ground nutmeg
      1   cup canned pumpkin
    1/2   cup buttermilk
      2   cups fresh *or* frozen cranberries, coarsely chopped
Oil for deep-fat frying
SPICED SUGAR:
      1   cup sugar
    3/4   teaspoon ground cinnamon
    1/4   teaspoon ground ginger
    1/8   teaspoon ground cloves
Dash ground nutmeg

In a large bowl, beat butter and sugar until crumbly, about 2 minutes. Add eggs, one at a time, beating well after each addition. Beat in vanilla.

   Combine flour, baking powder, salt, cinnamon, baking soda, ginger, cloves and nutmeg. Combine pumpkin and buttermilk. Add the flour mixture to the creamed mixture alternately with buttermilk mixture, beating well after each addition. Stir in the cranberries. Cover the dough and refrigerate overnight.

   Turn onto a lightly floured surface; roll to 1/2-in. thickness. Cut with a floured 2-1/2-in. doughnut cutter. Reroll scraps.

   In an electric skillet or deep fryer, heat oil to 375°. Fry doughnuts, a few at a time, until golden brown on both sides. Drain on paper towels. In a shallow bowl, combine the sugar, cinnamon, ginger, cloves and nutmeg; roll warm doughnuts in mixture.

Spiced Butter Cookies

PREP: 25 MIN. + CHILLING **BAKE:** 10 MIN./BATCH
YIELD: 6-1/2 DOZEN

Santa won't leave any crumbs on the plate when you put out these wonderful cookies. My mother passed down her recipe for the buttery, crisp cookies to me.

Carol Goss ★ Four Oaks, North Carolina

      1   cup butter, softened
      1   cup sugar
    1/4   teaspoon vanilla extract
  1-3/4   cups all-purpose flour
    1/2   cup cornstarch
      2   teaspoons baking powder
    1/2   teaspoon salt
    1/2   teaspoon ground cardamom
    1/2   teaspoon ground cinnamon
    1/4   to 1/2 teaspoon pepper
    1/4   teaspoon ground cloves
    1/4   cup heavy whipping cream
    2/3   cup chopped almonds

In a large bowl, cream butter and sugar until light and fluffy. Beat in vanilla. Combine the flour, cornstarch, baking powder, salt, cardamom, cinnamon, pepper and cloves; gradually add to the creamed mixture alternately with cream. Stir in almonds. Wrap in plastic wrap; refrigerate for 1 hour or until easy to handle.

   Shape into 3/4-in. balls; place 2 in. apart on ungreased baking sheets. Bake at 350° for 8-10 minutes or until edges begin to brown. Cool for 3 minutes before removing from pans to wire racks. Store in an airtight container.

Gingerbread House Sandwich Cookies

PREP: 1-1/2 HOURS + CHILLING
BAKE: 10 MIN./BATCH + COOLING
YIELD: ABOUT 2-1/2 DOZEN

These cute gingerbread houses are a fun activity to do with your children or grandkids. Let them fill and decorate the houses after the cookies have baked and cooled.

Lisa Speer ★ Palm Beach, Florida

1/2	cup butter, softened
1	cup packed brown sugar
1	egg
1/2	cup molasses
2	teaspoons vanilla extract
3	cups all-purpose flour
1	tablespoon ground ginger
2	teaspoons ground cinnamon
1-1/2	teaspoons baking powder
3/4	teaspoon baking soda
1/8	teaspoon salt

FILLING:

4	ounces cream cheese, softened
4	teaspoons half-and-half cream
1	teaspoon grated lemon peel
1	teaspoon lemon juice
1/8	teaspoon salt
3-1/3	cups confectioners' sugar

ICING:

1	cup confectioners' sugar
2	teaspoons lemon juice
1/4	teaspoon corn syrup
1	tablespoon water

Sprinkles of your choice

In a large bowl, cream butter and brown sugar until light and fluffy. Beat in the egg, molasses and vanilla. Combine the flour, ginger, cinnamon, baking powder, baking soda and salt; gradually add to creamed mixture and mix well. Divide dough into fourths. Refrigerate for 2 hours or until easy to handle.

On a lightly floured surface, roll one portion of dough into a 12-in. x 6-in. rectangle. Cut into twelve 3-in. x 2-in. rectangles. Starting from a short side of each rectangle, cut out roofs. Remove excess dough, reroll scraps and cut out three more houses. Repeat with remaining portions.

Place 1 in. apart on greased baking sheets. Bake at 350° for 8-10 minutes or until lightly browned. Cool for 2 minutes before removing to wire racks to cool completely.

In a large bowl, beat the cream cheese, cream, lemon peel, juice and salt until fluffy. Add confectioners' sugar; beat until smooth. Spread on the bottoms of half of the cookies; top with the remaining cookies.

For icing, combine the confectioners' sugar, lemon juice, corn syrup and water until smooth. Decorate cookies with icing and sprinkles. Let stand until set. Store in an airtight container in the refrigerator.

TO MAKE AHEAD: The dough can be made 2 days in advance; cover and refrigerate. Let stand at room temperature for 30 minutes before rolling out. The cookies can be baked 1 week ahead of time and stored in an airtight container at room temperature or frozen for up to 1 month.

Gingered Cranberry Scones

PREP: 20 MIN. **BAKE:** 20 MIN. **YIELD:** 1 DOZEN

I think scones are fabulous for breakfast or as a snack with tea in the afternoon. My Yuletide scones are flavored with crystallized ginger and bits of cranberry.

Gilda Lester ★ Millsboro, Delaware

2	cups all-purpose flour
1/2	cup quick-cooking oats
1/3	cup sugar
2-1/2	teaspoons baking powder
1/2	teaspoon baking soda
1/2	teaspoon salt
6	tablespoons cold butter
1	cup (8 ounces) sour cream
1	egg, lightly beaten
1/2	cup dried cranberries, coarsely chopped
1/4	cup crystallized ginger, chopped
2	teaspoons grated lemon peel
2	tablespoons heavy whipping cream
2	tablespoons coarse sugar

In a large bowl, combine the flour, oats, sugar, baking powder, baking soda and salt. Cut in butter until mixture resembles coarse crumbs. Whisk sour cream and egg; stir into crumb mixture just until moistened. Stir in the cranberries, ginger and lemon peel. Turn onto a floured surface; knead 10 times.

Divide dough in half; pat each into a 7-in. circle. Cut each into six wedges. Separate wedges and place on a greased baking sheet. Brush with cream; sprinkle with coarse sugar.

Bake at 375° for 20-25 minutes or until golden brown. Serve warm.

Creamy Pumpkin Bubble Ring

PREP: 1 HOUR + RISING **BAKE:** 25 MIN. + COOLING
YIELD: 1 RING (18 PIECES)

I adapted a recipe I saw many years ago on public television to create this caramel-coated pumpkin bread. It makes an impressive hostess gift or bake sale contribution. My young ones love to help by rolling the dough and cream cheese into balls.

Angela Coffman ★ Kansas City, Missouri

2-1/2 to 3 cups all-purpose flour
   1/2 cup sugar
     3 teaspoons active dry yeast
1-1/2 teaspoons ground cinnamon
     1 teaspoon salt
   1/4 teaspoon ground nutmeg
     1 cup canned pumpkin
   1/4 cup 2% milk
     1 egg
   1/2 cup packed brown sugar
   1/4 cup corn syrup
   1/4 cup butter, cubed
     1 cup chopped pecans
     1 package (8 ounces) cream cheese, cut into 18 pieces

In a large bowl, combine 2 cups flour, sugar, yeast, cinnamon, salt and nutmeg. In a small saucepan, heat the pumpkin and milk to 120°-130°. Add to dry ingredients; beat just until moistened. Add egg; beat until smooth. Stir in enough remaining flour to form a soft dough.

Turn onto a floured surface; knead until smooth and elastic, about 6-8 minutes. Place in a greased bowl, turning once to grease the top. Cover and let rise in a warm place until doubled, about 1 hour.

Meanwhile, in a large saucepan, combine the brown sugar, corn syrup and butter. Cook and stir over medium heat until sugar is dissolved. Pour half of the mixture into a greased 10-in. fluted tube pan; sprinkle with half of the pecans.

Punch dough down; divide into 18 pieces. Roll each piece into a ball. Flatten the balls and wrap each around a piece of cream cheese; pinch seams to seal. Place nine balls in prepared pan; top with remaining caramel mixture and pecans. Top with remaining balls. Cover and let rise for 30-45 minutes or until doubled.

Bake, uncovered, at 350° for 25-30 minutes or until lightly browned. Cool for 10 minutes before inverting onto a serving plate. Serve warm.

 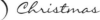

Enchanting ENDINGS

wrap and a damp towel to prevent it from drying out. Repeat layers nine times. Cut stack in half lengthwise, then cut widthwise, forming four rectangles.

Repeat with remaining phyllo on another baking sheet. Bake at 375° for 8-12 minutes or until golden brown. Cool on pans on wire racks. Crumble baked phyllo sheets into 1/2-in. pieces.

To serve, layer 1/2 cup crumbled phyllo, scant 1 tablespoon reduced wine, 2 teaspoons grated chocolate and 2/3 cup ricotta mixture in each of six martini glasses. Sprinkle with remaining chocolate and phyllo.

TO MAKE AHEAD: The ricotta mixture and crumbled phyllo can be prepared a day in advance. Cover and refrigerate ricotta mixture. Store phyllo in an airtight container.

Apple Pie with Walnut Topping

PREP: 20 MIN.   **BAKE:** 45 MIN. + COOLING
YIELD: 8 SERVINGS

Graham crackers add a sweet crunch to the streusel that tops this delightful apple pie. I enjoy it with a scoop of ice cream.

Jessica Bland ★ Riverton, West Virginia

 4   cups thinly sliced peeled tart apples
3/4   cup heavy whipping cream
 1   tablespoon quick-cooking tapioca
 1   tablespoon lemon juice
Pastry for single-crust pie (9 inches)
3/4   cup sugar
1/2   teaspoon ground cinnamon
1/4   teaspoon ground nutmeg
1/8   teaspoon salt
TOPPING:
1/2   cup graham cracker crumbs
1/2   cup packed brown sugar
1/4   cup all-purpose flour
1/4   cup chopped walnuts
1/4   cup butter, melted
1/2   teaspoon ground cinnamon

In a large bowl, combine the apples, cream, tapioca and lemon juice; let stand for 15 minutes.

Meanwhile, roll out pastry to fit a 9-in. pie plate. Transfer pastry to pie plate. Trim pastry to 1/2 in. beyond edge of plate; flute edges.

Combine the sugar, cinnamon, nutmeg and salt; add to apple mixture and toss gently to coat. Spoon filling into pastry. Bake at 375° for 35 minutes.

In a small bowl, combine the topping ingredients. Sprinkle over filling. Bake 10-15 minutes longer or until crust is golden brown and apples are tender. Cool on a wire rack.

Cannoli Martinis

PREP: 25 MIN.   **COOK:** 25 MIN.   **YIELD:** 6 SERVINGS

Showcase this dessert by serving it in martini glasses. Your taste buds will be delighted with this fabulous treat. There's a delicate crunch from the phyllo, a rich creaminess from the ricotta, a subtle wine flavor and a burst of chocolate. This creation is sure to have guests looking for seconds.

Deena Montillo ★ Framingham, Massachusetts

 3   cups ricotta cheese
 1   cup confectioners' sugar
4-1/2   teaspoons half-and-half cream
3/4   teaspoon vanilla extract
 3   cups dry red wine
 12   sheets phyllo dough
1/4   cup butter, melted
 1   bar (3-1/2 ounces) orange-flavored dark chocolate candy bar, grated

In a large bowl, combine the ricotta cheese, confectioners' sugar, cream and vanilla; cover and chill until serving.

Place wine in a large saucepan. Bring to a boil; cook until liquid is reduced to about 1/3 cup. Set aside to cool.

Place one sheet of phyllo dough on a baking sheet; brush with butter. Keep remaining phyllo covered with plastic

Berries & Swedish Cream Tartlets

PREP: 35 MIN. **COOK:** 10 MIN. + CHILLING
YIELD: 2-1/2 DOZEN

A friend of mine brought similar tartlets to a party we were both attending. I knew I just had to have the recipe. I modified it and now my family loves the dessert. Since the tartlets use mixed fresh berries, they are great year-round.

Maria Gruetzmacher ★ Stillwater, Minnesota

1-1/2	teaspoons unflavored gelatin
1	cup heavy whipping cream, *divided*
1/2	cup plus 4-1/2 teaspoons sugar, *divided*
1/2	teaspoon vanilla extract
1/2	teaspoon almond extract
1	cup (8 ounces) sour cream
1-1/2	cups mixed fresh berries
2	packages (1.9 ounces *each*) frozen miniature phyllo tart shells

In a small bowl, sprinkle gelatin over 1/4 cup heavy cream; let stand for 1 minute. In a small saucepan, heat 1/2 cup sugar and remaining heavy cream over low heat until mixture reaches 160°. Remove from the heat and pour over gelatin mixture, stirring to dissolve. Stir in extracts. Cool slightly; refrigerate for 10 minutes.

Stir in the sour cream until blended. Cover the filling and refrigerate overnight.

In a small bowl, toss berries with remaining sugar. Place 1 tablespoon cream mixture in each tart shell; top with berry mixture.

TO MAKE AHEAD: The Swedish cream needs to be made the day before and refrigerated overnight.

Editor's Note: These mini pastries can also be served in puff pastry shells. For six servings, bake frozen puff pastry shells according to package directions and cool. Fill shells with 1/3 cup Swedish cream and 1/4 cup of berries.

White Chocolate Latte Cups

PREP: 30 MIN. **COOK:** 20 MIN. + CHILLING
YIELD: 1-1/2 DOZEN

A smooth, rich caramel fills homemade chocolate cups for a decadent dessert. They are great for entertaining or potlucks.

- 1 cup (6 ounces) dark chocolate chips
- 2 teaspoons shortening

FILLING:

- 3 tablespoons sugar
- 3/4 cup heavy whipping cream
- 1/4 cup coffee liqueur
- 1 teaspoon instant espresso powder
- 14 ounces white baking chocolate, chopped

Chocolate-covered coffee beans

In a microwave, melt chocolate chips and shortening; stir until smooth. Using a narrow pastry brush, brush the inside of eighteen 2-in. foil muffin cup liners with 1/2 teaspoon melted chocolate. Refrigerate for 15 minutes or until firm. Repeat layers twice. Chill until set.

In a large heavy skillet, cook sugar over medium-low heat until melted and turns a golden amber color. Gradually stir in cream; cook and stir until sugar is dissolved. Add liqueur and espresso powder; stir until smooth. Stir in white chocolate until melted. Transfer to a small bowl; cover and refrigerate for 1-2 hours or until slightly thickened.

Carefully remove and discard foil liners from chocolate cups. Spoon or pipe filling into cups; garnish with coffee beans. Store in an airtight container in the refrigerator.

Sweet Potato Pound Cake with Marshmallow Frosting

PREP: 20 MIN.   **BAKE:** 55 MIN. + COOLING
YIELD: 16 SERVINGS

Sweet potatoes make tender spice cake so moist that you can dig into it without any frosting. I, however, like a little dollop of sweetness. So, I add a bit of frosting directly on each warm slice. The frosting melts into the cake, making it even more fabulous.

Emma Chapman ★ Springfield, Missouri

- 1   cup butter, softened
- 1   cup sugar
- 1   cup packed brown sugar
- 4   eggs
- 2   cups mashed sweet potatoes
- 2   teaspoons vanilla extract
- 3-1/4 cups all-purpose flour
- 2   teaspoons baking powder
- 1/2 teaspoon baking soda
- 1/2 teaspoon ground nutmeg
- 1/2 teaspoon ground cinnamon
- 1/8 teaspoon salt
- 1/2 cup 2% milk

MARSHMALLOW FROSTING:
- 1/2 cup butter, softened
- 1/2 cup confectioners' sugar
- 1/2 jar (3-1/2 ounces) marshmallow creme
- 1/4 teaspoon vanilla extract

In a large bowl, cream butter and sugars until light and fluffy. Add eggs, one at a time, beating well after each addition. Beat in sweet potatoes and vanilla.

Combine the flour, baking powder, baking soda, nutmeg, cinnamon and salt; add to the creamed mixture alternately with milk, beating well after each addition.

Transfer to a greased and floured 10-in. fluted tube pan. Bake at 350° for 55-60 minutes or until a toothpick inserted near the center comes out clean. Cool for 10 minutes before removing from pan to a wire rack to cool completely.

In a small bowl, cream butter and confectioners' sugar. Beat in marshmallow creme and vanilla. Serve warm cake with a dollop of frosting.

Holiday Treat Containers

These easy-to-make food containers are a fun way to present treats that guests can take home. They also are a simple way to serve snack mixes, nuts or popcorn at a party.

1. Fold a 12-in. square of double-sided paper in half diagonally to make a triangle.
2. Fold opposite sides in as shown, making sure the top edges are parallel with the bottom edge.
3. Fold the top layer down. If desired, wrap a ribbon around the container and tie. Place the treats inside the pocket.

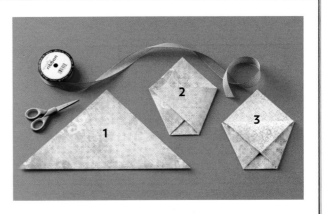

Cranberry Ginger Bark

(pictured at left)

PREP: 25 MIN. + CHILLING   **YIELD:** ABOUT 1-1/2 POUNDS

Need an item for a seasonal bake sale, cookie exchange or party? Try this treat. The crystallized ginger adds such a special touch to this lovely looking bark.

- 18 ounces white baking chocolate, chopped
- 2/3 cup dried cranberries
- 2/3 cup crystallized ginger, chopped
- 2/3 cup lightly salted cashews
- 2 ounces dark chocolate chips

In a microwave, melt white chocolate: stir until smooth. Combine the cranberries, ginger and cashews. Remove 2/3 cup and set aside. Stir remaining cranberry mixture into melted chocolate.

Spread onto a waxed paper-lined baking sheet. Sprinkle with reserved cranberry mixture. Refrigerate for 30 minutes or until firm.

In a microwave, melt dark chocolate chips; stir until smooth. Drizzle over candy. Chill until firm. Break into pieces. Store in an airtight container.

Apple Cranberry Upside-Down Cakes

PREP: 25 MIN.   **BAKE:** 15 MIN.   **YIELD:** 6 SERVINGS

Cornmeal gives this upside-down cake a unique texture. Apples, cranberries and pecans make a delicious alternative to the typical pineapple and cherries.

Margee Berry ★ White Salmon, Washington

- 2 medium tart apples, peeled and diced
- 1/3 cup packed brown sugar
- 1 teaspoon lemon juice
- 2 tablespoons butter
- 1/2 cup dried cranberries
- 1/3 cup chopped pecans
- 3/4 cup all-purpose flour
- 1/2 cup yellow cornmeal
- 1/3 cup sugar
- 1-1/2 teaspoons baking powder
- 1/2 teaspoon ground cinnamon
- 1/4 teaspoon salt
- 3/4 cup buttermilk
- 1/4 cup olive oil
- 1 egg

TOPPING:
- 1/2 cup heavy whipping cream
- 2 tablespoons sour cream
- 2 tablespoons confectioners' sugar

In a large skillet, cook the apples, brown sugar and lemon juice in butter over medium heat until apples are tender. Stir in cranberries and pecans. Place in six greased jumbo muffin cups. In a large bowl, combine the flour, cornmeal, sugar, baking powder, cinnamon and salt. In a small bowl, whisk the buttermilk, oil and egg. Stir into dry ingredients just until moistened. Pour over apple mixture.

Bake at 400° for 14-18 minutes or until a toothpick inserted near the center comes out clean. Carefully run a knife around edges of cakes to loosen. Cool for 3 minutes before inverting onto a serving plate.

In a small bowl, beat cream until it begins to thicken. Add sour cream and confectioners' sugar; beat until soft peaks form. Serve with warm cakes.

Cherry Chocolate Pecan Pie

PREP: 25 MIN. **BAKE:** 40 MIN. + COOLING
YIELD: 8 SERVINGS

*I'm a pie baker, and this is one my family frequently requests.
With the brandy-infused cherries and chocolate chips, it's an
awesome twist on a pecan pie.*

Sonya Labbe ★ Los Angeles, California

        3/4   cup dried cherries
        1/2   cup brandy
CRUST:
    1-1/4   cups all-purpose flour
        1   tablespoon sugar
        1/4   teaspoon salt
        1/4   cup canola oil
        3   tablespoons 2% milk
FILLING:
        1/3   cup butter, softened
    1-1/2   cups sugar
        3   eggs
        3/4   cup all-purpose flour
        1/8   teaspoon salt
        1   cup chopped pecans
        2   ounces semisweet chocolate, chopped
Chocolate whipped cream, optional

In a small bowl, combine cherries and brandy. Cover and
refrigerate for 1 hour.

In a small bowl, combine the flour, sugar and salt.
Combine oil and milk; using a fork, stir oil mixture into
flour mixture just until blended. Pat evenly onto the
bottom and up the sides of a greased 9-in. pie plate; set
aside. Drain cherries, reserving 1 tablespoon brandy; set
aside.

For the filling, in a large bowl, cream butter and sugar
until light and fluffy. Beat in eggs and reserved brandy.
Combine flour and salt; gradually add to creamed mixture.
Fold in the pecans, chocolate and cherries; pour into
prepared pastry.

Bake at 325° for 40-45 minutes or until golden brown.
Cover edges with foil during the last 15 minutes to prevent
overbrowning if necessary. Cool on a wire rack. Serve with
whipped cream if desired. Refrigerate leftovers.

CHOCOLATE WHIPPED CREAM: Beat 1/2 cup heavy whipping cream
until it begins to thicken. Add 2 tablespoons chocolate syrup and beat
until stiff peaks form.

Persimmon Pudding

PREP: 15 MIN. **BAKE:** 40 MIN. + COOLING
YIELD: 24 SERVINGS

*Fall is a wonderful time of year in the Midwest, and this
dessert is a favorite of mine during those months. This old-
fashioned pudding is moist, dense and firm. It's not like the
packaged pudding mixes.*

Judy Tharp ★ Indianapolis, Indiana

    1-1/2   cups all-purpose flour
        1   cup sugar
        1   cup packed brown sugar
        1   teaspoon baking powder
        1   teaspoon baking soda
        1/2   teaspoon ground cinnamon
        1/8   teaspoon salt
        2   cups mashed ripe Hachiya persimmon pulp
    1-1/2   cups buttermilk
        3   eggs
        1/4   cup butter, melted
        1   teaspoon vanilla extract
        1   teaspoon maple flavoring
Sweetened whipped cream

In a large bowl, combine the first seven ingredients. In
another large bowl, whisk the persimmon, buttermilk, eggs,
butter, vanilla and maple flavoring. Stir into dry ingredients
just until moistened.

Transfer to a greased 13-in. x 9-in. baking pan. Bake
at 325° for 40-45 minutes or until pudding begins to pull
away from sides of pan and center is firm. Serve warm with
whipped cream.

Bananas Foster Pie

PREP: 45 MIN. + CHILLING **YIELD:** 8 SERVINGS

I love peanut butter with banana, so it only made sense to me to make a pie with that combination. I also used the flavors of bananas foster to create this delectable pie.

Emily Hobbs ★ Ozark, Missouri

1-1/2   cups crushed vanilla wafers (about 45 wafers)
  1/4   cup butter, melted

FILLING:

  2   tablespoons butter
  1/3   cup all-purpose flour
  2/3   cup packed brown sugar
  3/4   teaspoon ground cinnamon
  1/4   teaspoon salt
  1/4   teaspoon ground nutmeg
  2   cups 2% milk
  4   egg yolks
  1/3   cup creamy peanut butter

  1   tablespoon dark rum
  1   teaspoon vanilla extract
  3   medium bananas
Whipped cream, caramel sundae syrup and chopped
      salted peanuts

Combine the wafer crumbs and butter; press onto the bottom and up the sides of a greased 9-in. pie plate. Bake at 350° for 8-10 minutes or until crust is lightly browned. Cool on a wire rack. In a large saucepan, melt butter. Stir in the flour, brown sugar, cinnamon, salt and nutmeg until smooth. Gradually add milk. Bring to a boil; cook and stir for 2 minutes or until thickened. Remove from the heat.

Stir a small amount of hot filling into egg yolks; return all to the pan, stirring constantly. Bring to a gentle boil; cook and stir 2 minutes longer. Remove from the heat. Stir in the peanut butter, rum and vanilla. Slice bananas into the crust; pour filling over top. Refrigerate for 3 hours or until set. Garnish as desired with whipped cream, caramel syrup and peanuts. Store leftovers in the refrigerator.

Fudge Fantasy Cake

(pictured at left)

PREP: 1 HOUR + CHILLING
BAKE: 25 MIN. + COOLING
YIELD: 12 SERVINGS

You'll catch everyone's attention when you present this showstopper. This exquisite chocolate cake tastes just as fabulous as it looks. Your guests are sure to say "wow!"

Jannine Fisk ★ Malden, Massachusetts

4	eggs
2	cups buttermilk
2	cups cold strong brewed coffee
1	cup canola oil
1	cup honey
2	teaspoons vanilla extract
3-1/2	cups all-purpose flour
3	cups sugar
1-1/2	cups baking cocoa
2	teaspoons salt
1-1/2	teaspoons baking soda
1	teaspoon baking powder

CHOCOLATE-COVERED STRAWBERRIES:

6	ounces semisweet chocolate, chopped
12	fresh strawberries

FILLING:

8	ounces semisweet chocolate, chopped
1	cup heavy whipping cream
1	teaspoon instant coffee granules

FROSTING:

1	cup butter, softened
1	package (2 pounds) confectioners' sugar
1-1/2	cups baking cocoa
1-1/4	cups half-and-half cream
2	teaspoons vanilla extract
3	cups sliced fresh strawberries

GARNISH:

1-1/2	cups crushed chocolate wafers

Chocolate curls

Line four 9-in. round baking pans with waxed paper; grease and flour the pans and paper. Set aside.

In a large bowl, beat eggs, buttermilk, coffee, oil, honey and vanilla until well blended. Combine flour, sugar, cocoa, salt, baking soda and baking powder; add to egg mixture and beat just until blended. Pour batter to prepared pans.

Bake at 350° for 25-30 minutes or until a toothpick inserted near center comes out clean. Cool for 10 minutes before removing from pans to wire racks to cool completely.

For strawberries, in a microwave, melt chocolate; stir until smooth. Dip strawberries in chocolate; allow excess to drip off. Place on waxed paper; let stand until set.

For filling, place chocolate in a small bowl. In a small saucepan, bring cream and coffee granules just to a boil. Pour over chocolate; whisk until smooth. Refrigerate, stirring occasionally, until ganache reaches a spreading consistency, about 45 minutes.

For frosting, in a bowl, beat butter, confectioners' sugar and cocoa until fluffy. Add cream and vanilla; beat until smooth.

Place one cake layer on a plate. Spread with 1/2 cup filling; arrange 1 cup sliced strawberries over filling. Repeat layers twice. Top with remaining cake layer; spread remaining filling over top. Frost sides and top edge of cake with 4 cups frosting. Press crushed wafers into sides of cake; pipe remaining frosting around edges. Top with chocolate curls and chocolate-covered strawberries. Store in the refrigerator.

Limoncello Tiramisu

PREP: 30 MIN. + CHILLING   **YIELD:** 16 SERVINGS

A lemon version of a traditional dessert? Yes. It's divine!

1/2	cup sugar
1/4	cup water
2	tablespoons limoncello

LEMON CURD:

1-1/2	cups sugar
1/3	cup plus 1 tablespoon cornstarch
1-1/2	cups cold water
3	egg yolks, lightly beaten
3	tablespoons butter, cubed
1/2	cup lemon juice
2	teaspoons grated lemon peel

CREAM FILLING:

1-1/2	cups heavy whipping cream
3/4	cup sugar
1	carton (8 ounces) Mascarpone cheese

ASSEMBLY:

3	packages (3 ounces *each*) ladyfingers, split
4	macaroon cookies, crumbled

In a small saucepan, bring sugar and water to a boil. Cook and stir until sugar is dissolved. Remove from the heat. Stir in limoncello; set aside.

For lemon curd, in another saucepan, combine sugar and cornstarch. Stir in water until smooth. Bring to a boil; cook and stir for 1 minute or until thickened. Remove from the heat.

Stir a small amount of hot mixture into egg yolks; return all to the pan, stirring constantly. Bring to a gentle boil; cook and stir 2 minutes longer. Remove from the heat. Stir in butter. Gently stir in lemon juice and peel. Cool to room temperature without stirring.

In a large bowl, beat cream until it begins to thicken. Add sugar; beat until stiff peaks form. Fold cheese and whipped cream into lemon curd.

Arrange a third of the ladyfingers on the bottom of a 9-in. springform pan. Drizzle with a third of the syrup; spread with a third of the filling. Repeat layers twice. Cover and refrigerate overnight. Carefully run a knife around edge of pan to loosen. Remove sides of pan. Sprinkle with cookies.

Candied Lemon Peel

PREP: 1-3/4 HOURS **COOK:** 50 MIN. + STANDING
YIELD: 1 POUND

This old-fashioned candy can also be used as a garnish for other desserts. The sweet-tart taste is delightful.

Betty Slivon ★ Sun City, Arizona

- 8 large lemons
- 2 cups sugar
- 2 cups water
- 1-1/2 cups superfine sugar
- 1-1/2 cups semisweet chocolate chips
- 2 tablespoons shortening

With a sharp knife, score each lemon, cutting peel into four wedge-shaped sections. Loosen and remove peel with a spoon (save fruit for another use).

Place peel in a large heavy saucepan and cover with cold water. Bring to a boil. Cover and cook for 30 minutes. Drain and repeat. Cool for 5 minutes. Carefully scrape off excess pulp from peel. Cut the peel into 1/4-in. strips.

In another saucepan, combine the sugar and water; cook and stir over medium heat until sugar is dissolved. Add the lemon strips. Bring to a boil. Reduce the heat; simmer, uncovered, for 50-60 minutes or until peels are transparent, stirring occasionally.

Using a slotted spoon, transfer strips to wire racks placed over a baking pan. Let stand for 1 hour. Sprinkle superfine sugar into an ungreased 15-in. x 10-in. pan. Sprinkle strips over sugar; toss to coat. Let stand for 8 hours or overnight, tossing occasionally.

In a microwave, melt chocolate chips and shortening; stir until smooth. Dip one end of each strip into chocolate mixture; place on waxed paper until set. Store in an airtight container for up to 2 weeks.

Apricot Eggnog Bars

PREP: 20 MIN. **BAKE:** 35 MIN. + CHILLING **YIELD:** 1 DOZEN

One year, I had a caroling party and served eggnog. I ended up with a lot left over. Since I did not want to toss out a half gallon of eggnog, I looked for a recipe to use it up. In the end, I took a little from several recipes I found and came up with this tasty treat.

Barbara Lento ★ Houston, Pennsylvania

- 1-1/2 cups crushed gingersnap cookies (about 30 cookies)
- 3/4 cup sliced almonds
- 1/2 cup butter, melted
- 9 ounces white baking chocolate, *divided*
- 3/4 cup chopped dried apricots
- 1 package (8 ounces) cream cheese, softened
- 2 teaspoons apricot brandy
- 2 cups eggnog
- 1 egg, lightly beaten

In a small bowl, combine the crushed cookie crumbs, almonds and butter. Press onto the bottom of an ungreased 11-in. x 7-in. baking dish. Bake at 350° for 8-10 minutes or until golden brown. Cool on a wire rack.

Chop 8 oz. white chocolate. In a small saucepan, melt chopped chocolate; cool. Sprinkle apricots over crust.

In a bowl, beat cream cheese until smooth. Beat in the melted chocolate and brandy. Gradually beat in eggnog. Add egg; beat on low speed just until combined. Pour over crust.

Place the baking dish in a larger baking pan; add 1 in. of boiling water to larger pan. Bake, uncovered, at 350° for 35-40 minutes or until the center is just set (mixture will jiggle).

Remove baking dish from water bath; cool on a wire rack. Cover and refrigerate for 2 hours or until firm. Chop and melt remaining chocolate; drizzle over top. Cut into bars. Refrigerate leftovers.

Cran-Apple Wontons a la Mode

PREP: 30 MIN. **BAKE:** 15 MIN. **YIELD:** 12 SERVINGS

These fancy wontons are a combination of a delicious array of flavors and textures. The crisp, flaky wontons go so well with the sweet, tender apples and vanilla ice cream.

Jamie Jones ★ Madison, Georgia

- 2 medium tart apples, peeled and finely chopped
- 1 cup fresh cranberries
- 1/2 cup packed brown sugar
- 2 tablespoons honey
- 1 teaspoon ground cinnamon
- 24 wonton wrappers
- 1 quart vanilla ice cream

Finely chopped toasted walnuts and additional honey

In a saucepan, combine the first five ingredients. Cook over medium heat until berries pop, about 15 minutes.

Place 2 teaspoons of cranberry mixture in the center of a wonton wrapper. Moisten edges with water; fold one corner diagonally over filling and press to seal. Repeat with remaining wrappers and filling. (Keep remaining wrappers covered with a damp paper towel until ready to use.)

Place wontons on greased baking sheets. Bake at 350° for 12-15 minutes or until golden brown. Divide warm wontons among 12 serving plates. Top each with a scoop of ice cream. Sprinkle with walnuts and drizzle with additional honey.

TO MAKE AHEAD: The wontons may be frozen for up to 3 months. Bake at 350° for 15-18 minutes or until golden brown.

Chocolate Pavlova

(pictured at left)

PREP: 20 MIN. **BAKE:** 45 MIN. + COOLING
YIELD: 8 SERVINGS

A mild chocolate-flavored meringue is topped with a fresh fruit mixture that's colored appropriately for the season.

- 4 egg whites
- 1 teaspoon red wine vinegar
- 1/4 teaspoon cream of tartar
- 1/4 teaspoon salt
- 1 cup sugar
- 2 tablespoons baking cocoa
- 1 ounce semisweet chocolate, finely chopped
- 1 cup fresh raspberries
- 1 cup sliced fresh strawberries
- 2 tablespoons orange liqueur, *divided*
- 1 cup heavy whipping cream
- 2 tablespoons confectioners' sugar
- 2 medium kiwifruit, peeled, halved and sliced

Place egg whites in a large bowl; let stand at room temperature for 30 minutes. Line a baking sheet with parchment paper; set aside.

Add the vinegar, cream of tartar and salt to egg whites; beat on medium speed until soft peaks form. Gradually beat in sugar, 1 tablespoon at a time, on high until stiff glossy peaks form and sugar is dissolved. Fold in cocoa and chocolate.

Spread into a 9-in. circle on prepared pan, forming a shallow well in the center. Bake at 250° for 45-55 minutes or until set and dry. Turn off oven and do not open door; leave meringue in oven for 1 hour.

In a small bowl, combine raspberries and strawberries. Drizzle with 1 tablespoon liqueur; toss gently to coat. In a small bowl, beat cream until it begins to thicken. Add confectioners' sugar and remaining liqueur; beat until soft peaks form.

Top meringue with berries. Arrange kiwi over berries; top with whipped cream. Refrigerate leftovers.

Orange-Glazed Cake

PREP: 30 MIN. **BAKE:** 40 MIN. + COOLING
YIELD: 12 SERVINGS

When I take a bite of this cake, it brings back marvelous memories from my childhood. Each luscious, moist piece is just bursting with orange flavor.

Deborah Forrest ★ Ocean Springs, Mississippi

- 2 medium oranges
- 1 cup butter, softened
- 1-3/4 cups sugar, *divided*
- 3 eggs, *separated*
- 1-3/4 cups all-purpose flour
- 1 teaspoon baking powder
- 1 teaspoon baking soda
- 1/2 teaspoon salt
- 1 cup (8 ounces) sour cream
- 1 medium lemon

Grease and lightly flour a 10-in. fluted tube pan; set aside.

Finely grate the peel from the oranges; set aside. In a large bowl, cream butter and 1 cup sugar until light and fluffy. Add egg yolks, one at a time, beating well after each addition. Stir in reserved orange peel. Combine the flour, baking powder, baking soda and salt; add to the creamed mixture alternately with sour cream, beating well after each addition.

In another large bowl, beat egg whites until stiff peaks form; fold into batter. Transfer to prepared pan. Bake at 325° for 40-45 minutes or until a toothpick inserted near the center comes out clean.

Meanwhile, squeeze juice from the oranges and lemon. In a small saucepan, combine the juices with the remaining sugar. Bring to a boil. Reduce heat; simmer, uncovered, for 20-25 minutes or until mixture is reduced by half. Remove from the heat.

Cool cake for 10 minutes before inverting onto a wire rack. Cool 10 minutes longer. Place rack on waxed paper. Brush warm cake with glaze.

Milky Way Fudge

PREP: 10 MIN. + CHILLING **YIELD:** ABOUT 1-1/2 POUNDS

If you're busy but would still like to make something special for the holidays, try this fudge. It uses candy bars and is cooked in the microwave. It takes mere minutes to make.

Arla Docherty ★ East Moline, Illinois

- 1 teaspoon butter
- 1 can (14 ounces) sweetened condensed milk
- 2 cups (12 ounces) semisweet chocolate chips
- 3 Milky Way candy bars (2.05 ounces *each*), chopped
- 1 teaspoon vanilla extract

Line a 9-in. square pan with foil and grease the foil with butter; set aside.

In a large microwave-safe bowl, combine the milk, chocolate chips and candy bars. Microwave, uncovered, on high for 1 minute; stir. Microwave at additional 15-second intervals, stirring until smooth. Stir in vanilla. Spread into prepared pan. Refrigerate for 1 hour or until firm.

Using foil, lift fudge out of pan; cut fudge into 1-in. squares. Store in an airtight container in the refrigerator.

Peppermint Candy Cheesecake

PREP: 50 MIN. **BAKE:** 55 MIN. + CHILLING
YIELD: 16 SERVINGS

I use this peppermint cheesecake as a dramatic centerpiece on my table. For our family, it's a traditional Christmas dessert.

Linda Stemen ★ Monroeville, Indiana

1-1/2	cups graham cracker crumbs
1/3	cup butter, melted
1/4	cup sugar

FILLING:

5	packages (8 ounces *each*) cream cheese, softened
1	cup sugar
1	cup sour cream
2	tablespoons all-purpose flour
1	teaspoon vanilla extract
5	eggs, lightly beaten
30	peppermint candies, crushed

Red food coloring, optional

TOPPING:

1	cup heavy whipping cream
1/4	cup confectioners' sugar

Additional crushed peppermint candies

Place a greased 10-in. springform pan on a double thickness of heavy-duty foil (about 18 in. square). Securely wrap around pan. In a bowl, mix cracker crumbs, butter and sugar. Press onto bottom of prepared pan. Place on a baking sheet. Bake at 350° for 8-10 minutes or until set. Cool on a wire rack.

In a large bowl, beat cream cheese and sugar until smooth. Beat in the sour cream, flour and vanilla. Add eggs; beat on low speed just until combined. Fold in crushed candies and a few drops of red food coloring if desired. Pour over crust. Place springform pan in a large baking pan; add 1 in. of hot water to larger pan.

Bake at 350° for 55 to 65 minutes or until center is just set and top appears dull. Remove springform pan from water bath. Cool on a wire rack for 10 minutes. Carefully run a knife around edge of pan to loosen; cool 1 hour longer. Refrigerate overnight. Remove sides of pan.

In a small bowl, beat cream until it begins to thicken. Add sugar; beat until stiff peaks form. Pipe around edge of cheesecake and sprinkle with additional crushed candies.

Golden Walnut Caramel Squares

PREP: 40 MIN. **COOK:** 40 MIN. + CHILLING
YIELD: 6-1/2 DOZEN

Rich, walnut-packed caramel tops a buttery crust in this decadent candy.

Marie Rizzio ★ Interlochen, Michigan

1	cup all-purpose flour
3	tablespoons sugar
1/2	cup cold butter
1/3	cup semisweet chocolate chips

CARAMEL LAYER:

1-1/3	cups sugar
1	cup butter, cubed
1	cup heavy whipping cream
1/3	cup corn syrup
2-1/2	cups chopped walnuts
1	ounce unsweetened chocolate, chopped

Line a 9-in. baking pan with foil and grease the foil; set aside.

In a large bowl, combine flour and sugar. Cut in butter until mixture resembles coarse crumbs. Press into prepared pan; prick crust with a fork. Bake at 350° for 18-22 minutes or until set and edges begin to brown.

Immediately sprinkle with chocolate chips. Allow chips to soften for a few minutes, then spread over crust; set aside.

In a large heavy skillet over medium-low heat, cook sugar until melted. Do not stir. Reduce heat to low; cook for 5 minutes or until golden brown.

In a large saucepan, combine the butter, cream and corn syrup. Slowly pour in cooked sugar. Cook and stir over medium heat until a candy thermometer reads 240° (soft-ball stage). Remove from the heat; stir in walnuts. Pour over prepared crust.

In a microwave, melt chocolate; stir until smooth Drizzle over caramel layer. Cover and refrigerate for 2 hours or until firm. Using foil, lift candy out of pan. Gently peel off foil; cut candy into squares.

Editor's Note: We recommend that you test your candy thermometer before each use by bringing water to a boil; the thermometer should read 212°. Adjust your recipe temperature up or down based on your test.

Salted Soft Caramels

PREP/TOTAL TIME: 30 MIN.   **YIELD:** 2-1/2 DOZEN

Velvety smooth homemade caramels are sprinkled with kosher salt to create a sweet-salty sensation. Best of all, these caramels don't call for each to be wrapped in waxed paper or plastic wrap. The hot caramel is poured into cute candy cups instead.

Kathryn Conrad ★ Milwaukee, Wisconsin

- 1/2 cup heavy whipping cream
- 2 tablespoons plus 1-1/2 teaspoons butter
- 1/4 teaspoon kosher salt
- 3/4 cup sugar
- 2 tablespoons water
- 2 tablespoons light corn syrup

Smoked *or* kosher salt

Arrange 30 paper or foil candy cups on a baking sheet. Spritz each cup with cooking spray; set aside. In a small heavy saucepan, bring the cream, butter and salt to a boil; keep warm.

In a large heavy saucepan, combine the sugar, water and corn syrup; cook until sugar is dissolved, stirring occasionally. Bring to a boil; cook, without stirring, until mixture turns a golden amber color, about 4 minutes.

Gradually stir in the cream mixture. Cook and stir over medium heat until a candy thermometer reads 247°.

Remove from the heat. Pour into prepared liners (do not scrape saucepan). Sprinkle with salt. Let stand until firm, about 2 hours.

Editor's Note: We recommend that you test your candy thermometer before each use by bringing water to a boil; the thermometer should read 212°. Adjust your recipe temperature up or down based on your test. You could also top with toasted nuts, candied ginger or candied flowers.

By using candy cups, you eliminate the chore of individually wrapping each caramel in waxed paper or plastic wrap. Pour the hot caramel into cups that are coated with cooking spray. Top as desired. The cooled caramels will pop right out of the cups.

Cherry Whoopie Pies

PREP: 30 MIN.   **BAKE:** 10 MIN./BATCH + COOLING
YIELD: 3 DOZEN

Red velvet cake is so good that I decided to create whoopie pies out of packaged cake mix. The individual pies are filled with velvety cream cheese frosting. Your family is sure to love my dessert, which is also ideal for bake sales and potlucks.

Lesley Marie Boylan ★ Centerville, Iowa

```
 1    package (18-1/4 ounces) red velvet cake mix
 3    eggs
1/2   cup canola oil
 1    teaspoon almond extract
36    maraschino cherries, halved
```
FILLING:
```
3/4   cup cream cheese frosting
2/3   cup whipped topping
1/2   cup chopped maraschino cherries
```

In a large bowl, combine the cake mix, eggs, oil and extract; beat on low speed for 30 seconds. Beat on medium for 2 minutes.

Drop by heaping teaspoonfuls 2 in. apart onto greased baking sheets. Top each with a cherry half. Bake at 350° for 8-10 minutes or until edges are set. Cool for 2 minutes before removing to wire racks to cool completely.

For filling, beat frosting and whipped topping until blended; fold in chopped cherries. Spread filling on the bottoms of half of the cookies; top with remaining cookies. Store in the refrigerator.

TO MAKE AHEAD: The cookies can be baked the day before assembly. Store in an airtight container.

Italian Flan

PREP: 20 MIN.   **BAKE:** 1 HOUR + CHILLING
YIELD: 8 SERVINGS

This rich, silky custard has a hint of coffee flavor and is draped with a luscious caramel sauce. It is a divine ending to a holiday meal or as a treat at a simple coffee and dessert get-together with friends.

Mariela Petroski ★ Helena, Montana

```
3/4   cup sugar
 3    tablespoons water
 1    can (14 ounces) sweetened condensed milk
 1    cup heavy whipping cream
 4    eggs
1/2   cup whole milk
 2    tablespoons Amaretto
 2    teaspoons instant espresso powder
```
Whipped cream and chopped hazelnuts

In a large heavy saucepan over medium heat, combine sugar and water. Cook stirring occasionally until sugar begins to melt. Using a pastry brush dipped in cold water, wash down the sides of the pan to eliminate sugar crystals. Cook without stirring until amber brown, about 8 minutes.

Quickly pour into an ungreased 9-in. round baking pan, tilting to coat bottom of pan. Place pan in a large baking pan; let stand for 10 minutes.

In a blender, combine the condensed milk, cream, eggs, milk, Amaretto and espresso powder. Cover and process for 1 minute or until well blended. Slowly pour into prepared baking pan.

Add 1 in. of hot water to larger pan. Bake, uncovered, at 325° for 1 to 1-1/4 hours or until center is just set (mixture will jiggle). Remove baking pan from water bath; cool for 1 hour. Cover and refrigerate overnight.

To serve flan, run a knife around edge of pan; invert onto a rimmed serving dish. Garnish with whipped cream and hazelnuts.

Pumpkin-Toffee Cake Roll

(pictured at left)

PREP: 30 MIN. **BAKE:** 15 MIN. + COOLING
YIELD: 12 SERVINGS

This cake roll is a must-have for our family parties. The decadent whipped cream filling has specks of toffee and a mild rum flavor. It's so scrumptious.

Betty Fulks ★ Onia, Arkansas

6	eggs
3/4	cup cake flour
1-1/2	teaspoons ground cinnamon
1-1/4	teaspoons ground ginger
3/4	teaspoon ground allspice
1/8	teaspoon salt
1/3	cup sugar
1/3	cup packed brown sugar
2/3	cup canned pumpkin

Confectioners' sugar

FILLING:

1	teaspoon unflavored gelatin
2	tablespoons dark rum
1	cup heavy whipping cream
3	tablespoons confectioners' sugar
1/3	cup plus 1/2 cup toffee bits, *divided*
1/2	cup caramel sundae syrup

Additional confectioners' sugar

Separate eggs. Place egg whites in a large bowl; let stand at room temperature for 30 minutes. Line a greased 15-in. x 10-in. x 1-in. baking pan with waxed paper; grease the paper and set aside. Sift flour, cinnamon, ginger, allspice and salt together twice; set aside.

In a large bowl, beat yolks until slightly thickened. Gradually add sugars, beating on high speed until thick. Beat in pumpkin. Gradually add flour mixture to yolk mixture and mix well.

With clean beaters, beat egg whites until stiff peaks form. Gradually fold into batter. Spread into prepared pan.

Bake at 350° for 15-18 minutes or until cake springs back when lightly touched. Cool for 5 minutes. Invert onto a kitchen towel dusted with confectioners' sugar. Gently peel off waxed paper. Roll up cake in the towel jelly-roll style, starting with a short side. Cool completely on a wire rack.

For filling, in a small saucepan, sprinkle gelatin over rum; let stand for 1 minute. Heat over low heat, stirring until gelatin is completely dissolved. Remove from the heat; set aside.

In a large bowl, beat cream until it begins to thicken. Add confectioners' sugar; beat until stiff peaks form. Fold in rum mixture and 1/3 cup toffee bits.

Unroll cake; sprinkle with 1/4 cup toffee bits. Spread filling over cake to within 1/2 in. of edges. Roll up again. Place cake seam side down on a serving platter. Dust with the additional confectioners' sugar. Drizzle with caramel syrup; sprinkle with the remaining toffee bits. Refrigerate until serving.

Sweet Potato Pecan Pie

PREP: 30 MIN. **BAKE:** 40 MIN. + COOLING
YIELD: 8 SERVINGS

The graham cracker crust for this heavenly pie is a nice change from a pastry crust. The coconut and pecan crumb topping makes it extra-special.

Heather Hunsaker ★ Austin, Texas

1-3/4	cups graham cracker crumbs
3	tablespoons brown sugar
1/2	teaspoon ground cinnamon
1/2	cup butter, melted

FILLING:

1-1/2	cups mashed sweet potatoes
1	cup apple butter
3/4	cup evaporated milk
3	eggs
1/2	cup packed brown sugar
1	teaspoon ground cinnamon
3/4	teaspoon ground nutmeg
1/2	teaspoon salt
1/2	teaspoon vanilla extract
1/8	teaspoon ground ginger

TOPPING:

1-1/4	cups chopped pecans
1/2	cup flaked coconut
1/3	cup packed brown sugar
1/4	cup quick-cooking oats
1/4	cup all-purpose flour
1/2	teaspoon ground cinnamon
1/3	cup cold butter, cubed

Combine the first four ingredients; press onto the bottom and up the sides of a greased 9-in. pie plate. Bake at 350° for 8-10 minutes or until crust is lightly browned. Cool on a wire rack.

In a large bowl, combine the filling ingredients. Pour into crust. Bake for 30 minutes.

Meanwhile, in another bowl, combine the pecans, coconut, brown sugar, oats, flour and cinnamon. Cut in butter until mixture resembles coarse crumbs. Sprinkle over pie; bake for 10-15 minutes longer or until a knife inserted near the center comes out clean and topping is golden brown. Cool completely on a wire rack. Refrigerate leftovers.

White Chocolate Bread Pudding with Tart Cherry Sauce

PREP: 35 MIN. **BAKE:** 25 MIN.
YIELD: 12 SERVINGS (2 CUPS SAUCE)

The flavor of this rich, indulgent bread pudding is reminiscent of eggnog. It is served with a bright cherry sauce, which makes it so good!

Shawn Osborne ★ Vinton, Virginia

2	cups dried cherries
2	cups cherry juice blend
1/2	cup sugar
1	loaf (1 pound) French bread, cut into 1-inch cubes
3	cups heavy whipping cream
10	ounces white baking chocolate, coarsely chopped
1	cup 2% milk
1/2	cup sugar
1	teaspoon ground cinnamon
1	teaspoon ground nutmeg
6	eggs, lightly beaten

White baking chocolate curls

In a large saucepan, bring the cherries, juice and sugar to a boil, stirring occasionally. Reduce heat; simmer, uncovered, for 5 minutes. Remove cherries with a slotted spoon; set aside. Return liquid to a boil; cook until reduced to about 3/4 cup. Return cherries to pan; cool.

Place bread cubes in a greased 13-in. x 9-in. baking dish. In a large saucepan, combine the cream, white chocolate, milk, sugar, cinnamon and nutmeg. Cook and stir over medium-low heat until chocolate is melted.

Stir a small amount of mixture into eggs; return all to the pan, stirring constantly. Pour mixture over bread cubes. Bake, uncovered, at 350° for 25-30 minutes or until a knife inserted near the center comes out clean. Serve warm with cherry sauce and chocolate curls.

Wrapped Up
FOR THE
HOLIDAYS

Southern Hospitality Basket

Add a bit of Southern flavor to the holidays with this gift basket filled with some of the region's favorites: Sweet Tea Concentrate, Pimiento Cheese Spread, Sweet and Spicy Barbecue Sauce, Salt-Free Seafood Seasoning and Southern Pecan Candy.

Pimiento Cheese Spread

PREP: 10 MIN. + CHILLING   **YIELD:** 1-1/4 CUPS

A classic Southern comfort food, this cheese spread is served as an appetizer with crackers, corn chips or celery. It also can be spread between two slices of bread for sandwiches or used as a topping for hamburgers and hot dogs.

Eileen Balmer ★ South Bend, Indiana

- 1-1/2 cups (6 ounces) shredded cheddar cheese
- 1 jar (4 ounces) diced pimientos, drained and finely chopped
- 1/3 cup mayonnaise
Assorted crackers

In a small bowl, combine the cheese, pimientos and mayonnaise. Refrigerate the spread for at least 1 hour. Serve with crackers.

Sweet & Spicy Barbecue Sauce

PREP: 30 MIN.   **COOK:** 35 MIN.   **YIELD:** 1-1/2 CUPS

I've never cared that much for store-bought barbecue sauce. I like to just make things from scratch, including this spicy, red-brown sauce. You'll find it clings well when you slather it on grilled meat.

Helena Georgette Mann ★ Sacramento, California

- 1 medium onion, chopped
- 1 tablespoon canola oil
- 1 garlic clove, minced
- 1 to 3 teaspoons chili powder
- 1/4 teaspoon cayenne pepper
- 1/4 teaspoon coarsely ground pepper
- 1 cup ketchup
- 1/3 cup molasses
- 2 tablespoons cider vinegar
- 2 tablespoons Worcestershire sauce
- 2 tablespoons spicy brown mustard
- 1/2 teaspoon hot pepper sauce

In a large saucepan, saute onion in oil until tender. Add garlic; cook 1 minute. Stir in the chili powder, cayenne and pepper; cook 1 minute longer.

Stir in the ketchup, molasses, vinegar, Worcestershire sauce, mustard and pepper sauce. Bring to a boil. Reduce heat; simmer, uncovered, for 30-40 minutes or until sauce reaches desired consistency. Cool for 15 minutes.

Strain sauce through a fine mesh strainer over a large bowl, discarding vegetables and seasonings. Store in an airtight container in the refrigerator for up to 1 month. Use as a basting sauce for grilled meats.

Southern Pecan Candy

PREP: 15 MIN.   **COOK:** 40 MIN. + COOLING
YIELD: ABOUT 2 POUNDS

Unlike traditional pralines, this recipe is spread in a pan, then cut into squares. It is loaded with pecans and has the same sweet taste as pralines. The candy was in my mother's recipe collection and dates back to 1941.

June Moffett ★ Santa Ana, California

- 1 teaspoon butter plus 1/4 cup butter, cubed
- 3 cups sugar, *divided*
- 1 cup half-and-half cream
- 1/8 teaspoon baking soda
- 1/2 teaspoon vanilla extract
- 1 pound chopped pecans, toasted

Line a 13-in. x 9-in. pan with foil and grease the foil with 1 teaspoon butter; set aside. In a large heavy skillet over medium-low heat, cook 1 cup sugar until melted. Do not stir. Reduce heat to low; cook for 5 minutes or until golden brown.

In a large saucepan, combine cream and remaining sugar. Slowly pour in cooked sugar. Cook and stir over medium heat until a candy thermometer reads 236° (soft-ball stage). Transfer to a large bowl; stir in remaining butter and baking soda. Cool until mixture reaches 110°.

Add vanilla. Beat until smooth and thickened, about 2 minutes. Stir in pecans. Quickly spread into prepared pan; cool completely. Using foil, lift candy out of pan. Discard foil. Store candy in an airtight container.

Editor's Note: We recommend that you test your candy thermometer before each use by bringing water to a boil; the thermometer should read 212°. Adjust your recipe temperature up or down based on your test.

Salt-Free Seafood Seasoning

PREP/TOTAL TIME: 10 MIN.   **YIELD:** 2 TABLESPOONS

Why buy seafood seasoning when you can easily assemble this tasty blend? Use it in all your favorite seafood recipes, from steamed shrimp to crab cakes.

David Cook ★ Taste of Home Online Community, Georgia

- 5 cardamom pods
- 6 bay leaves
- 4 whole cloves
- 1 tablespoon celery seed
- 1 tablespoon whole peppercorns
- 1 teaspoon paprika
- 1/2 teaspoon mustard seed
- 1/4 teaspoon ground mace

Remove seeds from cardamom pods; place in a blender. Add the remaining ingredients; cover and process for 1-2 minutes or until crushed. Store in an airtight container in a cool dry place for up to 1 year.

Sweet Tea Concentrate

PREP: 30 MIN. + COOLING
YIELD: 20 SERVINGS (5 CUPS CONCENTRATE)

Sweet iced tea is a Southern classic, and this is a fabulous recipe for tea lovers or for a party. The concentrate will make 20 servings.

Natalie Bremson ★ Plantation, Florida

2	medium lemons
4	cups sugar
4	cups water
1-1/2	cups English breakfast tea leaves *or* 20 black tea bags
1/3	cup lemon juice

EACH SERVING:

1	cup cold water

Ice cubes

Remove peels from lemons; save fruit for another use.

In a large saucepan, combine sugar and water. Bring to a boil over medium heat. Reduce heat; simmer, uncovered, for 3-5 minutes or until sugar is dissolved, stirring occasionally. Remove from the heat; add tea leaves and lemon peels. Cover and steep for 15 minutes. Strain tea, discarding tea leaves and lemon peels; stir in lemon juice. Cool the concentrate to room temperature.

Transfer to a container with a tight-fitting lid. Store in the refrigerator for up to 2 weeks.

To prepare tea: In a tall glass, combine water with 1/4 cup concentrate; add ice.

Teacher's Coffee Bag

At Christmastime, teachers often receive many presents. Have your child give something their teacher can enjoy and use. Plus, when you help your child prepare this gift, you'll be teaching him or her about recycling and being green. This Green Coffee Bag (directions on page 165) is made from recycled coffee bags and contains coffee-flavored goodies: French Vanilla Cappuccino Mix and Almond Coffee Walnuts. Add a coffee mug, and your child's teacher will be ready for a relaxing evening at home.

French Vanilla Cappuccino Mix

PREP/TOTAL TIME: 20 MIN.   **YIELD:** 1 SERVING

I've had this coffee mix recipe for many years and actually found it in a cookbook from a craft show. My family enjoys it so much that when I make up a batch it disappears almost immediately.

Tammy Fleury ★ Escanaba, Michigan

1-1/2   cups instant hot cocoa mix
1   jar (8 ounces) powdered French Vanilla nondairy
    creamer
1   cup nonfat dry milk powder
1   cup confectioners' sugar
1/2   cup sugar
1/2   cup instant coffee granules
ADDITIONAL INGREDIENT (for each serving)
1   cup hot water
Sweetened whipped cream and baking cocoa

In a large bowl, combine the first six ingredients. Store in an airtight container in a cool dry place for up to 2 months. Yield: 16 servings (4 cups total).

To prepare cappuccino: Place 1/4 cup mix in a coffee mug. Add 1 cup hot water; stir until combined. Top with whipped cream; sprinkle with baking cocoa.

Almond Coffee Walnuts

PREP: 40 MIN. + STANDING **YIELD:** 3 DOZEN

Set these out at a party for guests to nibble on. They also look nice on a tray of cookies. The subtle coffee flavor blends well with the almond paste and walnuts.

James Korzenowski ★ Fennville, Michigan

- 2/3 cup almond paste
- 2 tablespoons coffee liqueur
- 1 teaspoon instant espresso powder
- 72 walnut halves
- 6 ounces semisweet chocolate, chopped
- 1 teaspoon shortening

In a small bowl, combine the almond paste, liqueur and espresso powder. Spread about 1/2 teaspoon mixture on the flat side of half of the walnuts. Top with remaining walnuts, forming a sandwich.

In a microwave, melt chocolate and shortening; stir until smooth. Dip one end of sandwiches in chocolate; allow excess to drip off. Place on waxed paper; let stand until set. Refrigerate leftovers.

Green Coffee Bag

Use two 12-oz. or larger recycled coffee bags and two 20-in. lengths of 1-in.-wide coordinating grosgrain ribbon.

1. Cut straight across the bottom of each coffee bag as close as possible to the sealed edge. Carefully pull apart the seam that runs up the back of each coffee bag to open the bags, making two flat pieces. Wipe the inside of each bag with soapy water. Let dry.

2. With desired design centered, cut a 7-1/2- x 11-1/2-in. piece from each bag. With right sides facing and edges matching, sew sides together with a 1/4-in. seam. Finger-press the seams to one side. Turn about 1 in. to wrong side along top edge. Topstitch close to cut edge for hem. Stitching from side seams to side seams, sew the bottom edges together with a 1/4-in. seam.

3. Align side and bottom seams to form a triangle and sew a seam at opposite ends to form a flat bottom. See Fig. 1 at right. Use a paper punch to make two holes where desired in front and back of bag. Thread opposite ends of a ribbon piece from inside to outside through holes on front of bag for handles. Tie an overhand knot about 1 in. from each end to secure the handle. Repeat on back of bag.

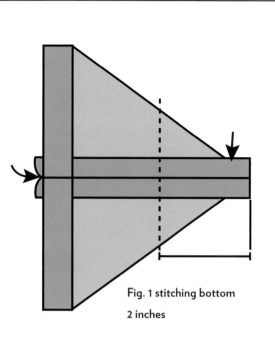

Fig. 1 stitching bottom

2 inches

Crafter's Note: Coffee bags are very durable and can be joined and sewn just like fabric to make pieces of any size. Carefully peel the freshness seal from the inside of the bag. If removing the seal damages the bag, leave it in place.

Romantic Fireside Picnic Basket

For a special couple, fix up a picnic basket that they can enjoy by a crackling fire. Featured in this basket are Ranch Cheese Spread, Sun-Dried Tomato Goat Cheese Spread, Rosemary Wheat Crackers and French Kiss Truffles. Add a bottle of wine, two wine glasses and a few Pinecone Fire Starters (directions on page 168) to create a gift just for the two of them.

Sun-Dried Tomato Goat Cheese Spread

PREP/TOTAL TIME: 15 MIN.   **YIELD:** 1 CUP

This simple recipe combines sweet and savory sun-dried tomatoes, tangy goat cheese and fresh herbs to make a truly magnificent spread. It's so flavorful, and it tastes perfect with a glass of red wine.

Sarah Agrella ★ Mountain View, California

1/3	cup oil-packed sun-dried tomatoes
2	garlic cloves, peeled and halved
1	tablespoon minced fresh basil
1	tablespoon minced fresh parsley
8	ounces fresh goat cheese, cubed

Assorted crackers

Drain tomatoes, reserving 2 teaspoons oil. In a small food processor, combine the garlic, basil and parsley. Cover and process until blended.

Add the goat cheese and reserved sun-dried tomatoes and oil. Cover and process until smooth. Chill until serving.

Rosemary Wheat Crackers

PREP: 20 MIN.   **BAKE:** 10 MIN./BATCH + COOLING
YIELD: 4 DOZEN

No one will believe you whipped up these delightful rosemary-scented crackers. They are easy to make and much better than store-bought.

Nancy Mueller ★ Menomonee Falls, Wisconsin

1-1/4	cups all-purpose flour
3/4	cup whole wheat flour
1	teaspoon sugar
1/2	teaspoon salt
1/2	teaspoon dried rosemary, crushed
1/4	cup olive oil
1/2	cup 2% milk
1-1/2	teaspoons kosher salt, *divided*

In a small bowl, combine the flours, sugar, salt and rosemary. Gradually add oil, tossing with a fork to combine. Add milk; toss with a fork until mixture forms a ball. Turn onto a lightly floured surface; knead 8-10 times.

Divide dough into three equal portions. On a greased baking sheet, roll out one portion into a 9-in. x 8-in. rectangle, about 1/16 in. thick. Sprinkle with 1/2 teaspoon kosher salt. Using rolling pin, gently press salt into dough. Prick holes in dough with a fork. Score dough into 16 pieces. Repeat with remaining dough.

Bake at 400° for 9-11 minutes or until edges are lightly browned. Immediately cut along the scored lines. Cool completely on baking sheets. Store in an airtight container.

French Kiss Truffles

PREP: 45 MIN. + CHILLING   **YIELD:** 32 SERVINGS

These truffles are so impressive that they won first place at the Wisconsin State Fair. These two-tone creamy candies combine an orange-flavored white chocolate with milk chocolate.

Gerry Cofta ★ Milwaukee, Wisconsin

8	ounces white baking chocolate, chopped
2/3	cup heavy whipping cream, *divided*
1/2	teaspoon grated orange peel
1/4	teaspoon orange extract
8	ounces milk chocolate, chopped

COATING:

12	ounces semisweet chocolate, chopped

Additional milk and white baking chocolate, melted

Place white chocolate in a small bowl. In a saucepan, bring 1/3 cup cream just to a boil. Pour over white chocolate; whisk until smooth. Stir in orange peel and extract.

Place milk chocolate in another small bowl. In the same saucepan, bring the remaining cream just to a boil. Pour over milk chocolate; whisk until smooth. Cool both mixtures to room temperature, stirring occasionally. Refrigerate until firm.

To form centers, take 1-1/2 teaspoons of each chocolate mixture and shape into a two-tone ball, about 1 in. round. Place on waxed paper-lined baking sheets; cover and refrigerate for at least 1 hour.

In a double boiler or metal bowl over simmering water, whisk the semisweet chocolate until smooth. Dip truffles in chocolate; allow excess to drip off. Return to baking sheets; drizzle with additional chocolate as desired. Refrigerate until set. Store in an airtight container in the refrigerator.

Ranch Cheese Spread

PREP: 15 MIN. + CHILLING **YIELD:** 3-1/4 CUPS

This is a real crowd-pleaser. You just can't go wrong with ranch flavor and cheese. This delectable dip is perfect for vegetables or crackers.

Jenna Marty ★ Las Vegas, Nevada

- 1 package (8 ounces) cream cheese, softened
- 1 cup (8 ounces) sour cream
- 1/2 cup mayonnaise
- 2 cups (8 ounces) shredded cheddar cheese
- 2 green onions, chopped
- 1 envelope ranch salad dressing mix

Assorted crackers *and/or* fresh vegetables

In a large bowl, beat the cream cheese, sour cream and mayonnaise until smooth. Stir in the cheddar cheese, onions and dressing mix. Transfer to a small bowl. Refrigerate for at least 1 hour. Serve with crackers and/or vegetables.

TO MAKE AHEAD: The cheese spread can be made a day in advance.

Pinecone Fire Starters

Gather pinecones from your yard and let dry or purchase a bag of them from a craft store. For colored flames, purchase chemicals mentioned below. We dyed the wax to match the color of the flame. Purchase desired colors of candle dye. Only burn one color in the fireplace at a time.

For colored flame: Fill a bucket with 1/2 gallon of hot water. Add only one of the following to the water: For a yellow flame, add 1 cup table salt; for a yellow-green flame, add 1 cup borax (found in the laundry aisle); for a violet flame, add 1 cup salt substitute (potassium); for a white flame, add 1 cup Epsom salt. Soak the pinecones in the desired solution for 8 hours. Remove and let dry until fully opened. Dip pinecones in wax as directed below.

To coat with wax: In double boiler over low heat, melt clear wax and add desired color of candle dye. Remove wax from heat source and pour it into a tall tin can. Using tongs, dip a pinecone into melted wax until completely covered. Remove pinecone and place on foil-lined baking sheet. Let stand until wax sets. Repeat dipping in wax until desired look is achieved.

Dog Lovers' Bowl

Don't forget man's best friend when handing out presents this season. Fido likes to chew on special snacks, too. Here, a purchased ceramic bowl is packed with homemade Ginger Dog Biscuits, a Festive Collar (directions on page 170) and, for his owners, some People Party Mix.

Ginger Dog Biscuits

PREP: 30 MIN.   **BAKE:** 20 MIN.   **YIELD:** 2-1/2 DOZEN

Treat your own pooch or a friend's pet to these special dog treats. The biscuits are soft and have a hint of spices.

Megan and Natalie Stanson ★ Frazeysburg, Ohio

- 4 cups all-purpose flour
- 2 cups whole wheat flour
- 1/4 cup ground ginger
- 2 teaspoons ground cinnamon
- 1 teaspoon ground cloves
- 1 cup water
- 1 cup molasses
- 1/2 cup canola oil

In a large bowl, combine the first five ingredients. Stir in the water, molasses and oil (dough will be stiff). On a floured surface, roll dough to 1/4-in. thickness. Cut with a 3-in. bone-shaped cookie cutter.

Place 2 in. apart on ungreased baking sheets. Bake at 325° for 20-25 minutes or until set. Cool on a wire rack. Store in an airtight container.

People Party Mix

PREP: 25 MIN. **COOK:** 10 MIN. + STANDING **YIELD:** 9 CUPS

Sweet, salty, crunchy and flavored with peanut butter—how popular this will be. It's sure to be snatched up quickly.

- 9 cups Corn Chex
- 1 cup peanut butter chips
- 1/2 cup creamy peanut butter
- 1/4 cup butter, cubed
- 1 teaspoon vanilla extract
- 1-1/2 cups confectioners' sugar
- 1 jar (4.1 ounces) Bac-O's bacon flavor bits

Place cereal in a large bowl; set aside. In a large heavy saucepan over low heat, melt the chips, peanut butter and butter; stir until smooth. Remove from the heat; stir in vanilla. Pour over cereal mixture and toss gently to coat.

Place confectioners' sugar in a large resealable plastic bag; add bacon bits and cereal mixture. Close bag and shake to coat. Spread onto waxed paper; let stand until set. Store in airtight containers for up to 2 weeks.

Festive Collar

Cut a 1/2-in.-wide strip of white fake fur equal to the measurement of the dog's neck. Use white thread and hand-sew seven silver bells evenly spaced down the center of the white fur strip.

Cut two pieces of 1-1/2-inch-wide red double-faced satin ribbon—a longer piece about four times the measurement of the dog's neck and a shorter piece equal to the measurement of the dog's neck. Following the manufacturer's instructions, fuse a strip of no-sew fusible web to the center of shorter ribbon piece. Let cool.

Remove paper from fusible web. With edges even, fuse shorter ribbon piece to center of longer ribbon piece. Let cool. Glue wrong side of white fur strip centered along right side of fused red satin ribbon section. Let dry. Wrap collar around dog's neck and tie ribbon ends in a bow. Trim excess ribbon ends to desired length.

Yuletide Brunch Basket

Use a classic mixing bowl to wrap up all the fixings for a leisurely brunch. This basket contains Whole Grain Pancake Mix and Cinnamon Cream Syrup. If you like, embellish the basket with a colorful dish towel, oven mitts, wire whisk or spatulas.

Cinnamon Cream Syrup

PREP/TOTAL TIME: 20 MIN.　**YIELD:** 1-2/3 CUPS

This versatile cinnamony sauce is great on ice cream, especially for the holidays. It also makes a delightful topping for pancakes or waffles.

April Madsen ★ Elko, Nevada

　1　cup sugar
1/2　cup light corn syrup
1/4　cup water
3/4　teaspoon ground cinnamon
1/2　cup evaporated milk
Ice cream

In a small saucepan, combine the sugar, corn syrup, water and cinnamon. Bring to a boil over medium heat, stirring constantly; boil for 2 minutes, without stirring. Remove from the heat. Let stand for 5 minutes.

Stir in evaporated milk. Serve warm or cold with ice cream. Refrigerate leftovers.

Whole Grain Pancake Mix

PREP: 20 MIN.　**COOK:** 5 MIN./BATCH
YIELD: 8 PANCAKES PER BATCH

I found this basic recipe in my local newspaper and tweaked it for our family. It has all of the convenience of commercial pancake mix, plus it is packed with whole grains. The mix makes light and fluffy pancakes.

Dorcas Byler ★ Brevard, North Carolina

　10　cups whole wheat flour
　　2　cups buttermilk blend powder
1-1/2　cups buckwheat flour
　　1　cup sugar
　1/3　cup baking powder
　　2　tablespoons baking soda
　　2　tablespoons salt
1-1/2　cups quick-cooking oats

ADDITIONAL INGREDIENTS:
　　1　egg, lightly beaten
　1/2　cup water
　　2　tablespoons canola oil

In a large bowl, combine the first seven ingredients. Place oats in a food processor; cover and process until ground. Stir into flour mixture. Divide mixture among five airtight containers. Store for up to 6 months. Yield: 15 cups.

To prepare pancakes: Pour 1 cup mix into a large bowl. In a small bowl, whisk the egg, water and oil; stir into pancake mix just until moistened. Pour batter by 1/4 cupfuls onto a greased hot griddle. Turn when bubbles form on top; cook until second side is golden brown.

Backpack Care Package

Show how much you care by sending your college student back to school with a new backpack filled with "survival" items. Pack it with fun and quick-to-make homemade treats, such as Apple Cinnamon Granola, Banana Chocolate Breakfast Drink Mix, Chicken and Rice Soup Mix, Hot Buttered Rum Party Mix and Coconut-Curry Popcorn Seasoning.

Coconut-Curry Popcorn Seasoning

PREP/TOTAL TIME: 10 MIN. **YIELD:** 6 SERVINGS

The sweet-salty combination is really great on snacks. Sprinkle the unique seasoning over buttered popcorn for a fantastic treat.

- 1 cup flaked coconut, toasted
- 2 tablespoons sugar
- 2 tablespoons curry powder
- 1/2 teaspoon salt

ADDITIONAL INGREDIENT FOR POPCORN:
- 1 package (3.3 ounces) butter-flavored microwave popcorn

Place coconut in a food processor; cover and process until finely chopped. Add the sugar, curry powder and salt; cover and process until blended. Store in an airtight container for up to 3 months. Yield: 4 batches (1/2 cup total).

To prepare popcorn: Pop popcorn according to package directions. Immediately sprinkle with 2 tablespoons seasoning; shake to coat.

Hot Buttered Rum Party Mix

PREP: 10 MIN. **COOK:** 5 MIN. + COOLING
YIELD: 2 QUARTS

A spicy mix of crisp cereal, soft marshmallows and rum extract makes this a delicious treat to nosh on while studying with friends or watching a movie.

Susan Tite ★ China, Michigan

- 4 cups Honey Nut Chex
- 2 cups Cinnamon Chex
- 1/4 cup butter, cubed
- 1/4 cup packed brown sugar
- 2 tablespoons honey
- 1 teaspoon rum extract
- 3/4 teaspoon ground cinnamon
- 1/2 teaspoon ground nutmeg
- 1/4 teaspoon ground cloves
- 2 cups miniature marshmallows

In a large microwave-safe bowl, combine cereals; set aside. In a small microwave-safe bowl, combine the butter, brown sugar and honey. Microwave, uncovered, on high for 2 minutes, stirring once. Stir in the extract and spices; pour over cereal mixture and toss to coat.

Cook, uncovered, on high for 3 minutes, stirring after each minute. Let cool slightly. Stir in marshmallows. Spread onto waxed paper to cool completely. Store the mix in an airtight container.

Apple Cinnamon Granola

PREP: 20 MIN. **BAKE:** 30 MIN. + COOLING **YIELD:** 6 CUPS

Granola is healthier than many snacks and can be stored at room temperature. This crunchy treat is great as is or as a topping for yogurt or as a breakfast cereal with milk.

Rebekah Radewahn ★ Wauwatosa, Wisconsin

- 2-1/2 cups old-fashioned oats
- 1/2 cup oat bran
- 1/2 cup sliced almonds
- 1/3 cup thawed apple juice concentrate
- 1/3 cup canola oil
- 1/3 cup honey
- 1 cup puffed rice cereal
- 1 cup dried apples, chopped
- 1/2 cup toasted wheat germ
- 1-1/2 teaspoons ground cinnamon
- 1/2 teaspoon ground nutmeg
- 1/2 cup raisins

In a large bowl, combine the oats, oat bran, and almonds; set aside. In a small saucepan, combine the concentrate, oil and honey. Cook and stir over medium heat for 2-3 minutes or until heated through. Remove from the heat; stir in the cereal, apples, wheat germ, cinnamon and nutmeg. Pour over oat mixture and toss to coat.

Transfer to two greased 15-in. x 10-in. x 1-in. baking pans. Bake at 300° for 30-35 minutes or until golden brown, stirring every 15 minutes. Cool on wire racks. Stir in raisins. Store in an airtight container.

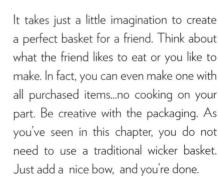

Making a Special Food Basket

It takes just a little imagination to create a perfect basket for a friend. Think about what the friend likes to eat or you like to make. In fact, you can even make one with all purchased items...no cooking on your part. Be creative with the packaging. As you've seen in this chapter, you do not need to use a traditional wicker basket. Just add a nice bow, and you're done.

Chicken and Rice Soup Mix

PREP/TOTAL TIME: 10 MIN.   **YIELD:** 1 SERVING

The recipient of this gift will have one hearty bowl of soup that will get rid of the chills on a blustery winter day. Suggest adding a salad or roll for a satisfying meal.

Edie DeSpain ★ Logan, Utah

2	tablespoons uncooked instant rice
1-1/2	teaspoons reduced-sodium chicken bouillon granules
1	teaspoon dried celery flakes
1	teaspoon dried parsley flakes
1/4	teaspoon dried minced onion
1/8	teaspoon pepper

ADDITIONAL INGREDIENTS:
3/4	cup boiling water
1	can (5 ounces) chunk white chicken, drained

In a small bowl, combine the first six ingredients. Transfer to a small spice jar. Store in a cool dry place for up to 6 months. Yield: 4 tablespoons.

To prepare soup: Place soup mix in a small microwave-safe bowl. Pour boiling water over mix; cover and let stand for 5 minutes. Stir in chicken. Microwave, uncovered, on high for 1-2 minutes or until heated through.

Banana-Chocolate Breakfast Drink Mix

PREP/TOTAL TIME: 10 MIN.   **YIELD:** 1 SERVING

For breakfast on the go, this beverage will get the day off to a delicious start.

5	cups nonfat dry milk powder
1	package (3.4 ounces) instant vanilla pudding mix
1	package (3.4 ounces) instant banana cream pudding mix
1/3	cup baking cocoa
1/4	cup confectioners' sugar
1/4	cup ground flaxseed

ADDITIONAL INGREDIENT (for each serving):
1	cup ice water

In a large bowl, combine the first six ingredients. Store in an airtight container in a cool dry place for up to 3 months. Yield: 10 servings (5 cups mix).

To prepare breakfast drink: Place 1/2 cup drink mix and 1 cup ice water in a jar with a tight-fitting lid; shake for 1-2 minutes or until slightly thickened.

Deck
THE HALLS

Selection and Care of Fresh Christmas Trees

In the 1800s, German settlers introduced Christmas trees to American culture...a custom that has been thoroughly embraced. In fact, many of us have more than one tree adorning our home during the holiday season.

Today, fresh trees are as popular as ever—25-30 million are sold annually. Whether it's a 3-foot table topper or a 10-foot showstopper, the tree is the centerpiece of holiday decorating. Here are a few pointers to help keep a fresh tree looking its best during the season.

Decide where you are going to place the tree, making sure it will be away from heat sources, such as fireplaces, heaters, radiators, heating vents and sunny windows.

Go Green

Before you toss your fresh tree to the curb, check with your city to see if they have a Christmas tree recycling program. Many areas will have a special pickup for used Christmas trees and will chip them for mulch.

Determine the size of the tree you need. Not only make note of the height, but also the width. The room may accommodate a 7-foot tree, but will the space comfortably hold a tree that is about 5-1/2 feet in diameter? When determining the height, allow about 18 inches for the tree topper and tree stand.

Selection of the tree is a personal preference. Some of the more popular trees are balsam fir, Douglas fir, Fraser fir, noble fir, Scotch pine, Virginia pine and white pine. Do you want a slender tree or classic Christmas tree shape, sparse or dense branches, a pronounced pine aroma or mild scent, green or blue-green needles?

Check for dryness. Hold your hand loosely around a branch and pull your hand toward the tip, letting the branch slip through your fingers. On a fresh tree only a few needles will come off. Another quick test is to bump the trunk of the tree on the ground; the green needles should not fall off the tree (a few fallen brown needles are alright).

Look for a tree that has a straight trunk. Avoid those with a split trunk, a wilted look, musty odor or wrinkled bark.

Needles No More

Do you hate cleaning up pine needles from your Christmas tree? Purchase a Scotch pine. They have excellent needle retention, even when the tree is dry.

Now that you've picked the perfect tree, keep it as fresh as possible by following these guidelines.

• Cut off 1/4 to 1 inch from the cut end of the trunk—just cut straight across the trunk. Then immediately place the tree in water.

• Use a stand that fits the tree, don't trim the trunk down. Also use a stand that holds water.

• Check the water daily. An average tree can absorb from a quart to a gallon of water a day. The water level should be above the end of the trunk. If it falls below the, a sap seal may form over the cut and interfere with the tree's ability to absorb water properly.

• If necessary, a tree can be stored in a cool, dry location, away from wind or sun. Just check the water level in the stand and refill as needed.

Flower Wreath

CRAFT LEVEL: BEGINNER

FINISHED SIZE: Wreath measures about 2-1/2 feet wide x 3 feet high with an 8-inch inner diameter.

Adorn a wall, door or mantel with this airy wreath that boasts both feminine grace and rustic charm. The flower petals are quick and easy to create using a die-cutting machine, and the snowflake centers add a glittering touch that will make your holidays sparkle.

Associate Editor Amy Glander

MATERIALS:

8-inch to 10-inch grapevine wreath

White spray paint

The Wizard™ Embossing and Die Cutting System (Spellbinders)

Heartfelt Creations Perfect Petals Dies (product number HCD 704)

Six 8-1/2-inch x 11-inch sheets of light blue vellum

Six 8-1/2-inch x 11-inch sheets of light green vellum

Scissors or paper trimmer

Glue dots

Pliers

Large snowflake brads

DIRECTIONS:

1. Paint grapevine wreath using white spray paint. Let dry.

2. Set up The Wizard™ Embossing and Die Cutting System following the manufacturer's instructions.

3. Using Heartfelt Creations Perfect Petals dies and light blue vellum, cut 36 large petals, 18 medium petals and 18 small petals. Follow the process again to create the same number of petals in light green. This should yield enough petals to create three blue flowers and three green flowers. Cut any additional petals as desired.

4. Slightly crease each petal in half lengthwise to create dimension.

5. Cut six 1/2-inch squares from leftover vellum to serve as the bases for flowers. Place a glue dot in the center of a square and arrange 12 large flower petals around it in a circle. Add a second glue dot on top of the first and arrange six medium-sized petals to create a second layer. Add a third glue dot and arrange six small petals to create a third layer.

6. Follow the same process for each additional flower until you have six flowers or the desired number to fit on your wreath.

7. Use pliers to clip the prongs off backs of the snowflake brads or bend the prongs to lie flat against the backs. Use a glue dot to secure a snowflake brad to the center of each flower.

8. Use glue dots to adhere the flowers around the inner circumference of the wreath.

Crafter's Note: See spellbinderspaperarts.com for The Wizard™ Embossing and Die Cutting System by Spellbinders. See heartfeltcreations.us for Heartfelt Creations Perfect Petals Dies.

Folded Fabric Star Ornament

Craft Level: BEGINNER

FINISHED SIZE: Including hanger, ornament measures about 6-1/2 inches high x 4 inches across.

This ornament came to mind when I was thinking of projects to make as presents. The next year I got requests for more, and have even created extras to sell at winter bazaars. The fabric ornaments offer many exciting design possibilities—it all depends on your fabric choices. You can use mottled prints, lamé, sheers, velvet...just about anything you like.

Ashley Gibbon
Black Mountain, North Carolina

MATERIALS:

44-inch-wide fabrics—1/4 yard of metallic silver solid and 1/8 yard each of purple or pink solid and mottled black print

3-inch Styrofoam ball

About 400 straight pins

Measuring tape or ruler

Iron and ironing surface

Glue gun and glue sticks

Quilter's marking pen or pencil

Quilter's ruler

Rotary cutter and mat (optional)

Scissors

DIRECTIONS:

Cutting:

1. From purple or pink solid, cut twenty-eight 2-in. squares, one 1-in. square, one 6- x 1-in. strip and one 1-1/4- x 11-in. strip.

2. From mottled black print, cut twenty-eight 2-in. squares, one 1-in. square and one 1- x 11-in. strip.

3. From metallic silver solid, cut sixty-four 2-in. squares.

Folded Triangles:

1. Referring to Fig. 1 at far right, fold each 2-in. purple or pink and black square in half with wrong sides together and press fold. Fold down each end to form a triangle and press.

2. Turn iron temperature down and test iron on a scrap of silver fabric to make sure iron will not damage it. When appropriate temperature is reached, make all silver squares into triangles the same as before.

Front:

1. For first round, place the 1-in. purple or pink square right side up on one side of Styrofoam ball. Insert a pin into each corner of square. Open one purple or pink triangle and insert a pin through the center point. Insert the pin into the center of the purple or pink square on the ball and push the pin into the ball as far as it will go. Referring to Fig. 2 at far right, refold the square into the pressed triangle with center folds on top. Pin down the corners to keep the triangle secure, pushing the pins into the ball as far as they will go. Attach three more purple or pink triangles to the ball in the same way, positioning them so the center points and the sides of the four triangles meet.

2. For second round, referring to Fig. 3 at far right, open a silver triangle and pin the center a scant 1/4 in. out from the center point of an attached purple or pink triangle, placing the pin along the center edges of the purple or pink triangle. Refold the square into the pressed triangle and pin. In the same way, add a silver triangle over the other three purple or pink triangles. Referring to Fig. 3 for position, pin four more silver triangles 1/4 in. out from the center points of purple or pink triangles, placing pins along the purple or pink side seam and overlapping the first set of silver triangles. The center area should look like an eight-pointed purple or pink star.

3. For third round, referring to Fig. 4 at far right, pin eight black triangles in place, positioning the center points 1/8 in. out from the center points of each silver triangle and adding them in the same way the silver triangles were added in round 2.

4. For fourth round, referring to Fig. 5 at far right, pin eight silver triangles so the center points are 1/4 in. out from the intersection of the silver triangles in step 2.

5. For fifth round, pin eight purple or pink triangles, positioning the center points 1/8 in. out from center points of each silver triangle in step 4 and placing the pins along center edges of silver triangles.

6. For sixth round, pin eight silver triangles, positioning the center points at the intersection of silver triangles in step 4.

7. For seventh round, pin eight black triangles, positioning the center points 1/8 in. out from the center points of each silver triangle in step 6 and placing the pins along the center edges of silver triangles.

8. For eighth round, pin eight silver triangles, positioning the center points at the intersection of the silver triangles in step 6. (Half of the Styrofoam ball should now be covered.)

Back:

1. Turn ball over and pin the 1-in. black square to the ball, positioning the black square directly opposite the 1-in. purple or pink square on the front.

2. Follow directions for rounds 1 through 8, reversing the positions of the purple or pink and black folded triangles, and making sure the center folds on the second ball half are aligned with the center folds on the first side so the second side mirrors the first.

Hanger and Border:

1. Fold and press the 6- x 1-in. purple or pink solid strip in half lengthwise with wrong sides together for hanger. Open and turn under the long raw edges 1/4 in. to the inside fold of the strip and press, making a 1/2-in.-wide folded strip. Using glue gun, glue folded edges together. Set aside.

2. Fold and press 1/4 in. to the wrong side along each long edge of the 1-1/4- x 11-in. purple or pink strip, making a 3/4-in.-wide strip. Open strip and place

it right side down around center of the ball, covering the raw edges and pins of round 8. Pin strip in place, positioning the pins along the folds of the strip.

3. Fold raw edges of purple or pink strip toward the center along the creased fold. Glue raw edges in place. Let dry.

4. Fold the hanger in half with the raw edges matching to create a loop. Secure raw edges of hanger to ball on purple or pink border seam with pins and glue. Let dry.

5. Fold 1/4 in. to the wrong side along each long edge of the 1- x 11-in. black strip and press, making a 1/2-in.-wide strip for border. Turn under one short end to hide raw edge.

6. Starting at hanger and beginning with raw edge, center and glue black border right side up over purple or pink border. Overlap ends, covering hanger ends. Let dry.

FIG. 1 Forming folded triangles

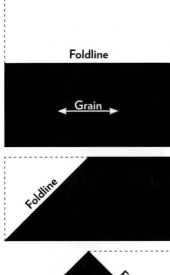

Foldline

←→ **Grain**

Foldline

Foldline

FIG. 2 Positioning first triangle

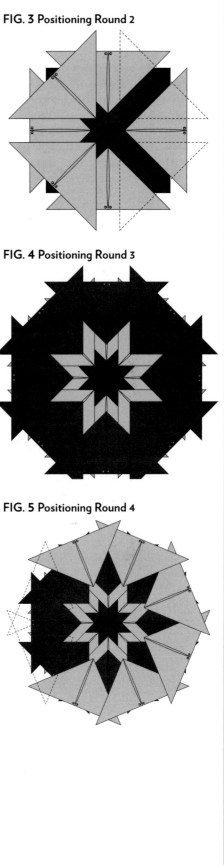

FIG. 3 Positioning Round 2

FIG. 4 Positioning Round 3

FIG. 5 Positioning Round 4

Fleur-de-lis
Paper Ornaments

CRAFT LEVEL: QUICK & EASY

FINISHED SIZE: Each ornament measures about 3-1/4 inches across.

I wanted to send my relatives an ornament that could be easily mailed, and one that was finished on both sides. I experimented with some of my crafting materials and created these festive trims. I plan to make larger versions of these to decorate my home.

Caroline Sanderson ★ Greenfield, Wisconsin

MATERIALS (FOR ONE):

Scraps or one 4-inch square each of three different coordinating colors of metallic card stock for outer circle, inner circles and fleur-de-lis design

2-1/2-inch and 1-7/8-inch circle punches

Two 1/2-inch-diameter pop dots

7/8-inch Fleur-de-lis paper punch (EK Success paper punch shown)

8-inch length of gold or silver metallic thread for hanger

Glue stick

Large hand-sewing needle

Scissors

DIRECTIONS:

Outer Circle:

1. Punch a 2-1/2-in. circle from metallic card stock for outer circle.

2. Punch six to eight fleur-de-lis designs from another color of card stock for outer circle.

3. Glue the fleur-de-lis designs evenly spaced around the outer edge card stock circle, alternating the sides as shown in the photo to the left.

Inner Circle:

1. Punch two 1-7/8-in. circles from the same or another color of card stock for inner circle on each side of ornament.

2. Punch 10 or 12 fleur-de-lis designs from another color of card stock for inner circles.

3. Glue five or six designs evenly spaced around each of the two small circles as before.

Assembly:

1. Use a pop dot to adhere the smaller circles to opposite sides of the large circle.

2. Use hand-sewing needle to make a hole in the outer edge of the large circle.

3. Thread metallic thread through hole and knot ends together to form a hanging loop. Trim ends close to knot.

Hats by the Mantel

Add a touch of whimsy to a fireplace with nontraditional "stockings." We found these fanciful, inexpensive Santa-shaped hats at a national drugstore chain. Any pointed hat should work. We used curtain rings with clips and stocking holders to hang the hats to the mantel. You can also string a ribbon across the mantel and attach with clip-style clothespins.

Use the hats as a room decor, in place of stockings or fun party favors. Simply add some goodies to the hats so guests have a sweet remembrance of your event.

Stocking Sachet

CRAFT LEVEL: BEGINNER

FINISHED SIZE: Stocking measures about 3-1/4 inches across x 3-1/4 inches high without hanging loop.

This spicy sachet with whole cloves and cinnamon oil has the aroma of Christmas baked goods. Hang it on the tree as a fragrant decoration, add it as cute embellishment to a gift package or place it in a lingerie drawer.

Taste of Home Craft Editor Jane Craig

MATERIALS:

Pattern shown on right

Tracing paper and pencil

Two 4-1/2-inch squares of unbleached muslin

Two 4-1/2-inch squares of gold metallic mesh fabric

Matching all-purpose thread

1 tablespoon of whole cloves

1-1/2 tablespoons of uncooked white rice

Cinnamon potpourri oil (optional)

10-inch length of gold metallic six-strand embroidery floss

Large-eye hand-sewing needle

Two 2-1/2-inch lengths of 1/4-inch-wide gold metallic ribbon

4-inch length of artificial mini holly garland with red berries

Glue gun and glue sticks

Standard sewing supplies

DIRECTIONS:

Stocking:

1. Trace the pattern below onto tracing paper with pencil. Cut out pattern.

2. With edges matching, place one square of muslin on a flat surface. Center the two squares of gold metallic mesh fabric on top. Center remaining square of muslin on top of gold metallic mesh fabric. Pin as needed to hold.

3. Pin stocking pattern to layered fabrics and cut out, cutting through all layers.

4. Remove pattern and sew around curved edges with a 1/4-in. seam, leaving top open. Clip curves and turn stocking right side out.

5. Combine whole cloves and rice in a small bowl. Stir in a few drops of potpourri oil if desired. Pour mixture into stocking.

6. Turn raw edges of top of stocking about 1/2 in. to the inside. Sew across top of stocking, stitching from seam to seam about 1/4 in. from fold to close.

Hanging Loop:

1. Thread metallic floss onto needle. Insert needle through top edge on back seam of stocking, leaving a long tail. Insert needle from inside to outside of seam, leaving a loop. Remove needle, leaving a long tail of floss. Tie ends of floss in a double overhand knot.

2. For the tassel, trim ends about 1 in. from knot.

Finishing:

1. Fold each length of gold metallic ribbon in half, making a "V" shape. Glue fold to hold. Glue one to center front and center back of top of stocking.

2. Wrap and glue holly garland around top of stocking.

Sachet Stocking Pattern

Trace 1—tracing paper
Cut as directed in instructions

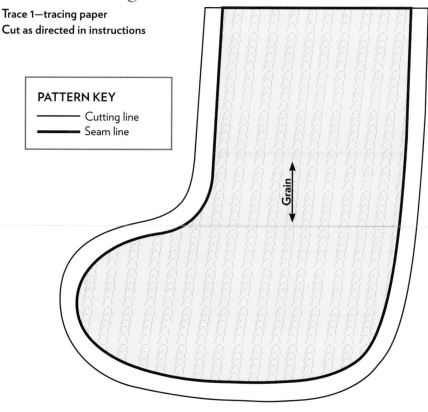

PATTERN KEY
— Cutting line
— Seam line

Grain

Gallery Glass Protective Sealer

Tweezers

Straight pin or needle

1-inch flat paintbrush

Ruler

Scissors

DIRECTIONS:

1. Place leading blank sheet smooth side up on a flat surface.

2. Apply an even coat of each desired color of glass paint in 1-in. wide x 4-in. long strips to leading blank. Use straight pin or needle to break any bubbles. Let set until colors darken and strip is dry.

3. Peel the strips off the leading blank and use scissors to cut the strips into small pieces as shown in photo at left.

4. Use tweezers to place the different color shapes flat side down on the ornament as desired, leaving about 1/8 in. between each.

5. Use paintbrush to apply a thin coat of protective sealer to entire ornament. Hang until completely dry.

6. Apply another coat of sealer in the same way and let dry.

Crafter's Notes: Before you start, make sure the ornaments and the color strips are clean and completely dry. Wrap ornaments in wax paper to store.

Fun & Simple Ornaments

To easily customize clear glass ornaments, add some confetti or various sizes of brightly colored scrap paper to the interior. You could even use your old, cut-up Christmas cards! Shake the ornament gently to spread around the paper pieces then hang on your tree. This easy ornament decoration is a great activity to do with the kids!

Mosaic Ornaments

CRAFT LEVEL: BEGINNER

FINISHED SIZE: Varies by size of ornament.

Every year I arrange the same ornaments on the tree. Well, last year I decided to make my own. I sat down at my drafting table, and by trial and error came up with my own unique designs.

Renee Glowe ★ Clayton, Wisconsin

MATERIALS (FOR ONE):

Clear glass ornament in desired shape and size (3-inch round and 4-inch teardrop ornaments shown)

Gallery Glass paint in colors of choice (Royal Blue, Blue Diamond and White Pearl shown on round ornament; Emerald Green, Ruby Red, Glitter Gold and Gold Sparkle shown on teardrop ornament)

8-inch x 10-inch sheet of Gallery Glass Leading Blank

Manger Star Ornament

CRAFT LEVEL: BEGINNER

FINISHED SIZE: Star ornament measures about 4-1/2 inches across.

The inspiration for this decoration came from my neighbor's pecan tree and the squirrels that eat the pecans. I found the empty pecan shells on my lawn and thought they looked like cradles. From that idea, I designed this ornament. You can also attach a fastener on the back and use it as a pin.

Carolyn Brannon ★ Atlanta, Texas

MATERIALS:

Pattern on bottom-right

Tracing paper and pencil

Two 5-inch squares of mottled yellow print fabric

All-purpose thread to match fabric

One whole pecan shell

Nail clippers

Small hammer

Tweezers

Glue gun and glue sticks

Metallic gold thread

Red six-strand embroidery floss

Polyester stuffing

10mm wood bead for head

15mm oval bead for body

1/2-inch x 8-inch strip of white solid fabric for body

Six artificial red berry sprigs

18-inch length of 1/4-inch-wide green satin ribbon

Two 12-inch lengths of 1/8-inch-wide dark green satin

Ribbon

Standard sewing supplies

DIRECTIONS:

Star:

1. Trace pattern at right onto tracing paper with pencil.

2. Layer the two 5-in. squares of yellow mottled fabric with right sides facing and edges matching. Pin star pattern to layered fabric.

3. With matching thread, sew on pattern line, leaving an opening for turning.

4. Trim excess fabric, leaving a narrow seam allowance outside stitching.

5. Turn star right side out and stuff softly. Turn raw edges of opening in and hand-sew opening closed.

Cradle:

1. Use hammer to crack pecan shell.

2. Use nail clippers to make an opening in the shell for the cradle and tweezers to remove the pecan.

Baby:

1. Glue hole-side of wood bead for head to hole-side of bead for body together for baby. Let dry.

2. For hair, wrap red embroidery floss around your finger. Remove loops from finger and tie in the center. Cut loops open. Glue hair to wood bead. Let dry.

3. Wrap oval bead for body with white fabric strip. Glue as needed to hold. Let dry.

Straw:

1. Wrap an 8-in. length of gold metallic thread around two fingers. Slip loops off fingers and tie in the center with another length of gold metallic thread. Repeat to make another straw bundle.

2. Crisscross bundles and glue centers together. Let dry.

Assembly:

1. Glue straw to the inside of the cradle and baby to straw. Let dry.

2. Glue berry sprigs to center front of fabric star.

3. Tie each length of green ribbon into a bow. Glue bows to center of berry sprigs. Let dry.

4. Glue cradle above bows. Let dry.

5. Thread hand-sewing needle with an 8-in. length of gold metallic thread. Attach thread to top of star for hanging loop.

Manger Star Ornament Pattern

Trace 1—tracing paper
Cut as directed—yellow mottled fabric

PATTERN KEY	
———	Cutting line
··········	Leave open

Grain

Leave open

Diorama Christmas Globe

CRAFT LEVEL: QUICK & EASY

FINISHED SIZE: Ornament measures about 4 inches across x 4-1/2 inches high.

Use this globe as a cute tabletop accent or make several and place them on a fireplace mantel. Bring your kids along when you shop for the miniature Christmas items, and let each child pick out something that they would like in their own diorama.

Taste of Home Craft Editor Jane Craig

MATERIALS:

Plaid Silver Extreme Glitter

White acrylic paint

Small flat paintbrush

Foam plate or palette

Clear drying craft glue

Diamond Dust Glitter

4-inch Styrofoam ball

Tablespoon

Metal canning jar rings—wide-mouth and regular

Miniature Christmas items (sleigh, gift, reindeer and two pine trees shown)

12-inch length of silver rope ribbon

Low-temperature glue gun and glue sticks or glue for Styrofoam

Scissors

DIRECTIONS:

1. Following the manufacturer's instructions, paint entire outside of Styrofoam ball with Silver Extreme Glitter. Let dry.

2. Place white paint on foam plate or palette. Using flat brush and white, paint outside of regular-size metal canning jar ring. Let dry.

3. Apply glue to outside of the white canning jar ring. While glue is still wet, sprinkle on glitter. Shake off excess glitter. Let dry.

4. Press wide-mouth canning jar ring into one side of Styrofoam ball to make an indentation for opening in ball. Use spoon to follow indentation and to hollow out the ball, leaving the wall of the ball about 1/2 in. thick.

5. Glue items inside ball where desired.

6. Glue silver trim around outside of opening. Trim excess.

7. Glue ball ornament to top of glitter-covered metal ring to display.

Pillow Cover

CRAFT LEVEL: BEGINNER

FINISHED SIZE: Pillow cover measures about 17-1/2 inches square.

Here's a simple way to add a touch of seasonal flair to your home. Purchase some holiday fabric that complements your decor and make slipcovers for your throw pillows. Conveniently, the covers do not take up much room when you store them.

Taste of Home Craft Editor Jane Craig

MATERIALS:

1 yard of 44-inch-wide fabric for pillow cover

18-inch square of muslin or other lightweight fabric for lining front of pillow

All-purpose thread to match fabric

18-inch square of lightweight cotton quilt batting

Quilter's ruler

Rotary cutter and mat

14-inch square pillow form

Standard sewing supplies

DIRECTIONS:

1. From fabric for pillow cover, cut one 18-in. square for front of pillow and two 12- x 18-in. rectangles for pillow back.

2. Place 18-in. square of lining fabric on a flat surface. Center batting on top. Then place 18-in. square of fabric for pillow front right side up on top of batting. Pin as needed to hold. Stitch around outside edges with a scant 1/4-in. seam.

3. Press one long edge of each rectangle for pillow back 1/4 in. to wrong side. Fold and press 1 in. to wrong side and sew close to first fold for hem.

4. Place pillow back rectangles wrong side up on right side of pillow top with outside edges matching and hemmed edges of pillow back pieces overlapping.

5. Sew around outside edges with a 1/4-in. seam.

6. Trim away excess quilt batting in seam close to stitching to reduce bulk. Clip corners.

7. Turn pillow top right side out and press seams.

8. Topstitch 1-1/2 in. from outside edges of pillow top.

9. Insert pillow form.

Outdoor Streamer

CRAFT LEVEL: BEGINNER

FINISHED SIZE: Outdoor ornament measures about 13 inches wide x 15 inches long.

Add a few baubles to the outside of your house with large shatterproof ornaments. We've cascaded a few with ribbon to create an eye-catching streamer.

Taste of Home Craft Editor Jane Craig

MATERIALS:

Three different sizes of shatterproof ornaments

Craft wire

Drill with bit to accommodate wire

Needle-nose pliers

Artificial boxwood spray

Large silver beads to decorate

Purple wire edge ribbon

Silver ribbon (expandable wire mesh ribbon shown)

Low-temperature glue gun and glue sticks

Scissors

DIRECTIONS:

1. Carefully remove the ornament caps from each ornament.

2. Drill a hole though the center bottom of each ornament.

3. Use needle-nose pliers to make a small closed loop at one end of the wire.

4. Thread the other end of the wire through the smallest ornament.

5. Attach boxwood to the top of the ornament as shown in photo at left. Wrap a length of silver ribbon around wire and tie a small bow.

6. Thread second largest ornament on wire and add boxwood and silver ribbon as before. Repeat with largest ornament.

7. Form end of wire into a hanging loop.

8. Glue silver beads to boxwood where desired.

9. Tie purple ribbon into a bow. Begin at base and layer three loops of decreasing size on both sides. Form a circular loop at top. Secure with wire around center. Cover wire with a small piece of ribbon. Shape bow and trim ends as desired. Secure to top of ornament with wire.

Welcome Basket

CRAFT LEVEL: QUICK & EASY

FINISHED SIZE: Basket measures about 20 inches wide x 20 inches high.

Dress up an outside door with a basket brimming with seasonal greenery and sparkling ornaments. This decoration will be a standout from the typical wreath.

Taste of Home Craft Editor Jane Craig

MATERIALS:

Natural woven basket with offset handle (basket shown measures about 11 in. across x 14 in. high)

White spray paint

Floral foam to fill basket

Four artificial pine sprays

Three artificial green glitter fern stems

Five assorted color glitter ball sprays

Three purple glitter picks

Three green glitter curly sprays

2-1/2-inch-wide green glitter wire-edge ribbon

Wire cutters

Scissors

DIRECTIONS:

1. Following the manufacturer's instructions, spray paint basket white. Let dry.

2. Fill basket with floral foam.

3. Starting at the back and cutting stems as needed, insert pine sprays, green glitter fern stems, glitter ball sprays and purple picks. Fill in open spaces with green curly sprays.

4. Wrap ribbon around basket and tie ends in a bow in the front. Trim ribbon ends as desired. Place by or hang on door.

Seasonal Lamp Shade

CRAFT LEVEL: QUICK & EASY

FINISHED SIZE: Shade shown measures about 7 inches high x 6 inches across without bead trim. Size will vary depending on shade used.

Spread Christmas joy to any room with a simple-to-make lamp shade. If you have multiple lamps in a room, replace each shade with a seasonal treatment.

Taste of Home Craft Editor Jane Craig

MATERIALS:

Self-adhesive lamp shade to cover

Fabric to cover shade

Beaded trim—amount needed to go around bottom of shade

Craft glue

Scissors

DIRECTIONS:

1. Follow instructions that come with the shade to cut and adhere fabric to the shade.

2. Trim and glue fabric over the top and bottom edges of the shade

3. Glue beaded trim to inside bottom edge of shade. Trim excess.

Framed Sentiments

CRAFT LEVEL: BEGINNER

FINISHED SIZE: Frames measure 7-1/2 inches wide x 9-1/2 inches high.

Looking for a letter-perfect way to deck the walls this year? Try this fun, easy project calling for large chipboard letters and black frames. Spell any holiday word or phrase of your choice…you're sure to make a statement!

Associate Editor Amy Glander

MATERIALS:

One 6-inch chipboard letter J

One 6-inch chipboard letter O

One 6-inch chipboard letter Y

Green spray paint

Three 7-1/2-inch x 9-1/2-inch black wall frames with double pane glass (see Crafter's Note)

Glass cleaner and cloth

DIRECTIONS:

1. Select three 6-inch chipboard letters to spell JOY or a word of your choice. (As many frames as letters are needed.) Paint each letter using green spray paint. Let dry.

2. Thoroughly clean glass panes with glass cleaner and cloth. Let dry.

3. Center letters between glass panes. Close hinges on frames to secure letters in place. Hang frames on wall in the appropriate order to spell JOY.

Crafter's Note: Any style of double pane glass wall frames and chipboard letters may be used. Be sure that your frames are slightly larger than your letters for the best fit.

Angel Table Topper

CRAFT LEVEL: BEGINNER

FINISHED SIZE: Angel measures about 6 inches across x 10-1/4 inches high.

Let a heavenly angel watch over the festivities from a perch in your home. This little darling also fits nicely on a desk, end table or tucked by a lamp.

Taste of Home Craft Editor Jane Craig

MATERIALS:

9-inch x 22-inch piece of fabric for dress and 9-inch x 3-inch piece for arms

Matching all-purpose thread

1-1/4-inch wooden doll bead and wooden clothespin

9-inch tall Styrofoam cone shape

4-inch circle of felt

1/2-inch gold star button

16-inch length of 1/4-inch-wide gold metallic ribbon

30-inch length of gold metallic wire edge cut from wire-edge ribbon or gold metallic bow wire

12-inch length of 2-inch-wide gold sheer wire-edge ribbon

Black permanent marker

Powdered cosmetic blush and cotton swab

Glue gun and glue sticks

Craft scissors

Standard sewing supplies

DIRECTIONS:

Doll Base:

1. Cut 1-1/2 inches from the top of the cone, leaving a 7-1/2-in.-tall cone.

2. Glue felt circle to bottom of cone. Let dry.

3. Insert clothespin into hole in wooden bead for head.

4. Press clothespin into top of cone shape, making a 10-in.-tall shape.

Dress:

1. Fold the 9- x 22-in. piece of fabric in half crosswise with right sides facing. Sew the short ends together with a narrow seam.

2. Fold 1/4 in. to wrong side along one long edge and sew in place for hem.

3. Sew a gathering stitch about 1/2 in. from remaining raw edge.

4. Turn fabric piece right side out and slip over angel's head. Draw up gathering thread and fasten off around top of clothespin. Adjust as needed so fabric is even with bottom of cone and seam is centered in the back.

5. Wrap a 12-in. length of 1/4-in.-wide gold ribbon around top of dress. Tie ends in a small bow in front.

6. Fold 3-in. x 9-in. strip of fabric for arms in half lengthwise with right sides facing. Sew the long edges together with a narrow seam. Turn tube right side out for arms. Fold arm piece in half crosswise and knot a 4-in. length of 1/4-in.-wide gold ribbon about 1/2 in. from raw edges to form hands. Trim ribbon ends close to knot.

7. Place arm piece around top of dress with hands in front. Spot-glue as needed to hold.

8. Remove shank from back of star button. Glue button to hands.

Head:

1. Glue Spanish moss to back sides and top of doll bead for hair, leaving an opening in the front for the face.

2. Use marker to add two small circles for eyes.

3. Use cotton swab and a circular motion to add blush for cheeks.

Halo:

1. Cut an 18-in. length of gold metallic wire edge or bow wire for halo.

2. Starting at one end, wrap wire around three times to form a 1-in. circle. Wrap remaining length of wire around the edge of circle.

3. Glue halo to top of the angel's head. Let dry.

Wings:

1. Fold the ends of the 12-in. length of 2-in.-wide gold metallic mesh ribbon in to the center, overlapping the ends about 1/2 in.

2. Wrap a 12-in. length of gold wire edge or bow wire around center and tie ends in a bow.

3. Glue wings to back of angel.

Painted Napkins

CRAFT LEVEL: BEGINNER

FINISHED SIZE: Design area measures about 2-1/2 inches across x 4 inches high. Each napkin measures about 20 inches square.

Add a bit of whimsy to a table setting with charming napkins. We created the napkins then added a shimmering tree. If you're artistic, paint your own original image on the napkins.

Taste of Home Craft Editor Jane Craig

MATERIALS:

Four 22-1/2-inch squares of white 100% or cotton-blend fabric

White all-purpose thread

Standard sewing supplies

Pattern shown at right

Tracing paper

Black permanent marker

Foam plate or palette

Dark green acrylic craft paint

Fabric medium

Glitter fabric paint—green and silver (Tulip Puffy Pens)

Small flat paintbrush

Red dimensional fabric paint (optional)

DIRECTIONS:

Napkins:

1. Fold and press 1/4 in. to wrong side on all sides of each fabric square for napkin. Fold and press another 1 in. to wrong side on all sides for hems.

2. To miter corners, open hem on one corner. Fold the corner to the wrong side and align the creases as shown in Fig. 1 at the right. Press fold to crease. Open. With right sides facing, align the crease as shown in Fig. 2. Sew in the crease. Trim seam, turn right side out and press. Repeat on all four corners and on all remaining napkins.

3. With matching thread, topstitch close to first fold of hem as shown in Fig. 3.

Painting:

1. Trace pattern below onto tracing paper with black marker.

2. Following the manufacturer's instructions, mix dark green acrylic paint and fabric medium. Using edge of flat brush and mixed paint add swirl design of tree. Let dry.

3. Use flat brush to add a thin coat of green glitter paint to the tree where desired. Let dry.

4. In the same way, add silver glitter paint where desired.

5. Use flat brush and silver glitter paint to add star to top of tree.

6. Use red dimensional paint to add ornaments if desired.

Painted Napkin Pattern

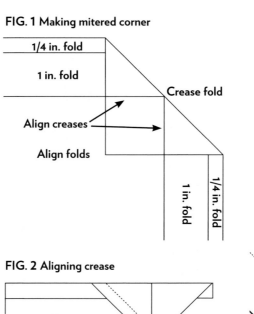

FIG. 1 Making mitered corner

1/4 in. fold

1 in. fold

Crease fold

Align creases

Align folds

1 in. fold

1/4 in. fold

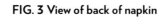

FIG. 2 Aligning crease

Align crease

Trim Seam

Sew

(Wrong side)

FIG. 3 View of back of napkin

1 in. fold

1/4 in. fold

1 in. fold

1/4 in. fold

PATTERN KEY

—— Fold line

•••••• Stitching

TREE PATTERN

Enlarge pattern 200%

Trace 1 as directed—tracing paper

Paint as directed

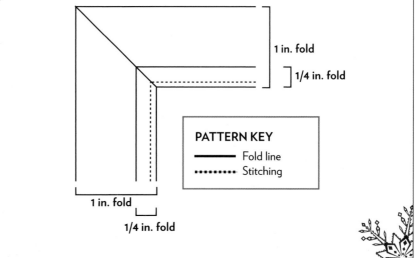

Fire & Ice Votives

CRAFT LEVEL: BEGINNER

FINISHED SIZE: 1 icy votive (4 inches in diameter and 8 inches high).

Guide guests to your door with the gentle glow of these cheerful lights.

Taste of Home Food Stylists

MATERIALS (FOR ONE):

Distilled water (freezes the clearest)

Two-liter bottles (rinsed)

Plastic bottles (smaller than the two-liter bottles)

Rocks

Decorations (ribbons, sticks, berries, ornaments, leaves, etc.)

DIRECTIONS:

1. Cut tops off the two-liter and smaller bottle.

2. Fill smaller bottle with rocks and place in center of two-liter bottle. Slowly fill two-liter bottle halfway with distilled water, making sure the smaller bottle doesn't float.

3. Place decorations in the water between bottles where desired.

4. Once decorated, slowly fill two-liter bottle with more water, then freeze.

5. Once frozen, remove rocks and smaller water bottle for an open area in the center to place the candle. Cut off outer layer of two-liter bottle. Place candle or battery operated lights in interior and display.

No-Fuss Napkin Rings

Instead of using traditional napkin rings, add a little holiday glamour to your table with these sparkling ideas.

- Use a wreath made of miniature sleigh bells strung on a wire.

- Tuck a favorite holiday photo or wish inside a plastic key chain and tie a napkin on with a bow. Have the key chains double as place cards by writing your guests' names inside of them.

- Glue lengths of wire-edge ribbon into circles. When dry, slip them over rolled napkins.

- Wrap beaded ribbon around a napkin then stuff the ends into a small seasonal cookie cutter.

- Add a twist of gold cord to a bright Christmas tree bulb.

6-1/2 yards of 1/4-inch-wide gold lamé Clover Quick Bias Fusible Tape (quick bias fusible tape is washable when stitched in place)

Standard sewing supplies

DIRECTIONS:
CUTTING:

1. From large holly print, cut one 10 in. square and four 5 in. squares.

2. From small holly print, cut eight 5 in. squares.

3. From small green print, cut four 5 in. squares. Cut each of these in half once diagonally to make eight triangles.

QUILTING:

1. Place quilter's grid fusible side up on a large flat surface.

2. Referring to Fig. 1 at right, lay out the squares and triangles following the lines of the grid and making sure the edges of all pieces meet.

3. Following the manufacturer's instructions, fuse fabrics to quilter's grid. Trim away excess quilter's grid.

4. With a zigzag stitch that is less than 1/4-in. wide, sew around all squares and triangles; make sure the stitching catches the edges on each side of all pieces.

5. Place backing fabric wrong side up on a large flat surface. Center batting on top of backing. Center fused fabrics right side up on top of batting. Smooth out all wrinkles and baste as needed to hold.

6. With a straight stitch, sew over all zigzag stitching and 1/8 in. from outside edges of runner.

7. Trim batting and backing even with outside edges.

8. With a stitch that is less than 1/4-in. wide, satin-stitch around outside edges.

9. Fuse quick bias tape over all inside stitching lines and then around outside edges.

10. Topstitch along outside edges of the quick bias tape for a washable runner.

Quilted Table Runner

CRAFT LEVEL: BEGINNER

FINISHED SIZE: Runner measures about 14 inches wide x 42 inches long.

Dress up any table with a runner. Leave the runner on the table whether it is set for a meal or not, since it will add some color and interest to the room.

Taste of Home Craft Editor Jane Craig

MATERIALS:

44-inch-wide 100% cotton fabrics—1/2 yard of large holly print, 1/4 yard of small holly print, 1/4 yard of small green print and 1/2 yard of coordinating print for backing

1/2 yard of 45-inch-wide fusible nonwoven onpoint quilter's grid with 1-inch printed grid

All-purpose thread to match fabrics

18-inch x 46-inch piece of quilt batting

FIG. 1 Runner Layout
Illustrated at 25%

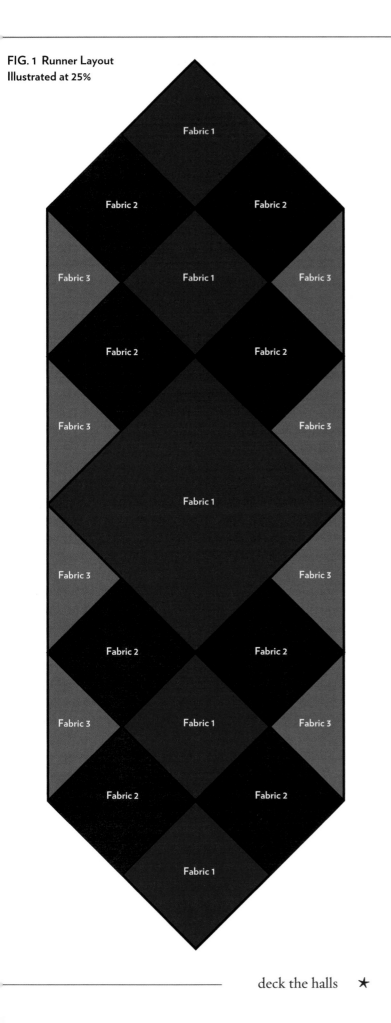

Fabric 1

Fabric 2   Fabric 2

Fabric 3   Fabric 1   Fabric 3

Fabric 2   Fabric 2

Fabric 3   Fabric 3

Fabric 1

Fabric 3   Fabric 3

Fabric 2   Fabric 2

Fabric 3   Fabric 1   Fabric 3

Fabric 2   Fabric 2

Fabric 1

Time in the Tub

Make a clean break by setting your tree stand inside a large metal washtub. The warm hue of this copper tub carries through the rest of the tree, which is trimmed with copper and gold ornaments. If you like, use a tub that has a silvery sheen, or choose a large urn, planter or kettle.

Ribbon Ornaments

CRAFT LEVEL: QUICK & EASY

FINISHED SIZE: Ribbon ornament measures about 4-1/4 inches across x 2-3/8 inches high.

Buy a spool of ribbon or use up leftover pieces to make a one-of-a kind ornament. Thin ribbons or leftover scraps can easily be glued together with fabric glue to make a delightful garland for your tree (shown at left).

Taste of Home Craft Editor Jane Craig

MATERIALS (FOR ONE):

25-1/2-inch length of grosgrain ribbon in width and color of choice

Fray check or fabric sealant

Measuring tape

Pencil

Fabric glue

Two spring clothespins

Silver metallic thread

Hand-sewing needle

Scissors

DIRECTIONS:

1. Apply fabric sealant to ends of ribbon to prevent raveling. Let dry.

2. Starting at one end, use pencil to mark the center of the ribbon at 2-1/2 in., 6-1/2 in., 10-1/2 in., 15-1/2 in. and 20-1/2 in.

3. Apply a thin line of glue across the ribbon at the 2-1/2-in. mark. Referring to Fig. 1 above, wrap the closest end of the ribbon to the mark to make a circle and hold. Wrap the remaining ribbon back and match the 6-1/2-in. mark to the previous mark, making sure the edges are aligned. Apply glue and hold as before. In the same way, match and glue the 10-1/2-in., 15-1/2-in. and 20-1/2-in. marks. Then glue the end of the ribbon to form a circle. Attach the two clothespins and let dry.

4. Thread hand-sewing needle with silver metallic thread. Stitch through top of ornament. Remove needle and tie thread ends in a knot for hanging loop.

FIG. 1 Forming ribbon ornament

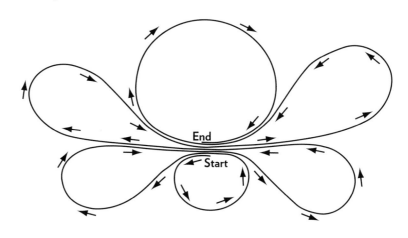

Gift of Greenery

Bursting from a gift box, you tree will fit right in with all of the surrounding Christmas presents. Simply cover a large empty cardboard box with wrapping paper and set your tree stand inside, arranging colorful tissue at the top.

Holiday Tags

CRAFT LEVEL: BEGINNER

FINISHED SIZE: Window wall frame measures 17-3/4 inches wide and 21 inches high. Tags vary in size.

Get scrap happy this season with a variety of heartfelt holiday tags and paper accents. The tags look adorable clipped to a frame like this one, but you can also hang them as ornaments on a Christmas tree, attach them to gifts, or send them to loved ones in lieu of traditional holiday cards.

Associate Editor Amy Glander

MATERIALS:

Assorted scrapbook papers, die cuts, stickers and rub-ons

Scissors or paper trimmer

Ornament punch

Tag punches

Photo corner rounder

Light blue velvet rickrack

Brown sheer ribbon

Dimensional foam adhesive

9-Clip Window Wall Frame (Pier 1 imports)

DIRECTIONS:

1. Use assorted scrapbook supplies to create a variety of tags in the colors and holiday paper collection of your choice.

2. Clip tags to window wall frame and display on mantel or shelf.

Paper Star
Tree Topper

CRAFT LEVEL: BEGINNER

FINISHED SIZE: Star measures about
7-1/2 inches wide x 7-1/2 inches high.

*Betsy Ross is best known for the part she
played in the birth of our nation, but few
people know that she developed an easy
folding technique for creating a perfect five-
point star. Follow the steps below to simply
create a paper star to adorn the top of
your evergreen.*

Associate Editor Amy Glander

Materials:

Scrapbook or specialty paper

Ruler

Scissors

Adhesive or double-sided tape

DIRECTIONS:

Create the star as directed in the
instructions that follow. Refer to the
diagrams as a guide.

1. Cut piece of paper to 8-1/2 inches x
10 inches.

2. Referring to Fig. 1 at right, fold
paper in half horizontally. Fold and
unfold in half both horizontally and
vertically to mark the centerlines
with creases.

3. Referring to Fig. 2a, with paper still
folded in half horizontally, fold corner
No. 1 right to meet the horizontal
centerline at point A. (Fold from the
top of the vertical creased centerline.)

4. Referring to Figs. 2b and 2c, fold
corner No. 1 left to meet the previously
folded outer edge.

5. Referring to Fig. 3a, fold corner
No. 2 to the left on top of corner No. 1.

6. Referring to Figs. 3b and 3c, fold
corner No. 2 to the right to meet the
previously folded outer edge.

7. Starting at corner No. 2, cut on an
acute angle as shown in the diagram.
Unfold the newly created star.

8. Follow steps 1-7 to create a second
star. Use adhesive or double-sided tape
to glue both stars together around the
edges. When gluing, leave an open gap
at the bottom of the stars to fit over the
top tree branch.

FIG. 1 First folds

FIG. 2 Folding left side

FIG. 3 Folding right side and cutting

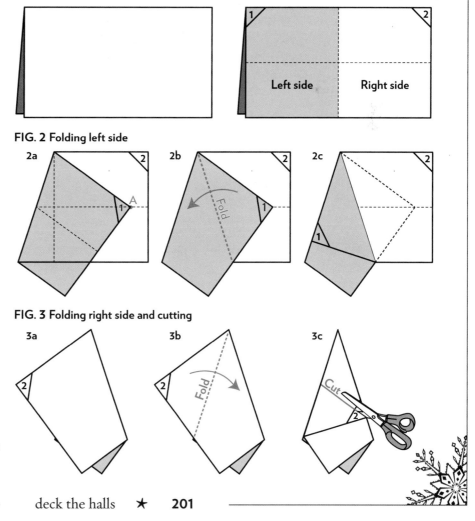

Joy Candle

CRAFT LEVEL: QUICK & EASY

FINISHED SIZE: Joy candle measures about 3 inches across x 8 inches high. Size will vary depending on size of candle used.

Add words of inspiration, such as joy, peace or hope, to create a little flourish to plain, store-bought candles.

Taste of Home Craft Editor Jane Craig

MATERIALS:

Pillar candle in size and color of choice

Dimensional glitter glue—silver or color of choice

1-1/2-inch-wide ribbon—silver metallic or color of choice

Scissors

DIRECTIONS:

1. Using silver dimensional glitter glue, write "Joy" around candle where desired. Let dry.

2. Tie ribbon around candle and tie ends in a bow. Trim ribbon ends as desired.

Gifts TO GIVE

Tissue Paper Ornament

CRAFT LEVEL: BEGINNER

FINISHED SIZE: Ornament measures about 3 inches across without hanging loop.

Change the look of the ornament by using different holiday patterned tissue paper. This can also make a fun weekend craft project for a child in middle school.

Taste of Home Craft Editor Jane Craig

MATERIALS:

3-inch Styrofoam ball

Patterned tissue paper (blue-and-white snowflake patterned paper shown)

Foam plate or palette

Small flat paintbrush

Matte finish decoupage medium or clear-drying craft glue

Clear glitter

Recycled ornament cap and wire

8-inch length of 1/4-inch-wide silver metallic ribbon

Craft glue

Scissors

DIRECTIONS:

1. Tear tissue paper into small pieces.

2. Use paintbrush to apply decoupage medium or clear-drying craft glue to a small area on exterior of Styrofoam ball. Place a piece of tissue paper on glue area. Apply more medium or glue over the top of the tissue paper piece. Continue adding tissue paper in this way, overlapping the pieces a bit until half of the ornament is covered. Let dry. Repeat on remaining half of ball.

3. Apply decoupage medium or clear-drying glue to entire ball. While it is still wet, sprinkle the clear glitter over entire ball. When dry tap off the excess glitter.

4. Apply the craft glue to bottom of ornament cap. Press cap firmly into top of ball. Let dry.

5. Thread ribbon through wire loop. Tie ends in a knot for hanging loop.

Paper Gift Box

CRAFT LEVEL: QUICK & EASY

FINISHED SIZE: Box measures about 3-1/2 inches wide x 3-1/2 inches high x 3-1/2 inches deep.

This special holiday box is the ideal container to hold a small gift, such as an ornament, cologne or jewelry. It can even be used for candy or cookies.

Taste of Home Craft Editor Jane Craig

MATERIALS:

Patterns on right

Scrapbook paper—one 12-inch-square piece for box bottom and one coordinating 12-inch-square piece for box lid

6-inch length of 1/4-inch-wide coordinating ribbon

Craft glue for paper

Ruler

Craft knife and cutting mat

Scissors

DIRECTIONS:

1. Enlarge patterns at right in color at 400%.

2. Cut out patterns following outlines of patterns.

Box Lid:

1. Following pattern outline, cut box lid from piece of scrapbook paper for box lid.

2. Place box lid on cutting mat. Use craft knife to cut a small "X" through lid where shown on pattern.

3. Fold paper with wrong sides together along red lines of pattern. Open flat.

4. Fold paper with right sides together along blue lines of pattern. Open flat.

5. Cut from A to B on each corner of the lid to make four flaps. Apply glue to right side of a flap and adhere it to inside of adjoining side. Repeat with remaining flaps.

6. Apply the glue to one blue shaded area of pattern and fold to inside over flaps. Let dry. Repeat remaining blue shaded area.

7. Apply glue to one red shaded area of pattern. Fold to inside of lid. Let dry. Repeat with remaining red shaded area.

8. Tie ends of ribbon together with an overhand knot, leaving a 1-3/4-in.-long loop. Cut excess. Thread fold of loop through slit from inside to outside of lid.

Box Bottom:

1. Following pattern outline, cut box bottom from piece of scrapbook paper for box bottom.

2. Fold paper with wrong sides together, following red lines of pattern.

3. Fold paper with right sides together, following blue lines of pattern.

4. Bring sides up and place lid on the box bottom.

Paper Gift Box Patterns

Use photocopier to enlarge patterns 400%

BOX BOTTOM PATTERN

Trace 1—tracing paper
Cut 1—scrapbook paper for box bottom

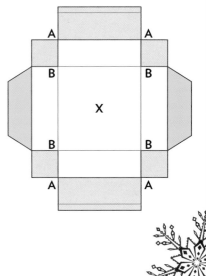

BOX LID

Trace 1—tracing paper
Cut 1—scrapbook paper for box lid

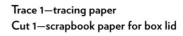

Paper Pieced Tree Place Mat

CRAFT LEVEL: BEGINNER

FINISHED SIZE: Place mat measures about 20-1/2 inches wide x 14-1/2 inches high.

Paper piecing is a technique used by quilters. Here it is used to create the tree pattern on this cheery place mat, which is made with classic Christmas reds and greens. You can change the fabric to fit any color scheme.

Taste of Home Craft Editor Jane Craig

MATERIALS:

Pattern on page 207

Tracing paper and pencil

44-inch-wide 100% cotton fabrics—one fat quarter (18-inch x 22-inch piece) each of ten different coordinating fabrics or 1/4 yard of dark green print for sashing and binding, and 1/8 yard each of green-and-red print for outer border, light green print for background of blocks, red print for cornerstones, brown print for tree trunks, red print, black bird print, green print, green holly print for pieced blocks and 1/2 yard of coordinating print for backing

All-purpose thread to match fabrics

Invisible monofilament thread for quilting

16-inch x 22-inch piece of lightweight quilt batting

Quilter's ruler

Rotary cutter and mat (optional)

Standard sewing supplies

DIRECTIONS:

Wash fabrics separately. If the water from any fabric is discolored, wash again until rinse water runs clear. Dry and press fabrics.

CUTTING:

1. From green and red print for outer border, cut two 3-1/2- x 7-1/2-in. pieces and two 3-1/2- x 14-1/2-in. pieces.

2. From dark green print, cut four 1- x 7-1/2-in. strips for sashing and inner border and two 1- x 14-1/2-in. strips for inner border. Also cut 2-1/2-in.-wide strips for binding to equal distance around place mat plus 12 in.

3. From red print, cut four 3-1/2-in. squares for corners.

4. From fabric for backing, cut one 16- x 22-in. piece for backing.

Foundation Pieced Tree Block (Make 3):

1. Cut one pattern apart on pattern lines, making pattern pieces 1 through 9.

2. Pin pattern pieces 1 through 9 right side up to right side of the different fabrics as directed or as desired.

3. Cut out shapes 1 through 9, cutting 1/2 in. outside pattern lines.

4. Place a fabric piece 1 right side up on section 1 of a paper pattern. Hold the pattern up to a light source to make sure the fabric is centered over the area. Pin fabric in place as shown in Fig. 1 below.

5. Place a fabric piece 2 and right side down on the first piece so the raw edges are matching as shown in Fig. 2 below. Hold the pattern up to a light source and flip the fabric over to make sure there is enough fabric on all edges of the number 2 pattern section. Flip the fabric back and pin to hold in place. Turn the pattern over. With a short straight stitch, sew on the pattern line between sections 1 and 2, extending stitching a couple of stitches beyond the pattern line. Remove pins and trim seam to 1/4 in. Open and press fabric 2 over section 2 as shown in Fig. 3 below.

6. In the same way add fabrics 3 through 9 to sections 3 through 9.

7. Baste just outside the outer line of the pattern.

8. With tree centered, trim block to an accurate 4-1/2- x 7-1/2-in. rectangle.

FIG. 1 Adding fabric 1
Pin fabric 1 to section 1

FIG. 2
Adding fabric 2

FIG. 3 Open and press
fabric 2 over section 2

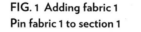

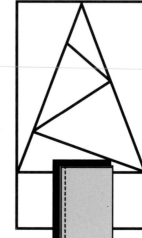

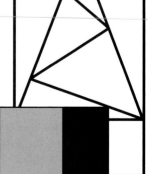

Sashing and Inner Border:

1. Layout pieced tree blocks right side up.

2. Sew a 1- x 7-1/2-in. sashing strip between the blocks and a same-size inner border to each end. Press seams toward strips.

3. Sew a 1- x 14-1/2-in. inner border strip to top and bottom edges. Press seams toward strips.

Outer Border:

1. Sew a 3-1/2- x 7-1/2-in. border strip to opposite sides of place mat. Press seams toward inner border strips.

2. Sew a 3-1/2-in. square to opposite ends of remaining border strips. Press seams toward squares. Sew a pieced strip to top and bottom edges of place mat. Press seams toward inner border strips.

Quilting:

1. Place backing piece wrong side up on a flat surface. Center batting on top of backing and pieced place mat on top of batting. Smooth out and baste as needed to hold layers together.

2. Thread sewing machine with mono-filament thread and stitch in-the-ditch of seams in pieced blocks, inner border and corner squares.

3. Trim excess batting and backing even with pieced top and square place mat.

Binding:

1. Sew narrow ends of binding strips together diagonally to make one long strip. Trim excess from seams and press seams open.

2. Fold one end of strip diagonally and press 1/4 in. to wrong side. Fold and press binding strip in half lengthwise with wrong sides facing.

3. Sew binding to front of place mat with a 1/4-in. seam, mitering corners and overlapping ends. Trim excess binding.

4. Fold binding to back of place mat, encasing raw edges and hand-sew fold to back and mitering corners. Hand-sew fold of binding to back of place mat.

Crafter's Note: If you've never done any paper piecing, we recommend that you do a test using scrap fabric before working on the final blocks.

Place Mat Pattern

Trace four tree patterns onto tracing paper with pencil, numbering each section of patterns as shown. Go over pattern lines of each with black permanent marker so pattern lines are visible on both sides. Follow instructions to piece blocks.

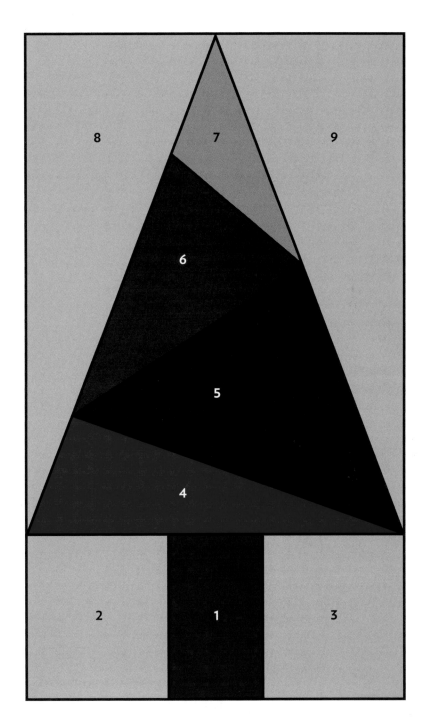

Let it Snow Card

CRAFT LEVEL: BEGINNER

FINISHED SIZE: Card measures about 5-1/2 inches wide x 4-1/8 inches high.

I enjoy making cards with a little some-thing extra, like with a part that stands out or moves. I liked this snowflake stamp and thought it would be nice if it would move as if it were snowing.

Lori Ditzler ★ Bloomingdale, Michigan

MATERIALS:

4-1/8-inch x 11-inch piece of white card stock

5-inch x 7-inch piece of light blue card stock

"Let it Snow" stamp (Anita's stamp shown)

Snowflake stamp (Stampin' Up! stamp shown)

Clear drying craft glue

Iridescent glitter

Embossing ink

White embossing powder

Heat gun

Decorative-edge scissors

Scissors

Ruler and pencil

Craft knife

DIRECTIONS:

1. Fold 4-1/8- x 11-in. piece of white card stock in half crosswise to make a card measuring 5-1/2-in. wide x 4-1/8 in. high.

2. From blue card stock cut a 5-1/2- x 4-1/8-in. piece.

3. Use decorative-edge scissors to trim about 1/8 in. from each edge.

4. Use craft knife to cut two 3-in.-long x 1/4-in.-wide slits 1 in. apart in blue card stock piece as shown in Fig. 1 at right.

5. From blue card stock, cut three 1/4- x 2-in. pieces. Fold each piece in thirds. Wrap two around the slit opening on left and the other one around other slit opening on right. Glue to hold the ends together to make sliders, being careful not to glue them to the openings so they will slide freely.

6. With embossing ink, stamp "Let it Snow!" to the right of the openings and immediately sprinkle on the white

FIG. 1 Cutting slits in blue cardstock

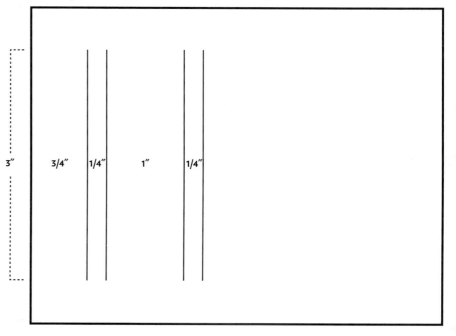

3" 3/4" 1/4" 1" 1/4"

embossing powder. Tap off excess and heat with heat gun until embossing powder melts. Let dry.

7. With embossing ink, stamp three snowflakes on remaining scrap of blue card stock and immediately sprinkle on white embossing powder. Tap off excess and heat with heat gun until embossing powder melts. Let dry. With snowflakes centered, cut out each as shown.

8. Glue a snowflake to each of the sliders on the openings, being careful not to glue the snowflakes to the back-ground so snowflakes can move up and down along the openings.

9. Apply random dots of glue to right side of blue card stock piece. While glue is still wet, sprinkle on iridescent glitter. Tap off excess glitter and let dry.

10. Place white card on a flat surface with fold at the left. Glue blue card stock piece right side up to center front of card.

Crafter's Note: Make sure your craft knife or cutter is sharp to make the slide slats smooth, not rough, so that the snowflakes slide easily.

Drinking Glass Charm/Bracelet

CRAFT LEVEL: QUICK & EASY

FINISHED SIZE: Each glass charm measures about 2 inches across.

One bracelet takes 20 to 30 minutes to make and is a great way to use up an accumulation of leftover small beads. Make each one unique and place them on straight-side drinking glasses when you're having a party. That way, your guests can find his or her glass after they put it down. You can also use these bracelets to dress up a pillar candle or as a bracelet for a young girl.

Sarah Farley ★ Menomonee Falls, Wisconsin

MATERIALS (FOR ONE):

Bracelet memory wire

Assorted beads in desired colors (assorted blue, red and green beads shown)

Wire cutters

Round-nose pliers

1-1/2-inch length of gold or silver small chain (optional)

Four silver head pins (optional)

DIRECTIONS:

1. Use wire cutters to cut about 4 loops of memory wire.

2. Using round-nose pliers, make a tight coil on one end of the memory wire.

3. String beads on memory wire in desired order, leaving enough room at the end to make another tight coil.

Hanging Accent (optional):

1. String a large bead on a head pin. Use round-nose pliers to make a loop at end of head pin and attach it to one end of chain.

2. String desired numbers and colors of beads on each head pin. Attach each to chain with a closed loop.

3. Attach end of chain to a loop on one end of the bracelet.

Christmas Gift Card Holders

CRAFT LEVEL: BEGINNER

FINISHED SIZE: Each gift card measures about 3 inches across x 4 inches high without hanging loop.

Gift cards are a popular holiday present and I, too, give them. I designed these paper holders so the cards would look festive when I handed them out.

Sandy Rollinger ★ Apollo, Pennsylvania

Note: Gift card holders will accommodate a standard credit card-size gift card.

MATERIALS (FOR BOTH):

1-inch circle punch

Ruler

Pencil

Bone folder (optional)

Paper crimper

Red and white card stock

Two 9-inch lengths of 1/8-inch-wide coordinating satin ribbon for hanging loops

Corsage pin, round toothpick or quilling tool for rolling paper strips

Straight pin or toothpick

Clear-drying craft glue

Scissors

MATERIALS (FOR ONE ORNAMENT GIFT CARD HOLDER):

2-inch circle punch

Patterned scrapbook paper for decorative band (red-green-and-white polka dot paper shown)

Three red e-beads

1/8-inch-wide light green and dark green quilling paper or construction paper cut into 1/8-inch-wide strips

MATERIALS (FOR ONE TREE GIFT CARD HOLDER):

Patterned scrapbook paper for decorative band (red-green-and-white diagonal stripe paper shown)

Light green quilling paper or construction paper cut into 1/8-inch-wide strips

Seven red e-beads

1/2-inch flat-back rhinestone star

DIRECTIONS:

Basic Quilling Instructions:

1. To roll paper, tear off a strip of 1/8-in.-wide quilling or construction paper to the length specified in the instructions.

2. Moisten one end of the strip slightly and press it onto the center of the corsage pin or toothpick. If using a quilling tool, place the paper end in the crevice.

3. Roll the remaining length of the strip tightly between your thumb and your forefinger, keeping strip's edges even.

4. Slide pin/toothpick/tool out and glue end in place, or allow coil to open to desired size, then glue end in place. Strive for uniformity between like shapes.

5. When gluing quilled shapes, use pin or toothpick to apply a small amount of glue.

Quilling Shapes (see Fig. 1 below):

1. Cut a 4- x 6-1/2-in. piece of red card stock.

2. Referring to photo on page 211, center gift card on wrong side of red card stock and fold sides over as shown. Use bone folder or ruler to sharply crease folds.

3. Open and use 1-in. circle punch to make a semicircle at the center top as shown.

4. Refold and glue overlap at back and bottom edge of gift holder. Place a book or other flat heavy object on top of gift holder and let dry.

5. Cut a 3-in. x 6-1/2-in. piece of polka dot scrapbook paper for decorative band. Wrap piece around gift card holder, leaving a margin of red showing at the top and bottom and overlapping excess in back. Glue as needed to hold.

6. Glue opposite ends of satin ribbon to back corners of gift card holder for hanger. Let dry.

7. From red card stock, punch a 2-in. circle.

8. Cut a 1- x 3-in. piece of white cardstock. Run through paper crimper. Glue crimped paper to center of red circle. Use scissors to trim excess even with edge of circle.

FIG. 1 Quilling Shapes:

Holly:

1. Cut a 4-in. strip of dark green paper. Roll paper into a tight coil without gluing end.

2. Slip coil off the tool and let it expand to 1/2 in. Glue the end and let dry.

3. Pinch the circle into a diamond shape as shown.

Bow:

1. Cut a 3-1/2-in. strip of light green paper for loops of bow. Fold and glue ends in to center to form loops. Let dry.

2. Cut a 2-in. strip of light green paper for streamers of bow. Fold strip in half and glue over center of loops.

Open Scroll:

1. Cut a light green strip as directed.

2. Crease strip at center.

3. Roll the remaining ends toward crease on the outside of paper as shown.

Ornament Gift Card Holder:

9. Glue three e-beads to center of white strip.

10. Make two quilled holly leaves as directed. Glue holly leaves to opposite sides of e-beads.

11. Make a light green bow as directed. Glue bow to center top of patterned paper.

Tree Gift Card Holder:

1. Follow steps 1-6 of ornament gift card holder, using striped scrapbook paper for decorative band instead.

2. To make triangle for tree, cut a 2- x 3-in. piece of white card stock. Draw a line from each corner to center of opposite short edge. Cut along marked lines. Run through paper crimper.

3. Cut a 4-, 5- and 6-in. length of light green quilling or construction paper. Form each length into an open scroll. Glue the small, medium and large scrolls to the top, center and bottom of the tree.

4. Glue seven e-beads to tree as shown.

5. Glue the tree to center front of the decorative band.

6. Glue rhinestone star to top of tree.

Decorate With Quilling

Use the simple quilling methods shown at left to embellish a variety of holiday packaging and decor items. With a few simple craft supplies, make a variety of quilled papers and add them to cards, gift bags, presents and even ornaments. Try combining unique paper color combinations for even more appeal.

Sweater Backpack

CRAFT LEVEL: INTERMEDIATE

FINISHED SIZE: Backpack measures about 13 inches across x 13-1/2 inches high.

I am inspired to make something new out of something old, and thrift store sweaters are one of my favorite things to recycle. This backpack was made from a sweater from South America with a llama pattern on it. I entered it in a local fair and won a blue ribbon and best of show for a large recycling project.

Laurel Beale ★ Valley Center, California

MATERIALS:

Two Adult-size recycled all-wool sweaters (Laurel used a print sweater and a coordinating solid color sweater)

Matching all-purpose thread

Magnetic purse closure

Four 1-1/4-inch metal D rings

1/2-inch x 40-inch coordinating cloth or leather strip for tie

1-1/4-inch coordinating button for flap

Standard sewing supplies

DIRECTIONS:

Felting:

1. To felt the sweaters, machine-wash them in hot water using laundry detergent, running them through a complete cycle that includes a cold rinse cycle. Without using detergent, repeat this process until the sweaters are felted as desired.

2. Smooth out wrinkles and place felted sweaters on a flat surface to dry. Check sweaters while drying and smooth out as needed.

Cutting:

1. From print sweater, cut two 14- x 15-in. pieces from body of sweater for front and back of backpack. From sleeves, cut two 3- x 10-in. strips and two 3- x 28-in. strips for the straps. (Strips may need to be joined to make the two 28-in.-long straps.) Also cut a 5-1/2- x 10-1/2-in. piece for the outside of the flap.

2. From solid sweater, cut a 5-1/2- x 10-1/2-in. piece for the lining of the flap. Also cut a 4- x 11-in. piece for the bottom of the backpack.

Straps:

1. Fold long edges of a 3-in.-wide strip for strap with wrong sides together and edges meeting in the center to make a 1-1/2-in.-wide strap. Pin as needed to hold. Sew down the center of the strap with a wide zigzag stitch, catching the edges of each side in the stitching. Repeat with remaining strap pieces to make two 10-in.-long straps and two 28-in.-long straps.

2. Round one end of each strap and overcast edges.

3. Thread two D rings on the rounded edge of each of the 10-in.-long straps. With wrong sides facing, fold rounded edge back 3 in. Sew ends in place on each strap to secure D rings.

Flap:

1. Following the manufacturer's instructions, attach one half of the magnetic purse closure to the right side of the solid (lining) flap piece centered 2 in. from one narrow end.

2. Pin the print and solid flap pieces together with right sides facing and edges matching. Sew pieces together with a narrow seam, rounding corners on the end with magnetic closure. Trim excess and turn flap right side out.

3. Topstitch 1/2-in. from edge of flap if desired.

4. Hand-sew button to right side of flap over magnetic closure.

Assembly:

1. Pin the two 14- x 15-in. pieces for the front and back of the backpack together with right sides facing and edges matching. Sew the long edges together with a 1/4-in. seam for sides of backpack. Overcast the raw edges.

2. Fold 1 in. along top edge to wrong side. Zigzag close to raw edge for the hem. (If fabric is too stiff, the hem can be omitted.)

3. Center the straight edge of the flap about 2 in. from the top back top edge of right side of backpack. Top stitch close to raw edge of flap and then stitch 3/4 in. from first row of stitching to form a channel.

4. Sew raw edge of straps with D rings centered along the raw edge of flap on the right side of back of the backpack.

5. Starting about 1/2 in. from sides of flap on back, cut four evenly spaced 1/2-in. slits in the front and back of the backpack for leather strip.

6. With wrong side of 28-in.-long straps facing right side of the back, pin straps 1-1/2 in. from side seams of back. Sew straps in place with a narrow seam.

7. Pin bottom piece to bottom edge of backpack with right sides facing, and side seams centered on the opposite short sides of bottom piece. Ends of straps will be sandwiched between the backpack and bottom piece. Sew the bottom piece to backpack with a 1/2-in. seam. Leave needle down at each corner, turn and realign raw edges as you continue to sew. Sew around a second time to reinforce the seam and then overcast raw edges. Turn backpack right side out.

8. Thread end of a long strap through both D rings on corresponding short strap. Then thread the end through just one of the D rings to secure. Repeat with remaining straps and adjust to desired length.

9. Starting at the front, thread the leather or cloth strip in and out of the slits and through the channel on the back of the backpack. Tie ends in front.

Crafter's Note: For recycled sweater projects, look for interesting sweaters at thrift stores or use an unused one from your closet.

Buttonhole Scarf

CRAFT LEVEL: BEGINNER

FINISHED SIZE: Scarf measures about 4 inches wide x 28 inches long.

I designed this scarf because I wanted a short one that would stay in place, keep my neck warm and could be tucked into my coat. The one end of the scarf goes through the buttonhole opening on the other end. It's a quick homemade item, great for gift giving.

Lois Westlund ★ Winfield, Illinois

MATERIALS:

6-ounce skein of Lion Brand Homespun yarn in color of choice

Size 6 (4mm) knitting needles

Stitch holder

Yarn or tapestry needle

Measuring tape

Scissors

GAUGE:

4 sts and 4 rows = 1 inch. Slight variations in gauge will change finished size a bit.

DIRECTIONS:

Cast on 15 sts.

K every row until piece measures about 27 in.

Next row: K 8 sts, place next 7 sts on stitch holder.

K the 8 sts on the needle for 4 in.

Place the 7 sts onto the needle and place the 8 sts on stitch holder. Cut the yarn, leaving an 8-in. tail. Make a loose knot in yarn to prevent raveling.

Leaving an 8-in. tail of yarn, attach yarn to the sts on the needle and k for 4 in.

Beginning at the edge of the 8 sts, k across all 15 sts.

K each row for another 3 in.

Bind off all sts.

Use yarn or tapestry needle to weave in all loose ends.

ABBREVIATIONS	
k	knit
st(s)	stitch(es)

Special Gifts

Use your pile of leftover yarn and half-used skeins to make several of these charming scarves. Don't be afraid to combine whatever colors you have on hand to create unique striped patterns.

Sparkling Tray or Charger

CRAFT LEVEL: QUICK & EASY

FINISHED SIZE: Use any size tray or charger. Our tray measures 11-1/2 inches x 17-1/2 inches; charger, 13 inches across.

My ornaments hold special memories for me of Christmases past, and I hate to throw them out, even when they are broken. I came up with this idea to repurpose those ornament pieces into a new colorful use.

Wendy Borchert ★ Whitefish Bay, Wisconsin

MATERIALS:

Tray or charger with recessed area

EnviroTex Lite (a pour-on acrylic polymer that dries clear—available at craft and hardware stores)

Broken colored-glass ornaments

Heavy plastic bag

Hammer

Bamboo skewer

DIRECTIONS:

1. Place broken ornaments in heavy plastic bag and use hammer to gently break into small pieces.

2. Sprinkle ornament pieces into recessed area of the tray or charger.

Arrange pieces as desired, with some pieces colored side up, and others with the inside silver or gold color showing.

3. Mix the EnviroTex Lite following the manufacturer's instructions. Working in a well-lit area, pour the EnviroTex Lite slowly into the tray or charger, completely covering the ornament pieces. Use skewer to break air bubbles, move or break pieces and push down any pieces that surface. Check to make sure the surface is completely smooth. Let dry on a firm, level surface until hardened.

Crafter's Note: Items are not heat-resistant. Wipe clean, but don't submerge in water.

Cozy Sweater Jacket

CRAFT LEVEL: INTERMEDIATE

FINISHED SIZE: Chest = 39-1/2 (41,43,45) inches.

Length = 26(27,29,31) inches.

Upper sleeve circumference = 17 inches.

Directions are given for size Small; changes for sizes Medium, Large and Extra Large are in parentheses.

This oversize sweater is great as a gift or for yourself. It's knitted in one piece, can be whipped up in just a day or two, and you can modify the design to include long sleeves or a shorter sweater with a zipper. It's a wonderful wrap to get snuggly warm on a cold day!

Sarah McFarland ★ Burdett, New York

MATERIALS:

5(6,6,8) 4-ounce 80-yard skeins of 2-ply-bulky weight yarn (Bear Farm Yarns Bulky 100% wool yarn in Cranberry shown)

Size 15 (10mm) 29-inch circular needle

Size J (6mm) crochet hook

Cable needle

Two 3-yard lengths of smooth contrasting color scrap yarn

Yarn or tapestry needle

Measuring tape

Scissors

Gauge:

Working in Stockinette stitch (k RS, p WS), 8.5 sts and 12 rows = 4 inches.

Special Stitches:

St st = Stockinette stitch

K all RS rows

P all WS rows

Garter st = garter stitch

K all rows

DIRECTIONS:

Cast on 40(44,48,52) sts.

Rows 1-12: K every row: 40(44,48,52) sts.

Row 13 (RS): (First inc row), k 8(9,10,11), yo, k 1, yo, k 6, yo, k 1, yo, k 8(10,12,14), yo, k 1, yo, k 6, yo, k 1, yo, k 8(9,10,11). This is the foundation row establishing the 8 places in which you will yo to add stitches, expanding front the neck into two front sections, sleeves and a back for your sweater: 48(52,56,60) sts.

Row 14 (WS): (Begin working in St st with garter st border): K 4, p across row including all yo sts in previous row, k last 4 sts: 48(52,56,60) sts.

Row 15 and all remaining RS rows: K across, working a yo on both sides of all single k sts as established in Row 13. (Front, sides, back and sleeves will get wider on each inc row.)

Row 16 and all remaining WS rows: K 4, p across, k last 4 sts.

Repeat Rows 15 and 16 until you have completed 14 sets of incs, ending with at WS row: 152(156,160,164) sts.

Separating Sleeves and Body:

(RS): K 23(24,25,26) sts to start of sleeve section. Do not break original yarn; with scrap yarn, bind off next 34 sts for first sleeve. Pick up original yarn and resume knitting; k 38(40,42,44) across back of sweater. Stop and use second piece of scrap yarn to bind off 34 sts for second sleeve. Resume knitting with original yarn across remaining 23(24,25,26 sts).

Continue working 84(88,92,96) sts on needle in St st with 4-st garter st border.

Center Back Cable:

Work until sweater measures 12 in. from base of neck or desired length to middle of back.

Row 1 (RS): K 38(40,42,44), place 2 sts on cable needle and hold to back of work, k 2, k 2 from cable needle, place 2 sts on cable needle and hold in front of work, k 2, k 2 from cable needle, k 38(40,42,44): 84(88,92,96) sts.

Rows 2-4: Work as established in St st: 84(88,92,96) sts.

Row 5 (RS): K 38(40,42,44 across to center 8 sts and reverse twists; place 2 sts on cable needle and put at front of work k 2, k 2 from cable needle, place 2 sts on cable needle and hold in back of work, k 2, k 2 from cable needle, k 38(40,42,44): 84(88,92,96) sts.

Remaining Rows:

Work in St st with 4-st garter st border until sweater measures about 22(24,26,28) in. from start or about 4 in. shorter than desired finished length, ending with a RS row.

Garter St Bottom Edging:

Rows 1-15: K each row. Bind off on last (WS) row.

Sleeves:

Carefully undo scrap yarn bind-off for one sleeve, placing 34 sts back on needle. Starting with a RS row, k seven rows. Bind off on next (WS) row. Repeat for other sleeve.

Finishing:

With RS facing and matching yarn, sew underarm seams together.

Tie Detail:

With a size J (6mm) crochet hook and matching yarn, chain 40 sts. Thread the chain through the center back cable and tie in back. Weave in all loose ends.

VARIATIONS (optional):

Long Sleeves:

Pick up the 34 sleeve sts, continue to

work in St st, decreasing 1 st at each end of every fourth row until 24 sts remain. Work until sleeve is 2 in. shorter than desired finished length, ending with a WS row. Starting with a RS row, k seven rows. Bind off on next (WS) row. Sew underarm seams together.

Bomber Jacket:

Follow instructions, omitting the center back cable. When sweater is about 13(14,15,16) in. long or desired length from base of neck, k the first and last 4 sts of every row and work k 2, p 2 ribbing on sts in between, continue in established pattern for 2 to 6 in. Finish sleeves using short or long version.

Add a Zipper:

Hand- or machine-sew a matching or contrasting zipper to the front. Use fabric glue to hold the zipper tape in place before sewing.

Belt:

With a size J (6mm) crochet hook and matching yarn, chain desired number of sts for belt. Thread the belt through the center back cable.

ABBREVIATIONS	
inc(s)	increase(s)
k	knit
p	purl
RS	right side
st(s)	stitch(es)
WS	wrong side
yo	yarn over

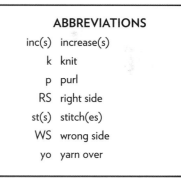

Craft glue

Ruler

Scissors

DIRECTIONS:

1. From white card stock cut one 2-7/8-x 5-in. piece for large tag and one 3/4- x 2-in. piece for small tag. Trim corners from adjoining sides on one narrow end of each to make tag shape. Use 1/4-in. punch to make a hole in trimmed end of large tag. Attach eyelet to trimmed end of small tag.

2. Use green ink pad and holly background stamp to stamp one side of the large and small gift tags. Apply ink to the top edges of the large gift tag to shade it.

3. Cut two 2-in. squares from dark green card stock. Glue the squares diagonally to from of gift tag as shown in photo on left. Glue "To: From:" sticker to bottom green square or use markers to write "To" and "From" and to add holly design.

4. Adhere "Holiday Greetings" sticker or write "Holiday Greetings" on front of small gift tag. Thread red-and-white polka dot ribbon through the eyelet and tie ends in a small bow. Glue one poinsettia or other small cutout to upper right corner. Adhere a small piece of foam mounting tape to back of remaining cutout and adhere it over the other cutout. Apply a long strip of mounting tape to the back of the small gift tag and adhere it to the top square.

5. Fold dark green ribbon in half and thread fold through hole in gift tag. Thread ends through loop and pull ends to secure ribbon to tag.

Crafter's Note: I keep an art journal of future ideas. My inspiration comes from nature, art fairs and trends in craft stores.

Holiday Greetings Gift Tag

CRAFT LEVEL: QUICK & EASY

FINISHED SIZE: Gift tag measures about 2-7/8 inches wide x 5 inches high without ribbon tie.

I'm a crafter and like to keep busy. After having minor surgery, I couldn't drive to the craft store, so I looked through my craft materials and decided to do a scrap project. I started with a tag for a wedding gift, then expanded to birthdays and holidays. Each one of my tags is unique. In an evening, you can easily make five tags.

Louise Getz ★ East Moline, Illinois

MATERIALS:

Dark green and off-white card stock

Holly or other background stamp

Dark green ink pad

1/4-inch round hole punch

Stickers—clear "Holiday Greetings" and "To: From:" or black, green and red markers

8-inch length of 1/8-inch-wide ribbon (red-and-white polka dot ribbon shown)

Two small cutouts (poinsettia cutouts shown)

One small silver eyelet and eyelet-setting tool

Foam mounting tape

10-inch length of dark green 1-1/4-inch-wide sheer wire-edge ribbon

Quilted Tote

CRAFT LEVEL: BEGINNER

FINISHED SIZE: Quilted tote measures about 17 inches wide x 13 inches high without straps.

Totes are so handy to carry all sorts of things from a laptop, exercise clothes, lunch or paperwork. Use your friend's favorite colors to make an exclusive tote just for her.

Taste of Home Craft Editor Jane Craig

MATERIALS:

18-inch x 44-inch piece of quilted fabric (purchased black-and-white print quilted fabric shown)

2-1/2 yards of 1/2-inch-wide purchased piping—red or color of choice

All-purpose thread to match fabrics

15-1/2-inch length of 3/4-inch-wide loop side of hook-and-loop tape

Four 17-inch lengths of 3/4-inch-wide metal carpenter's measuring tape

Craft scissors metal shears

Masking or duct tape

3 yards of 1-inch-wide woven belting—black or coordinating color

5-inch x 12-inch piece of plastic canvas for bottom of tote

Standard sewing supplies

DIRECTIONS:

1. From quilted fabric, cut one 18- x 30-in. piece for outside of tote. Cut two 3-1/2- x 18-in. strips for casings and one 7- x 10-in. piece for outside pocket.

2. Overcast edges of 7- x 10-in. piece for pocket. With right sides facing, sew piping 1 in. from one long edge of pocket piece. With raw edges matching, sew piping to opposite long edge. Fold seam allowances to wrong side.

3. Center pocket piece right side up on front of 18- x 30-in. piece for outside of tote with top edge about 3 in. from top raw edge of tote piece. Topstitch side edges to front of tote. Stitch in-the-ditch of the piping seam along bottom edge of pocket only.

4. Cut two 3-in. lengths of belting. Fold each in half crosswise. With raw edges matching, pin one to the center front top edge of the tote and one to the center back top edge of the tote.

5. With right sides facing and raw edges matching, sew piping to top edge of front and back of tote.

6. With right sides facing, pin a 3-1/2- x 18-in. casing strip to outside top edges of front and back of tote. Sew each in place, stitching just outside previous stitching and making sure piping is visible on the outside of the tote. Fold each casing strip in half, matching raw edges. Sew raw edges together, stitching on previous row of stitching. Overcast raw edges together.

7. Center and sew hook-and-loop tape below casing on back of tote.

8. Fold remaining belting piece in half crosswise. Mark fold.

9. Referring to Fig. 1 at right and starting and stopping at the center bottom, pin belting piece to outside of the tote. Making sure belting is not twisted, pin marked fold to other side of center bottom. With matching thread, topstitch the belting to the outside of the tote. Do not stitch through the casing on the front and back of tote.

10. Fold the tote in half crosswise and mark the fold at each side of the bottom of the tote. With raw edges matching and starting at the casing seam, sew piping to opposite sides of front of tote.

11. Use craft scissors to round the ends of each of the four pieces of carpenter's tape. Stack two lengths of carpenter's tape together with edges matching. Wrap each end with masking tape or duct tape. Repeat with remaining pieces of carpenter's tape.

12. With numbers facing the inside, slide a set into the front and back casings of the tote. Baste across ends to hold.

13. Fold tote in half crosswise with right sides facing. Sew side seams, stitching just inside previous piping stitching. Overcast seam.

14. For a flat bottom, align side and bottom seams forming a triangle as shown in Fig. 2 shown on right. With a straight stitch, sew across triangle about 1/4 in. from belting.

15. Turn tote right side out and place plastic canvas piece on bottom of tote.

FIG. 1 Attaching belting

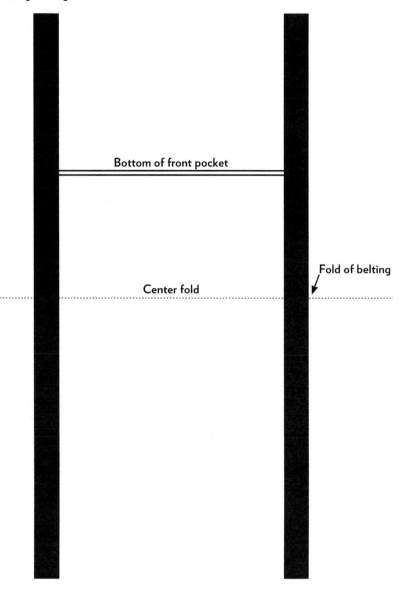

Bottom of front pocket

Center fold

Fold of belting

FIG. 2 Forming flat bottom of tote

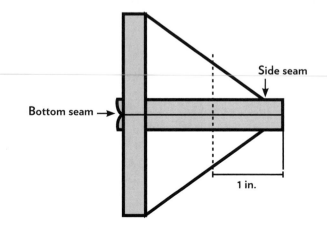

Side seam

Bottom seam →

1 in.

Organizer Pocket for Tote Bags

CRAFT LEVEL: BEGINNER

FINISHED SIZE: Pocket insert measures about 15 inches wide x 6-1/2 inches high.

If you are frequently rummaging in the bottom of your tote for a cell phone, credit cards, pen or wallet, here is a solution. This organizer will make it easier to find those objects and it can be attached to the top of tote bag. It's removable, so you can easy switch the organizer from one tote to another.

Taste of Home Craft Editor Jane Craig

MATERIALS:

1/2 yard of 44-inch-wide red or coordinating color canvas or heavy cotton fabric

1 package of 1/4-inch-wide double-fold bias tape—black or color of choice

15-1/2-inch length of 3/4-inch-wide hook side of hook-and-loop tape

Matching all purpose thread

Standard sewing supplies

DIRECTIONS:

1. From canvas or heavy cotton fabric, cut one 15- x 7-1/2-in. piece for the backing, one 15- x 6-in. piece for pocket section and two 2-1/4- x 4-in. pieces for center pocket flap.

2. Place 2-1/4- x 4-in. pieces for flap together with wrong sides facing and edges matching. With wider side of bias tape on top, slip tape over raw edge of pocket flap. With matching thread and a decorative stitch, sew bias tape in place. With matching thread, sew a 1/2 in. length of hook-and-loop tape to the center of the wrong side of the flap.

3. Fold and press 1/2 in. to wrong side along one long edge of 15- x 6-in. piece for pocket section. Cut a 1/2 in. length of hook side of hook-and-loop tape. With matching thread, sew piece to right side of pocket piece where shown.

4. For top hem, fold and press 1 in. to wrong side along one long edge of 15- x 7-1/2-in. piece for backing. Referring to Fig. 1 at right, center pocket section piece on top of backing piece with long

raw edges matching. Pin to hold. With matching thread and a straight stitch, sew channels for pockets where shown. Sew raw edge of pocket flap to center of pocket piece where shown and fold flap down to close.

5. Sew bias tape to side and bottom edges of pocket piece as before.

6. Center remaining length of hook-and-loop tape along top hem of pocket

piece. With matching thread, sew both long edges of hook-and-loop tape in place. Slip bias tape over top fold and sew thebias tape in place as before, wrapping ends to back. Center another piece of bias tape on top of the bottom row of stitching and sew it in place as before.

FIG. 1 Adding pockets

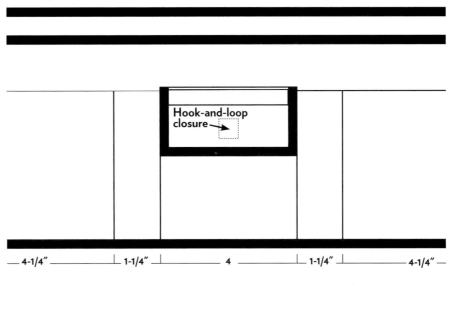

Hook-and-loop closure→

4-1/4"   1-1/4"   4   1-1/4"   4-1/4"

Cross-Stitched Snowman Tree Trimmer

CRAFT LEVEL: QUICK & EASY

FINISHED SIZE: Design area is 49 stitches high x 38 stitches wide. Excluding hanger, ornament is about 3-1/2 inches high x 2-1/2 inches wide.

I was looking at a roll of gift wrap when the pattern on the paper piqued my interest. The design featured funny snowmen in various poses. I thought I could cross-stitch those snowmen, so I adapted the idea and set about embroidering. Now I have this frosty fellow to trim a tree.

Darlene Polachic ★ Saskatoon, Saskatchewan

MATERIALS:

Chart on page 223

One 4- x 5-inch piece of antique white 16-count Aida cloth

DMC six-strand embroidery floss in colors listed on color key

Size 26 tapestry needle

One 4- x 5-inch piece of white 100% cotton or cotton-blend fabric for backing

White all-purpose thread

Polyester fiberfill

One 12-inch length of 1/8-inch-wide green satin ribbon

Standard sewing supplies

DIRECTIONS:

Cross-Stitching:

1. Zigzag or overcast edges of Aida cloth to prevent fraying.

2. Fold cloth in half lengthwise, then fold it in half crosswise and mark where folds intersect.

3. Draw lines across chart, connecting the arrows. Begin counting where lines intersect to locate first stitch of top row, then locate same spot on Aida cloth and begin stitching there for a centered design.

4. Each square on chart represents one set of fabric threads surrounded by four holes. Each stitch is worked over one set of threads with the needle passing through the holes.

5. The color and/or symbol inside each square, along with the color key, tells which color of six-strand embroidery floss to use for the cross-stitch. Wide lines on charts show where to work backstitches. See Fig. 1 at bottom right for stitch illustrations.

6. Use 18-in. lengths of six-strand floss. Longer strands tend to tangle and fray.

7. Separate the strands, then thread the tapestry needle with two strands for all cross-stitches and one strand for all backstitches.

8. To begin stitching, leave a 1-in.-long tail of thread on back of work and hold it in place while working the first few stitches around it.

9. To end stitching, run needle under a few stitches in back before clipping the embroidery floss close to work.

Assembly:

1. When stitching is complete, and only if necessary, gently wash stitched piece in lukewarm water. Press right side down on terry towel to dry.

2. Place stitched piece right side down on right side of backing fabric with edges matching.

3. Fold ribbon in half to make a hanging loop. Pin ends of ribbon between layers at top of snowman so ribbon loop is sandwiched between the layers.

4. With a tiny straight stitch and white thread, machine-sew around stitched design about 3/8 in. from outside edge of snowman as shown on chart. Catch the ribbon in stitching and leave an opening along the bottom edge for turning. If preferred, the piece can be backstitched by hand instead.

5. Trim the excess fabric, leaving a 1/4-in. seam allowance. Trim corners diagonally and clip curves. Turn ornament right side out and lightly stuff. Turn in raw edges and hand-sew closed.

CROSS-STITCHED SNOWMAN TREE TRIMMER CHART

COLOR KEY	DMC
⊡ White
◉ Holiday Red	321
◼ Light Holiday Green	701
⊠ Black Brown	3371
BACKSTITCH
— Black Brown	3371

FIG. 1

Backstitch   Cross-Stitch

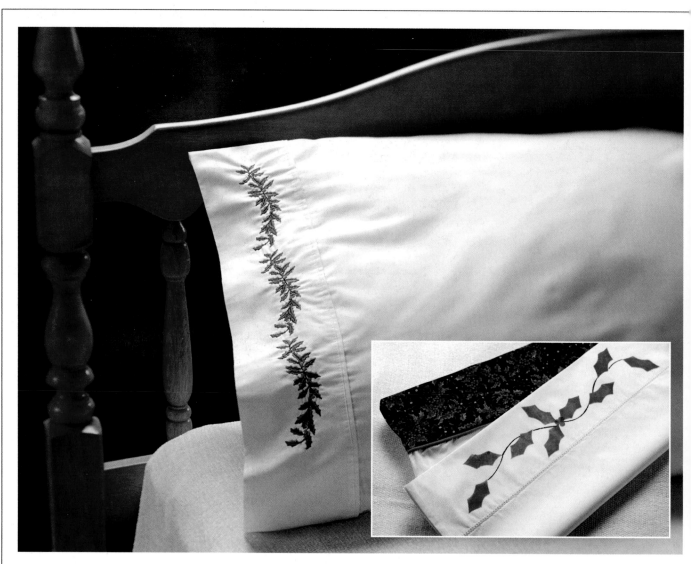

Pillowcases with a Holiday Look

CRAFT LEVEL: BEGINNER

FINISHED SIZE: Standard-size pillowcases shown.

Don't forget the bedroom when adding seasonal decor to a home. Here are three ways to add holiday merriment to pillowcases. Select one that matches your crafting skills or try all three for a pretty gift assortment.

Taste of Home Craft Editor Jane Craig

MATERIALS (FOR EMBROIDERED PILLOWCASE):

Standard-size white pillowcase

Embroidery thread for sewing machine in colors required for design

Embroidery stabilizer

Holly embroidery design

Standard sewing supplies

FINISHED SIZE: Design area measures about 1-1/2 high x 14-3/4 inches wide.

DIRECTIONS:

1. Following embroidery machine instructions, add stabilizer to background.

2. Embroider holly design across hem on one side of pillowcase.

MATERIALS (FOR FABRIC-TRIMMED PILLOWCASE):

Standard-size white pillowcase

18-inch x 22-inch piece or fat quarter of holly print fabric

Coordinating purchased 1/2-inch-wide piping trim

Matching all-purpose thread

Standard sewing supplies

FINISHED SIZE: Design area measures about 4-1/4 inches high x 37 inches wide.

DIRECTIONS:

1. Remove hem from pillowcase. Open hem to make a flat piece. Press removed piece. Using removed hem for pattern, cut a new hem from holly print fabric.

2. With raw edges matching and overlapping ends, sew piping to raw edge of pillowcase.

3. Sew short ends of holly fabric together with a narrow seam to make a large tube.

4. With piping trim sandwiched in between, pin one raw edge of tube to raw edge of pillowcase. Sew fabric in place with a narrow seam. Fold remaining raw edge 1/4 in. to wrong side. Hand-sew fold of fabric to inside of pillowcase, encasing raw edges.

MATERIALS (FOR STENCILED PILLOWCASE):

Standard-size white pillowcase

Pattern, shown above

Tracing paper and pencil

Plastic-coated freezer paper or stencil plastic and stencil adhesive

Craft knife and cutting mat

Scissors

Foam plate or palette

Acrylic craft paints—brown, dark green, light green and red

Fabric medium

Three small pieces of clean household sponge or three stencil brushes

Masking tape

Plastic covered cardboard

Small round paper punch

Iron and ironing surface

FINISHED SIZE: Design area measures about 3-1/2 inches high x 15-1/4 inches wide.

Pillowcase Pattern

**Use photocopier to enlarge pattern 200% or draw a 1-inch grid on freezer paper and draw pattern as shown
Trace as directed—tracing paper
Trace and cut as directed—plastic-coated freezer paper or stencil plastic**

DIRECTIONS:

1. Trace holly pattern, below, onto tracing paper three times with pencil.

2. Cut out and discard entire holly shapes from one tracing (A).

3. Cut out and discard shaded areas (stems) from second tracing, leaving holly shapes (B).

4. Cut out and discard berries from third tracing (C), leaving holly shapes and stems.

5. Trace each pattern onto plastic-coated freezer paper or stencil plastic. Cut out each as shown.

6. Lightly press plastic-coated side of freezer paper A (holly) to pillowcase hem. Or follow stencil adhesive directions to adhere stencil plastic pattern to hem. Slip plastic-covered cardboard into pillowcase to protect the other side of hem.

7. Place a small amount of each acrylic paint on foam plate or palette. Add fabric medium to each paint color, following manufacturer's instructions.

8. Dip a piece of household sponge into the light green paint. Dab excess paint off on paper towel. With a nearly dry sponge and an up-and-down motion, sponge-paint the holly leaves.

9. Dip a piece of household sponge into the dark green paint. In the same way, sponge-paint only the outer edges of the holly leaves. Let dry.

10. In the same way, place pattern B (stems) over stenciled holly leaves, lining up placement dots. Dip a piece of household sponge into the brown paint. Sponge-paint the stems between the holly leaves. Let dry.

11. Place pattern C (berries) over the stenciled holly leaves as before. Dip a piece of household sponge into the red paint. Sponge-paint the berries. Let dry.

Create a Stencil

Almost any design can be made into a stencil. Use the holly stencil instructions for this craft to create a Christmas tree, star or other simple design.

Registration dot •   • Registration dot

of the next two dcs] around, join with a sl st in top of beginning ch-3: 48 dcs.

Rounds 5-9: Ch 3, work 1 dc in each st around, join with a sl st in top of beginning ch-3: 48 dcs.

Round 10: Ch 1, sc in fp of the same st, [sc in bp of next st, sc in fp of next st] around, join with a sl st in beginning ch-1: 48 scs.

New Year's Streamers:

1. With colored yarn, ch 25, work 3 scs in second ch from hk and in each remaining ch. Fasten off, leaving a tail of yarn. Fasten tail of yarn to center top of hat.

2. Repeat to make streamers in different colors. Vary the length of the streamers by starting with from 10 to 25 chs.

Crafter's Note: You can change the color of the hat and streamer to fit the season.

ABBREVIATIONS

bp	back post
ch	chain
dc	double crochet(s)
fp	front post
sc(s)	single crochet(s)
sl st	slip stitch
st(s)	stitch(es)
[ ]	Instructions between brackets are repeated as directed.

Beanie Hat with Streamers

CRAFT LEVEL: QUICK & EASY

FINISHED SIZE: Hat has a circumference of about 12 inches.

The hats I design and crochet are donated to my area's local hospitals for their newborns. This hat is easy to do and takes about one evening to complete.

Dorothy Buick ★ Mahopac, New York

MATERIALS:

5 ounces lightweight pompadour yarn (see note)

Worsted-weight yarn—scraps or up to 5-yard lengths of yarn in desired colors (green, pink, purple, turquoise and yellow shown)

Size G/6 (4mm) crochet hook or size needed to obtain correct gauge

Yarn or tapestry needle

Scissors

Note: Larger hats can be made by using heavier yarns and larger crochet hooks. See finished size.

GAUGE: Using Size G hook and White Pompadour yarn 16 dcs and 8 rows = 4 inches.

DIRECTIONS:

With white, ch 3, join with sl st in first ch made to form a ring.

Round 1: Ch 3 (counts as first dc here and throughout), work 11 dcs in ring, join with a sl st in top of beginning ch-3: 12 dcs.

Round 2: Ch 3, work 1 dc in same st, work 2 dcs in each remaining st around, join with a sl st in top of beginning ch-3: 24 dcs.

Round 3: Ch 3, work 1 dc in same st, dc in next st, [work 2 dcs in next, 1 dc in next st] around, join with sl st in top of beginning ch-3: 36 dcs.

Round 4: Ch 3, work 1 dc in same st, work 1 dc in each of the next 2 sts, [work 2 dcs in next st, work 1 dc in each

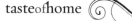

Warmest Wishes Card

CRAFT LEVEL: QUICK & EASY

FINISHED SIZE: Card measures about 4-1/4 inches wide x 5-1/2 inches high.

I used traditional Christmas red and green in this card and added a touch of blue with the mittens. The tree on the wire gives the card some dimension. The card stands up by itself, which is nice when it is displayed.

Lori Ditzler ★ Bloomingdale, Michigan

MATERIALS:

Card stock one 8-1/2-inch x 11-inch sheet or scraps each of green red and white

Rubber stamps assorted mini stamps for outside of card (candy cane, mitten and tree stamps shown), "warmest wishes" stamp or other message for outside of card, and "Joy to you and yours" or other message for inside of card

Ink pads—blue, green and red

5-inch length of 20-gauge gold craft wire

Craft glue for paper

Transparent tape

Ruler

Scissors

DIRECTIONS:

Cutting:

1. From green card stock, cut one 5-1/2- x 8-1/2-in. piece for outside of card.

2. From white card stock, cut two 5-1/8- x 1-1/8-in. pieces for sides on front of card and one 1-7/8- x 1-6/8-in. piece for stamped sign.

3. From red card stock, cut one 2-1/8-in. square for background of stamped sign.

Stamping:

1. Randomly stamp one side of each of the 5-1/8- x 1-1/8-in. white pieces with blue mittens, green trees and red candy canes.

2. Stamp the 1-7/8- x 1-6/8-in. white card stock piece with two blue mittens. Then using the red ink pad, stamp "warmest wishes" onto the piece.

3. Stamp a green tree on a scrap of white card stock.

Assembly:

1. Fold the short sides of the green card stock piece in to meet in the center, forming a 4-1/4-in. x 5-1/2-in. card with two side folds.

2. Glue a stamped white rectangle right side up to each side front of the card. Let dry.

3. Cut out the stamped green tree, leaving a small margin of white showing.

4. Wrap the center of the gold wire in a coil, leaving about 1-in. of straight wire at each end. Tape one straight end of the wire to the back of the tree cutout. Tape the other end of the straight wire to the back of the stamped white piece as shown in the photo.

5. Glue the stamped white piece right side up to the red 2-1/8-in. square, leaving a bit more space along the bottom edge of the red piece. Glue the assembled stamped square right side up to the left side of the card only. Let dry.

6. Stamp the inside of the card with the "Joy to you and yours" or other stamp of choice.

Dangle Bracelet

CRAFT LEVEL: QUICK & EASY

FINISHED SIZE: Bracelet measures about 7-1/2 inches long x 7/8 inch wide.

You can always make this bracelet in the recipient's favorite color with either a square or round bead. Or pick a color to match a special outfit for yourself!

Sarah Farley ★ Menomonee Falls, Wisconsin

MATERIALS:

Ten 20mm flat square red beads

Five gold eye pins

Five gold head pins

Fifteen size 11/0 gold seed beads

3-5/8-inch length of gold flat bar and link chain

Two gold jump rings

One gold lobster clasp

Round-nose pliers

Measuring tape

DIRECTIONS:

1. Separate the flat bar chain into five segments consisting of two bars with a link in the center.

2. Insert an eye pin into a flat square red bead. Use round-nose pliers to connect it with a closed loop to one end of a flat bar chain segment. Attach the other end of the eye pin to another flat bar segment with a closed loop. Repeat to join a total of five red square beads to five flat bar chain segments together. At one end, add a single bar link and a jump ring. At the other end, add a jump ring and the lobster clasp to make the bracelet about 7-1/2 in. long.

3. Place a seed bead, red square bead and two more seed beads on a head pin. Use round-nose pliers to attach the assembled beads to the center link between to flat bars of the bracelet with a closed loop. In the same way, attach the four remaining red beads and gold seed beads to the bracelet.

Crocheted Shrug

CRAFT LEVEL: INTERMEDIATE

FINISHED SIZE: Adult size Medium shown (length of finished crocheted piece measures about 20 inches, and width from sleeve end to sleeve end measures about 49 inches). Size can be changed by using a smaller or larger crochet hook (size G—Small; size I—Large; size J—X Large; size K—XX Large) or by working fewer or more rows and fewer or more stitches in each row.

Pretty and practical, this cozy crocheted shrug can be easily adapted to suit your needs. It's a project with endless possibilities! Vary the sleeve length for the season, and try other kinds of yarn for lots of different looks.

Josie Griego-Rabier ★ Saratoga, California

MATERIALS:

11 ounces/853 yards of worsted-weight yarn (Jo-Ann Sensations Berry Rainbow Boucle #1010 shown)

Size H/8 (5mm) crochet hook or size needed to obtain correct gauge

Yarn needle

Scissors

GAUGE: 11 sts and 10 rows = 4 inches. Check gauge to save time.

DIRECTIONS:
Ch 75 loosely.

Row 1: (RS): dc in fourth ch from hk and in each remaining ch across, turn: 73 dcs.

Row 2: Ch 1, sc in same sp, sc in each remaining st across, turn: 73 scs.

Row 3: Ch 3 for first tr, * FPtr around dc one row below next sc, dc in next sc; repeat from * across, (there will be a FPtr worked around every other dc in Row 1 and a dc in every other sc in Row 2) turn: 73 sts.

Row 4: Repeat Row 2.

Row 5: Ch 3 * Dc in next sc, FPtr around dc one row below next sc; repeat from * across, ending row with a dc in last 2 dcs, turn: 73 sts.

Row 6: Repeat Row 2.

Row 7: Ch 3 * FPtr around dc one row below next sc, dc in next sc; repeat from * across, turn: 73 sts.

Row 8: Repeat Row 2. Fasten off.

Row 9: (Sleeve): Ch 31 (new ch), with RS facing, dc in first sc, of Row 8, * FPtr around dc one row below next sc, dc in next sc; repeat from * across, ending row with a dc in last 2 dcs, (73 sts), ch 32 for other sleeve, turn.

Row 10: Sc in second ch from hk, sc in each ch and st across, turn: 135 scs.

Row 11: Ch 2 for first dc, dc in next 30 scs; * FPtr around dc one row below next sc, dc in next sc; repeat from * across to sleeve, dc in next 31 scs, turn.

Row 12: Repeat Row 2: 135 sts.

Rows 13-40: Repeat rows 3-6. Fasten off at end of Row 40, leaving a tail of yarn to sew sleeve edges together.

Row 41: (RS): Skip 31 sts, attach yarn with sl st in next st, ch 2, * dc in next sc, FPtr around dc one row below next sc; repeat from * across next 72 sts, ending row with a dc in last 2 dcs and leaving 31 sts unworked, turn: 72 sts.

Row 42: Repeat Row 2.

Row 43: Repeat Row 3.

Row 44: Repeat Row 2.

Row 45: (Reverse shaping for collar), ch 3, dc in next sc, * BPtr around dc one row below next sc, dc in next sc: repeat from * across, ending row with a dc in last 2 scs, turn.

Row 46: Repeat Row 2.

Row 47: Ch 3, * BPtr around dc one row below next sc, dc in next sc; repeat from * across, turn.

Row 48: Repeat Row 2.

Row 49: Repeat Row 45. Fasten off, leaving a tail of yarn to sew sleeve edges together.

ASSEMBLY:
Fold crocheted piece in half lengthwise with RS facing.

Use yarn needle and tails of yarn to sew side edges and underarm seams together. Weave in all loose ends.

EDGING:
Body:
Round 1: With RS facing, attach yarn with a sl st in sp between a side seam and next st. Ch 1, sc in same sp, sc between each dc around to beginning, join with a sl st. Fasten off.

Sleeve:
Round 1: With RS facing, attach yarn with a sl st in sp between underarm seam and next st. Ch 1, sc in same sp, work evenly around, working 2 scs in each dc, join with a sl st in beginning st. Do not turn.

Round 2: Ch 2, dc in each sc around, join with a sl st in top of beginning ch 2.

Round 3: Sl st into sp between next dc, ch 1, sc in same sp, sc between each dc around, join with a sl st in beginning st. Fasten off. Repeat around other sleeve.

ABBREVIATIONS	
ch	chain
dc(s)	double crochet(s)
hk	hook
sc(s)	single crochet(s)
sp	space
sl st	slip stitch
st(s)	stitch(es)
tr(s)	treble crochet(s)
BPtr	back post treble crochet
FPtr	front post treble crochet
RS	right side
WS	wrong side
*	Instructions following asterisks are repeated as directed.

RECIPE & CRAFT INDEXES

We've included three indexes for your convenience. The first is a complete alphabetical listing of all the recipes in this book. If you know the name of the recipe you need, simply turn to this index. The second index, the General Recipe Index, lists every recipe by food category, major ingredient and/or cooking method. For example, if you're looking for an appetizer recipe or one that uses beef, see this index. The last index can be used to find a craft. They're listed by title and type of craft.

Alphabetical Recipe Index

General Recipe Index

Craft Index

Share in the Magic of Christmas

Do you have a special recipe that has become part of your family's Christmas tradition? Do you have a special flair for decorating on a budget or making the most superb, original gifts? Those are the types of recipes, ideas and crafts we'd like to include in future **Taste of Home Christmas** books.

To submit a recipe, craft or decorating idea, print or type the information on a standard sheet of paper. Please be thorough and include directions, measurements and sizes of materials or equipment. Also include your name, address and daytime phone number, photo if available, and add a few words about yourself and your submission.

Send to **Taste of Home Christmas Annual**, 5400 S. 60th Street, Greendale WI 53129 (with a self-addressed stamped envelope if you'd like your materials returned). Or email your submissions and photos to **bookeditors@reimanpub.com** (write **Taste of Home Christmas Annual** in the subject line).